Later Greek Epic and the Latin Literary Tradition

Trends in Classics –
Supplementary Volumes

Edited by
Franco Montanari and Antonios Rengakos

Associate Editors
Stavros Frangoulidis · Fausto Montana · Lara Pagani
Serena Perrone · Evina Sistakou · Christos Tsagalis

Scientific Committee
Alberto Bernabé · Margarethe Billerbeck
Claude Calame · Kathleen Coleman · Jonas Grethlein
Philip R. Hardie · Stephen J. Harrison · Stephen Hinds
Richard Hunter · Giuseppe Mastromarco
Gregory Nagy · Theodore D. Papanghelis
Giusto Picone · Alessandro Schiesaro
Tim Whitmarsh · Bernhard Zimmermann

Volume 136

Later Greek Epic and the Latin Literary Tradition

Further Explorations

Edited by
Katerina Carvounis, Sophia Papaioannou
and Giampiero Scafoglio

DE GRUYTER

ISBN 978-3-11-153667-5
e-ISBN (PDF) 978-3-11-079190-7
e-ISBN (EPUB) 978-3-11-079198-3
ISSN 1868-4785

Library of Congress Control Number: 2022946453

Bibliographic information published by the Deutsche Nationalbibliothek
The Deutsche Nationalbibliothek lists this publication in the Deutsche Nationalbibliografie; detailed bibliographic data are available on the Internet at http://dnb.dnb.de.

© 2024 Walter de Gruyter GmbH, Berlin/Boston
This volume is text- and page-identical with the hardback published in 2023.
Editorial Office: Alessia Ferreccio and Katerina Zianna
Logo: Christopher Schneider, Laufen

www.degruyter.com

Contents

Abbreviations —— VII

Katerina Carvounis, Sophia Papaioannou, and Giampiero Scafoglio
Preface: Later Greek Epic and the Latin Literary Tradition —— 1

Ursula Gärtner
Latin and Later Greek Literature: Reflections on Different Approaches —— 7

Katerina Carvounis
The Poet as Sailor: Claudian between the Greek and Latin Traditions —— 31

Silvio Bär
Sinon and Laocoon in Quintus of Smyrna's *Posthomerica*: A Rewriting and De-Romanisation of Vergil's *Aeneid*? —— 55

Emma Greensmith
Odysseus the Roman: Imperial Temporality and the *Posthomerica* —— 75

Giampiero Scafoglio
Triphiodorus and the *Aeneid*: From Poetics to Ideology —— 101

Markus Kersten
ἄντρα περικλυτά: Revisiting Mythical Places in the Orphic *Argonautica* —— 123

Sophia Papaioannou
Pantomime Games in the *Dionysiaca* and Vergil's Song of Silenus —— 151

Helen Lovatt
Nonnus' Phaethon, Ovid, and Flavian Intertextuality —— 179

List of Contributors —— 207
General Index —— 209
Index Locorum —— 211

Abbreviations

Decleva Caizzi	Decleva Caizzi, F. (1966), *Antisthenis Fragmenta*, Milan.
EpGF	Davies, M. (1988), *Epicorum Graecorum Fragmenta*, Göttingen.
FGrH	Jacoby, F. (1923–1994), *Die Fragmente der griechischen Historiker*. Teil I-III (15 volumes), Berlin.
GDRK	Heitsch, E. (^{2}1963), *Die griechischen Dichterfragmente der römischen Kaiserzeit*, Göttingen.
Jocelyn	Jocelyn, H.D. (1967), *The Tragedies of Ennius. The Fragments edited with an Introduction and Commentary*, Cambridge (repr. with corr. 1969).
Manuwald	Manuwald, G. (2012), *Tragicorum Romanorum Fragmenta (TrRF)*. Volumen II. *Ennius*, Göttingen.
Merkelbach–West	Merkelbach, R./West, M.L. (1967), *Fragmenta Hesiodea*, Oxford.
PMG	Page, D.L. (1962), *Poetae Melici Graeci*, Oxford.
PMGF	Davies, M. (1991), *Poetarum Melicorum Graecorum Fragmenta*, Oxford.
Vahlen	Vahlen, I. (1903), *Ennianae poesis reliquiae, iteratis curis rec.*, Leipzig (Leipzig ^{3}1928; Amsterdam 1963, 1967).
Weissenborn–Müller	Weissenborn, W./Müller, H.J., *Titi Livi ab urbe condita libri* (Sammlung griechischer und lateinischer Schriftsteller mit deutschen Anmerkungen). 1. Band: Buch I (^{9}1908) und Buch II (^{8}1894), Nachdruck Dublin/Zurich 1969. 2. Band: Buch III (^{6}1900) und Buch IV/V (^{6}1896), Nachdruck Dublin/Zurich 1970.

Abbreviations of ancient authors and texts follow *L' Annee Philologique*.

Katerina Carvounis, Sophia Papaioannou, and Giampiero Scafoglio

Preface: Later Greek Epic and the Latin Literary Tradition

The idea of exploring later Greek epic alongside, and in the light of, Latin literature came up in May 2017, during dinner after a conference in the wonderful city of Athens: while talking about the presence of the Latin literary tradition in the Greek epic of the imperial period — a topic both intriguing and elusive, considering the different ways in which the 'presence' of some works in the subtext of others may be conceived —, we realised that it was worth engaging in this debate. All the more so, as the last two decades have witnessed a surge of interest in later Greek epic, both in the study of individual works and in their broader contexts, leading to the collapse of many prejudices that have long precluded a lucid and balanced approach to these literary texts.[1]

Reliable editions, modern annotated translations, and book-length studies on Quintus' *Posthomerica*, Triphiodorus' *Sack of Troy*, the Orphic *Argonautica*, and Nonnus' *Dionysiaca* have now made these poems considerably more accessible to scholars interested in ancient Greek literature, the evolution of the epic tradition, and Late Antiquity. In the past decade a series of well-attended international conferences on these authors and their respective contexts, among which the meetings on Quintus (Zurich, 2006; Cambridge, 2016) and the conference series 'Nonnus of Panopolis in Context' (Rethymno, 2011; Vienna, 2013; Warsaw, 2015; Ghent, 2018), have reignited systematic and in-depth study, and brought together scholars from a variety of traditions. The edited volumes resulting from these meetings, together with the *Brill's Companion to Nonnus of Panopolis* and the number of monographs on the *Posthomerica* and *Dionysiaca*

---

1 If we look back over the history of criticism on Quintus' *Posthomerica*, for instance, we realise that a correct analysis of its sources has long been hindered by an aesthetic prejudice, i.e. an undervaluation of the literary merit of the *Posthomerica*. Until recently, critics maintained that it would be unlikely for an 'epigonal author,' such as Quintus, to have practised creative and selective imitation of a Latin source: had he known Vergil's *Aeneid*, he would have undoubtedly imitated it in a more obvious way; therefore, if such plagiarism is not evident, Quintus did not know the *Aeneid*. This thread was started by Richard Heinze in his pivotal book *Virgils epische Technik* at the beginning of the 20th century (Heinze 1915, 63–81), and it was carried on fifty years later by Francis Vian in his seminal *Recherches sur les Posthomerica de Quintus de Smyrne* (Vian 1959, 55–85 and 96–101).

https://doi.org/10.1515/9783110791907-001

in the last few years, attest to this recent 'explosion' of scholarly interest in later Greek epic poetry.

Despite the proliferation of innovative work on late antique Greek epic in recent years, scholarship has not explored systematically the interaction of imperial Greek epicists with the Latin tradition. Comparative examinations of the Greek and the Latin literary traditions in the imperial period and in Late Antiquity are beginning to appear in this shifting landscape. Daniel Jolowicz's most recent monograph entitled *Latin Poetry in the Ancient Greek Novels* begins with an introductory chapter that puts forward evidence to support the claim that there was Greek engagement with Latin poetry in the early and high imperial periods,[2] and makes an overall compelling case that there were some, at least, Greek-speaking individuals in the imperial period who read Latin poetry.[3] Moreover, a volume entitled *Greek and Latin Poetry of Late Antiquity: Form, Tradition, and Context*, which has just been published, results from a conference held in Ghent in September 2016 and constitutes the first organised effort to bring together scholars working in the fields of late antique Greek and late Latin poetry. In their introduction, the volume editors (and organisers of the highly successful Ghent conference), Berenice Verhelst and Tine Scheijnen, underscore the significance of comparative study between the two literary traditions to trace and comprehend in depth the respective elaborate developments across a period of several centuries.[4]

The present volume narrows down this comparative examination to focus on Latin epic, which it aspires to analyse not only from a bilingual perspective but also under the assumption that the two traditions do not necessarily develop independently from, and ignorant of, each other. As both the Greek and the Latin epics of Late Antiquity are influenced by the same poetic rules and aesthetic principles, the admission of ongoing interaction, not always conscious, sought after, and sustained, between the Greek and the Latin epic traditions may help modern readers reconsider their understanding of 'Greek' or 'Latin' at a time when both have acquired new definitions.

---

[2] For this stated aim and purpose of his monograph see Jolowicz 2021, 2–3. Jolowicz 2021, 6–10, also examines some reasons why scholars have so far been reluctant to accept Greek engagement with Latin literature.
[3] Jolowicz 2021, 34.
[4] Verhelst/Scheijnen 2022, 1–10.

After reflection and exchange of ideas, and aware that the study of bilingual allusion in late antique poetry is only at the beginning, we organised a panel on *The Latin literary tradition and later Greek poetry* at the conference organised by the *Fédération internationale des associations d'études classiques* (FIEC), held in London in July 2019. The rich and lively debate that followed this panel encouraged us to continue along the path. Thus, we enrolled a small but enthusiastic group of experts with the shared aim to study in depth, and from different points of view, this complex yet stimulating topic.

In our approach, we tried to embrace the new trends in the study of Late Antiquity and to rephrase the issue commonly set by those who explore late antique intertextuality, who seek to prove if (and to what extent) Greek poets such as Quintus and Nonnus read, or not, Latin models like Vergil and Ovid.[5] There is evidence that Latin language and the major Roman poets were known, and even taught at school in late antique Egypt; but there is no way to determine if really a single Greek poet read and imitated a specific Latin model. The difficulties are many, starting from the (contemptuous?) silence that Greek poets keep on Latin poetry and the awkwardness of a comparison between works in different languages; but the *coup de grace* is the possibility that analogies between Greek and Latin texts derive from a common (Greek) model. We have chosen, therefore, to avoid going over arguments already stated by others, and not to dwell on explorations of textual and/or structural relationships between Greek works and (possible) Latin models; we have rather tried to analyse rela-

---

[5] The most important systematic, book-length contribution on the subject of possible influences from Latin literature on later Greek epic is the study by Ursula Gärtner in *Quintus Smyrnaeus und die Aeneis. Zur Nachwirkung Vergils in der griechischen Literatur der Kaiserzeit* (Gärtner 2005), where she carries out a careful analysis of a series of parallel passages, of various length between the *Aeneid* and the *Posthomerica*. For the large majority of these passages she acknowledges that she cannot prove uncontested direct influence of the former on the latter, but succeeds in making a convincing case for this influence in a dozen of the so-designated parallels; this seems sufficient to indicate that Quintus knew Vergil and appropriated his work selectively. There are, of course, various difficulties in accepting this influence; in a most recent discussion on the use of Latin models by later Greek authors, Agosti (2020) sensibly cautions against acknowledging allusions to Latin intertexts, especially Vergil and Ovid, too readily; he points out that knowledge of Latin language and literature does not necessarily mean conscious imitation of Latin texts. For Agosti, the late antique Greek authors were deeply indebted to the Greek tradition, and did not, therefore, feel the need to turn to Latin models, even though they might have known them. We may wonder, however, if imitation must necessarily be 'conscious,' if it is going to be acknowledged and thought worthy to be studied. Moreover, in a forthcoming paper the point is raised that even if a poet were familiar with a Latin model, he need not expect his readership to be familiar with it too (Maciver, forthcoming).

tionships that exist anyway, at least in a cultural dimension. We are less concerned, in other words, with the issue if and how Quintus and Nonnus came to know the great Latin epicists; we acknowledge that it is possible that the Greek poets of Late Antiquity were indeed familiar with crucial works of Latin poetry such as Vergil's *Aeneid* and Ovid's *Metamorphoses*, be it in the original or in translation, and that this familiarity was used in individual, creative ways.

Besides, we tried to enhance the interpretative perspective that we, as modern readers of ancient epic, forged and shaped, approaching the late antique poems as interfaces at the end of an ongoing interaction between the Greek and the Latin tradition — an interaction that may not necessarily be intentional or ascertainable. Thereby, we hope to have combined, or at least to have adopted alongside with each other and in mutual support, the authorial perspective and the informed readers' critical reception. We have tried to take into account in our inquiry the main exponents of later Greek epic, including the epyllion and a hexameter composition with epic subject matter, in order to outline a wide and varied overview of the subject. Thus, Emma Greensmith and Silvio Bär have focused on Quintus' relationship with the *Aeneid*, a relationship in which differences and omissions speak even more than analogies, with problematic implications of 'cultural policy'; and it is along the same lines that Giampiero Scafoglio has studied Triphiodorus' approach to Vergil. The latter's *Eclogue 6* is at the core of an emulative process that overcomes the boundaries of literary genre in Nonnus' *Dionysiaca*, as argued by Sophia Papaioannou. Helen Lovatt revisits Nonnus' treatment of the Phaethon narrative in the light of a sophisticated reception process of Ovid's celebrated account of the same story by the Flavian epicists. Markus Kersten, in turn, has dealt with the *Orphic Argonautica*, in which he has detected the use of some poetic features prominent in the treatment of myth in Latin epic poetry. The analysis of the metaphor of 'the poet as sailor' performed — in different ways and for different audiences — in both Greek and Latin language by Claudian has allowed Katerina Carvounis to explore the interaction between the two literary traditions from the specific point of view of a bilingual poet. Admittedly, our journey on mined ground starts from a healthy dose of scepticism, with the overview by Ursula Gärtner on previous research on the subject, which works as a reminder of the risks and limits of the voyage we have undertaken. It is hoped, nevertheless, that the new readings of select passages and themes in later Greek epic that are offered in this volume may be a step towards fruitfully considering these works alongside, or in the light of, Latin poetry.

Before 'setting sail' (to recall a metaphor that is the subject of one of the chapters in our volume), we wish to thank warmly all the contributors, as well as Philip Hardie and Dan Jolowicz, who participated in the FIEC 2019 panel which became somehow the first stage of our voyage. We would also like to thank the anonymous readers of the volume for their feedback and some thought-provoking comments; and the editors of the 'Trends in Classics — Supplementary Volumes' series, Franco Montanari and Antonios Rengakos, who championed this book. Not least, we thank in advance the readers who will approach our bold — and maybe sometimes reckless — arguments with the audacity and the *ouverture d'esprit* required to tune into and enjoy them.

Bibliography

Agosti, G. (2020), "Modelli latini per poemi greci? Sulla possibile influenza di autori latini sulla poesia epica tardoantica", in: A. Garcea/M. Rosellini/L. Silvano (eds.), *Latin in Byzantium I: Late Antiquity and Beyond*, Turnhout, 313–331.
Gärtner, U. (2005), *Quintus Smyrnaeus und die Aeneis. Zur Nachwirkung Vergils in der griechischen Literatur der Kaiserzeit*, Munich.
Heinze, R. (1915), *Virgils Epische Technik*. Third Edition, Stuttgart.
Jolowicz, D. (2021), *Latin Poetry in the Ancient Greek Novels*, Oxford.
Maciver, C.A. (forthcoming), "Homer without Vergil (and Ovid): *Erwartungshorizont* and Late Antique Greek Epic", Turnhout.
Verhelst, B./Scheijnen, T. (eds.) (2022), *Greek and Latin Poetry of Late Antiquity: Form, Tradition, and Context*, Cambridge.
Vian, F. (1959), *Recherches sur les Posthomerica de Quintus de Smyrne*, Paris.

Ursula Gärtner
Latin and Later Greek Literature: Reflections on Different Approaches

Abstract: The question of whether and how Greeks dealt with Latin literature during the imperial period and whether and how this might be reflected in Greek texts of this period has often been 'solved' or 'answered.' The present contribution reflects on methodological approaches without prejudice or the desire to promote a particular approach, and rather discusses (1) the advantages, problems, and limitations of each approach. To begin with (2), we briefly discuss the external criteria, i.e., the facts that can be used to draw conclusions about the general knowledge of Latin literature in the Greek-speaking world during the imperial period. The main part (3) concentrates on the internal criteria (text, sources, subtexts); we discuss the various approaches and methodology, such as *Quellenforschung*, intertextuality, reader-response theory or 'non-engagement.' A summary (4) attempts with caution to take stock of the issue.

Keywords: Latin literature and Greek readers; overview of methodological approaches; *Quellenforschung*; intertextuality.

ceterum et mihi vetustas res scribenti nescio quo pacto anticus fit animus
Liv. 43.13.2

1 Preface

Let me begin my contribution with a personal note. The question of whether and how Greeks dealt with Latin literature during the imperial period and whether and how this might be reflected in Greek texts of this period has accompanied me for over 25 years. And during this time — and of course even before that — the question has often been 'solved' or 'answered' emphatically by others, too; there has been talk of 'prejudice,' scholars have demanded the 'burden of proof' from the other side and have accused each other of methodological backwardness or errors. Others have changed their position or have avoided committing themselves from the outset.[1]

---

[1] See below, n. 77 and n. 84.

https://doi.org/10.1515/9783110791907-002

When I began my work on Quintus (accustomed to working with the concepts of intertextuality), I was quite alone with the idea that the *Aeneid* could be a subtext, not just a source for the *Posthomerica*, and I met with unanimous resistance to my original aim to start with this hypothesis. I therefore sought to identify the evidence base first, and so I tried to collect and discuss all possible parallels, discrepancies, and lines of motifs. This was not as exciting as I had hoped, but I thought it would be helpful for further studies.[2] On the other hand, delving into all the variations and connections of motifs on the fall of Troy meant that I became increasingly aware of the immense breadth of the subject and the huge gaps that opened up for us due to the loss of transmission, so that the scrupulous approach described above was the consequence, which forbade too quick assumptions regarding allusions, however they were to be defined.[3] I had ended my book with the statement that research into the literary techniques of the text was needed because there was still a lot to be done. I am therefore delighted that this has happened in recent decades and that the poet is receiving the respect he deserves. I myself have been following the question from a distance, but I was gratified to see that the issue is obviously still being examined with passion from new angles. In this respect, I gladly agreed to contribute to this volume with a review of, and reflections on, methodology.[4]

Before giving an overview, I would like to start with some general reflections.[5] The question whether Greek poets knew or even dealt with Latin literature was long considered absurd; it was almost accepted as law that these poets as well as their readers did not have to consider Latin works.[6] Today, on the

---

2 Most of the reviews took it exactly as it was meant; cf. Lovatt 2006; Bär 2006; Rochette 2006/2008; James 2006; Maciver 2009.
3 This was captured, perhaps most aptly, in the review by Lovatt 2006.
4 In part, this contribution is a revised version of the discussions in Gärtner 2013.
5 Cf. Gärtner 2013, 90–93.
6 Cf., e.g., Maas 1935, 385; Kroll 1902, 8–9: "Da konnte man es von den Hellenen nicht verlangen, daß sie der römischen Literatur irgendwelche Beachtung schenkten, und wirklich haben sie diese, insofern sie eine künstlerische Leistung darstellen wollte, so gut wie ganz ignoriert, auch dann noch, als römische Literatur Werke hervorbrachte, denen die gleichzeitige griechische nichts Ebenbürtiges an die Seite zu stellen hatte. Es war schlimm genug, daß man um der sachlichen Belehrung willen manche lateinisch geschriebenen Werke lesen mußte, wie es z. B. Dionysios von Halikarnaß und Plutarch mit römischen Historikern taten: aber Genuß bereitete ihnen diese Lektüre nicht und sie schränkten sie daher auf das notwendigste Maß ein. [...] Aber sich um die Belletristik, vor allem die Dichtung der Römer zu kümmern, durfte man einem Griechen nicht zumuten. Er hatte gar nicht das Bedürfnis, sich außerhalb der reichen Literatur des eigenen Volkes umzusehen, und hätte er es gewollt, so waren seine Sprachkenntnisse nicht ausreichend, um römische Poesie wirklich mit Genuß zu lesen." ("The Hellenes could not

other hand, it almost seems to have gone to the other extreme, for now the familiarity of Greek poets (and their readers) with, e.g., Vergil is often taken for granted and arguments turn to intertextuality: for instance, even the absence of traces of the *Aeneid* in the Greek epics is interpreted nowadays as an indication of deliberate disregard. We are all familiar with this approach when working on poetry where intertextual references are very clear and not in doubt (as the *Aeneid* and the *Iliad* and the *Odyssey*, or Lucan's *Bellum civile* and the *Aeneid*), but it becomes tricky when we talk about works where the relationships between them seem to be unknown.[7] Moreover, observations on individual authors are often generalised, but even if the genesis of these literary works is not locally restricted, it is of course culturally determined at the respective location. Furthermore, the expression 'later Greek poetry' can imply a misleading uniformity over a long period of time.[8] Therefore, we should be careful with expressions such as "the Greeks."[9] In addition, in many cases we know little about the empirical author and his or her audience at the time.[10] And finally, in the imperial period, we can consider one thousand years of literature, much of which is lost to us, so we should refer to direct allusion with caution.[11] In many cases the motifs have become standardised to *topoi* or simply form "noise,"[12] which can be recognised as a tradition, but can no longer be dissolved into single threads.

Finally, we must clarify the question: is it a question of whether the poets (and their recipients) had access to the Latin texts? Is it a question of knowledge

---

be expected to pay any attention to Roman literature, and in fact, in so far as it was intended to be an artistic achievement, they almost completely ignored it, even when Roman literature produced works such that contemporary Greek literature had nothing equal to put alongside. It was bad enough that some works written in Latin had to be read for the sake of factual instruction, as Dionysius of Halicarnassus and Plutarch did with Roman historians: but they did not enjoy this reading and therefore reduced it to the bare minimum. [...] But a Greek could not be expected to concern himself with fiction, especially Roman poetry. He did not feel the need to look outside the rich literature of his own people, and if he wanted to, his knowledge of the language was not sufficient to read Roman poetry with real pleasure." — my translation).
7 See below, 18–23.
8 Cf. Carvounis/Hunter 2008, 3: "Despite some special cases of intertextuality (Quintus and Triphiodorus, for example), the glib way in which we have been writing of 'later Greek (hexameter) poetry' misleadingly suggests a far greater chronological and generic affiliation than actually exists on the Greek side [...], and respecting difference will be one of the great challenges for the serious study of this poetry."
9 Cf. Whitmarsh 2010, 1–16.
10 For the question of the author see below, 19–21.
11 See below, 13–14.
12 Cf. Hinds 1998, 19: "the variety of kinds of background noise which can get in the way of the rigorous study of 'direct imitations.'"

(which can per se hardly be proved or denied) or use, i.e., of adoption in terms of expression, form, or content, for example, while leaving the role of the reader open? Is it a matter of tracing intertextual references in the stricter sense, such as those that are evident in the relationship between the *Aeneid* and the *Iliad*? Is, for instance, the *Aeneid* a subtext that the (implied) reader had to be able to recall? Do we privilege the reader and ask how one might understand the text after having read the *Aeneid*? Or is it simply a matter of proving that the Greek texts were affected by contemporary politics and culture, which were also determined or influenced by the Romans in the Greek-speaking world?[13]

Therefore, the present contribution will reflect on methodological approaches without prejudice or the desire to promote a particular approach. Rather, the advantages, problems, and limitations of each approach will be discussed.[14] In most cases the *Posthomerica* of Quintus Smyrnaeus is used as an example. As far as the possible reception of Latin literature is concerned, for reasons of space we will limit our focus to Vergil. To begin with (2), we will briefly discuss the external criteria, i.e., the facts that can be used to draw conclusions about the general knowledge of Latin literature in the Greek-speaking world during the imperial period. The main part (3) will concentrate on the internal criteria (text, sources, subtexts); we will discuss the various approaches and methodology, such as *Quellenforschung*, intertextuality, reader-response theory, or 'non-engagement.' A summary (4) attempts with caution to take stock of the issue.

---

13 For a broader approach see the volume edited by Schubert 2013a.
14 No comprehensive research report can be given in the following, especially as research on the *Posthomerica* has increased over the last 20 years. Only works which can stand for the individual directions or which could represent new approaches will be selected.

2 External criteria: On the diffusion and the importance of Latin language and literature in the Greek-speaking world during the Imperial Period

Much research has been undertaken — especially in recent decades — regarding the knowledge of Latin language and literature among the Greek-speaking population of the Roman empire during the imperial period. The results will not be repeated here.[15] Scholars have established that Vergil and his works were known in the Greek-speaking world, at least by name. One could read the texts in the original as well as in translation, and this is particularly evident in the eastern provinces of the coast of Asia Minor, Syria, Palestine, and Egypt. Furthermore, we do have references to reading Vergil in the works of Greek authors.

However, the material or the results themselves have not actually changed across this body of research. It is rather the interpretation that changes. And here one cannot avoid the impression that the findings are not very clear, a realisation that is also imprinted in the interpretations: depending on the direction of the research, the rare bilingual papyri, for instance, are taken as evidence for more widespread reading of Vergil, or statements about knowledge of Latin or about reading Vergil are not interpreted as exceptions worth mentioning, but as confirmation of possible acquaintance with Latin literature. Nowadays several critics tend to see this material as proof that an interaction with Latin literature on a larger scale is at least conceivable, if not to be taken for granted,[16] but sceptical voices remain.[17]

---

15 Cf., e.g., Hahn 1906; 1907; 1912; Reichmann 1943; Fisher 1982; Schmitt 1983, 554–586; Irmscher 1984; 1985; 1986; Rochette 1990; 1993; 1994; 1995a; 1995b; 1997, with comprehensive bibliography; Tilg 2010, 271–297; Bechert/Wildgen 1991; Myers-Scotton 1993; Wenskus 2001, 70–72; Adams/Janse/Swain 2002; Adams 2003; Cribiore 2003/4, 111–118; Gärtner 2005, 13–22; Hidber 2006, 237–254; Cribiore 2007, 47–66; Nesselrath 2013; Schubert 2013a; Szabat 2015, 256–258; Carvounis 2019, lvii–lxv; Jolowicz 2021, 1–34.
16 This is the starting point in this volume.
17 Cf. Nesselrath 2013, 306–307: "ferner sind vor allem seit dem 3. Jh. n. Chr. mehrere [...] Initiativen festzustellen, die Latein auch auf höherer Bildungsstufe [...] im Osten etablieren und konsolidieren wollen. Überblickt man jedoch die konkreten Ergebnisse dieser Bemühungen, soweit sie uns noch feststellbar sind, wirken sie aufs Ganze gesehen eher mager. [...] doch fällt es [...] sehr schwer, diese beiden Autoren [sc. Claudian; Ammianus Marcellinus] nicht als Aus-

3 Internal criteria: Texts, sources, subtexts? The various approaches, their advantages, problems, and limitations

3.1 Preliminary remarks: Quintus Smyrnaeus' *Posthomerica*

The question of Quintus Smyrnaeus' interaction with Latin works has been thoroughly discussed and has generated more controversy than probably any other epicist.[18] His *Posthomerica* is a good example of how the methodological approach has changed, and with what success.

Here are some notes to introduce this text: critics nowadays generally agree that this epic in 14 books, which was intended to bridge the gap between the *Iliad* and the *Odyssey* and is today usually referred to as *Posthomerica*, was written at the end of the 3rd century CE. The Homeric epics are of course regarded as subtexts, and they are also constantly present through vocabulary, language, syntax, formulaic verses, similes, typical scenes, etc. The same applies more or less to Apollonius Rhodius' *Argonautica*. But there are also clear allusions to other genres such as tragedy (Aeschylus, Sophocles, and Euripides). The incorporation of Alexandrian poetics is important, as has been convincingly demonstrated in recent research.[19]

---

nahmen zu betrachten, die die Regel bestätigen." ("In addition, since the 3rd century CE in particular, there have been several [...] initiatives that aim to establish and consolidate Latin in the East at a higher educational level [...]. However, if we take a look at the concrete results of these efforts, as far as we can still detect them, they appear rather meagre on the whole. [...] but it is [...] very difficult not to regard these two authors [sc. Claudian; Ammianus Marcellinus] as exceptions that confirm the rule." — my translation); Schubert 2013b, 269: "Enfin, les papyrus littéraires montrent certes une présence des auteurs latins en Égypte romaine, mais le niveau de connaissance reste assez rudimentaire: on se concentre sur des auteurs scolaires et l'impact sur la composition de textes grecs ne se fait sentir que dans des cas exceptionnels." ("Finally, although the literary papyri show a presence of Latin authors in Roman Egypt, the level of knowledge remains rather rudimentary: the focus is on school authors and the impact on the composition of Greek texts is only felt in exceptional cases." — my translation).

18 For an overview on Triphiodorus, Nonnus, Colluthus, Musaeus, *Oracula Sibyllina*, and other works cf., e.g., Gärtner 2013, 101–113.

19 Cf., e.g., Bär 2009; Maciver 2011; 2012a; 2012b; Greensmith 2018.

3.2 *Quellenforschung* I: The *Aeneid* as a 'source'

For a long time, the main question focused on establishing the poet's literary sources. The topic itself, the Trojan War, had been known for more than a thousand years before the *Posthomerica* and had been shaped by literature again and again. If one considers that we have lost countless works that dealt with Troy, one can recognise certain strands or traditions of motifs, but an argument based solely on source analysis quickly reaches its limits. One has to point out, for instance, that it is unclear whether or until when and where the Epic Cycle was still known, and if so, in what form.[20] *Posthomerica* 11, 12, and 13 covering the destruction of Troy have always been the centre of attention, with critics tending to recognise references to the second book of the *Aeneid*. Intertextual references to the *Aeneid* were identified in the subtext of the character profile of individual figures such as Penthesileia (Camilla), and sometimes also a Vergilian colouring was observed to underwrite the overall representation of these heroes. The following sources were suggested as the origins for the content: a mythological manual in the manner of Ps-Apollodorus or Proclus, which Quintus filled and enlivened by using poetry,[21] or Hellenistic epics or epyllia about the Trojan War,[22] although this is purely hypothetical because we have no traces of them. Had they been widely disseminated, one would have expected to find references to such works in Servius or Macrobius, for example. Macrobius' statement (*Sat.* 5.2.4) that everyone would know that the second book of the *Aeneid* was written following "Peisander" *ad verbum paene*[23] has confused readers since antiquity. Peisander of Laranda, however, did not write his *Heroikai Theogamiai*, a comprehensive epic on world history in 60 books, until the first decades of the 3rd century CE. It is easy to agree with Keydell, who suspected that Macrobius made an error here in the chronological order.[24] It is more sensible, however, to refrain from speculation about possible lost sources.

---

20 Cf. Gärtner 2005, 28–29; Bär 2009, 78–84; Bär/Baumbach 2015.
21 Cf. Keydell 1963, 1273.
22 Vian 1959; 1963–9, *passim*, was particularly imaginative here; he suspected not only a Hellenistic representation of Penthesileia, but also a Hellenistic *Iliupersis* influenced by the cyclic *Thebais*, or a Hellenistic *Thebais* and Hellenistic *Nostoi* as models.
23 However, one should also consider the role of the speaker Eustathius and of the statement in the dialogue.
24 Perhaps Keydell's 1935a, 1975, 5, solution was a "simplification illusoire," according to Vian 1959, 99; however, Vian's thesis was equally unconvincing: he believed he had found in this Peisander, the author of the lost Hellenistic common source for Quintus and Vergil.

The disregard for Quintus' creative abilities as an epic poet meant that his poetry was often regarded as almost exclusively limited to imitation. As a result, parallels in expression, motifs, and scenes furnished arguments to corroborate this methodology of imitation. The researchers who argued against a knowledge of the *Aeneid* explained these similarities as a result of drawing on one or more common sources. Factual divergences and differences in narrative style were used as arguments against knowledge; the possibility that Quintus consciously wanted to distance himself had not even been considered[25] or had been rejected as "not methodical," as Norden put it.[26] The researchers who asserted that Quintus had 'used' the *Aeneid* pointed out above all the literal parallels — which are, in some cases, striking even between the two different languages. In fact, earlier critics, especially Noack, had argued that there are correspondences to be found even outside the second book of the *Aeneid* which is thematically related to the narrative of the *Posthomerica*.[27] Becker wanted to corroborate methodologically the approach that embraced the direct interaction with the *Aeneid*, and hoped to weaken the thesis of the common source, by pointing out that even in a work recognised by others as a "safe common source," identical deviations in Quintus and Vergil from this very source could be found, which he explained by the "dependence" of the Greek author on the Latin text; at least he agreed that Quintus did not follow his models "slavishly."[28]

These source-critical approaches are often viewed with disdain today.[29] Actually, *Quellenforschung* and modern approaches of intertextuality are often not that far apart. Of course, the sole question of what exactly one text takes over from another is, from today's point of view, unproductive. Yet, one must at least be thankful for the way the parallels have been worked out, even though anyone who in the past had focused on identifying all the variations of a certain motif, and their connections and differences, nowadays would not hasten to speak of direct relationships.

---

25 Cf. Köchly 1853, XIII–XV.
26 Norden 1901, 329 n. 1.
27 Cf. Heyne 1832; Kehmptzow 1891; Noack 1892.
28 Becker 1913.
29 Cf. Most 2016.

3.3 *Quellenforschung* II: Structural comparison: The *Aeneid* as a 'model'

The following approach was also committed to *Quellenforschung*. Here, the focus was not limited to details and also included the structures of the respective narratives. Kroll and Heinze, for example, argued against Quintus' knowledge of the *Aeneid*, on the grounds that the later poet had not incorporated in his text the typical Vergilian narrative characteristics. The view that Quintus often deviates even when Vergil offers "an excellent narrative" which "an imitator should not have passed by" is symptomatic of this approach.[30] According to this line of thinking, Quintus would usually offer the inferior and therefore earlier version of the narrative.[31]

Another argument against familiarity with the *Aeneid* was the complexity of the Vergilian representations and the fact that similar motifs were sometimes spread over two different passages in the *Aeneid*. Critics argued that the Greek poet did not possess the poetic ability to put the two passages 'back' together again if he had recourse to the *Aeneid*.[32] Thus the lost Hellenistic epics and other texts once again were suggested as possible common sources.[33] Vian went even further, in refuting a direct interaction and explaining parallels either by independent reception of common models not recognised by scholars before (Homer, Apollonius, Theocritus, etc.) or, in cases where he did not succeed in identifying these models, by postulating other common sources that had not been preserved.[34] Following Kroll's earlier arguments, he justified this methodologically as follows: "Si QS s'inspirait de l'*Énéide*, la loi de l'imitation épique l'obligerait ici de suivre scrupuleusement son modèle."[35] Interestingly, scholars who sought to explain the peculiarities of Vergil's composition advanced similar arguments. Zintzen's view is representative: "Eine gemeinsame Vorlage

---

[30] Kroll 1902, 162–167; Heinze 1915. They referred, e.g., to the episodes of Sinon, Laocoon, the Wooden Horse, the death of Coroebus, and the death of Priamus.
[31] Cf. Leone 1968; 1984.
[32] Cf., e.g., the presentation of the *testudo* in Quint. Smyrn. 11.358–366 and *Aen.* 2.438–444 and 9.505–518. The parallels to Vergil's second depiction are closer, although the latter does not deal with the conquest of Troy but with the fight for the camp in Italy; cf. Gärtner 2005, 114–132; Greensmith in this volume, 92–95.
[33] See above; cf. Knight 1932a; 1932b.
[34] Vian 1959, 95–109; and *passim*. He argued above all for Hellenistic epics which were in a complicated relationship of dependence; cf. n. 22.
[35] Vian 1959, 57 ("If QS was inspired by the *Aeneid*, the law of epic imitation would oblige him here to scrupulously follow his model." — my translation).

beider kann man nur postulieren, wenn man zugleich einräumt, daß entweder QS oder Vergil selbständig geändert hat."[36] The decisive factor for him was, "ob Färbung und Darstellung bei QS in verwandten Szenen sich sinnvoll aus der vergilischen Schilderung entwickelt zu erkennen geben."[37] He therefore rejected a direct interaction with Vergil's text. For Zintzen and others, Vergil had changed the common source drastically, whereas Quintus reproduced the material in a way which could be traced.

Those in favour of 'knowledge' argued methodologically in the same way but they believed they had found Vergilian characteristics in expressions, motifs, or structures, as Noack did;[38] or later Duckworth, who stressed the similar narrative technique of "foreshadowing and suspense";[39] and also Buchheit, who pointed out Vergilian characteristics in the Aeolus scene (14.474–487; Verg. Aen. 1.34–87).[40] Keydell is certainly one of the main representatives of this trend; his opinion has been influential because he presented it in renowned reference works,[41] and he was able to identify a greater number of parallels. He even went a step further in the interpretation of those passages as he explained the mixture of parallels and differences through the poet's way of working: the basis for Quintus' work was not an earlier epic, but a mythological manual. The poet then filled this brief framework by referring back to well-known poems, including the *Aeneid*. Erbse followed this approach and 'methodically' demanded the burden of proof from those who fundamentally denied the knowledge or attributed clear parallels to a possible common source.[42] Ferrari, too, questioned *the* common Hellenistic source by directing the alleged 'laws of imitation' against the very advocates of this thesis: for according to Vian's arguments, the common source should have resembled Quintus' version so much that one wondered why Quintus had taken on the task again.

On my part, I felt obliged to take the source-critical investigations into account, to compile as many presumed parallels as possible and to treat each passage chronologically in the narrative sequence of the *Posthomerica* before

---

36 Zintzen 1979, 39 ("A common source for both can only be postulated if one admits at the same time that either QS or Vergil has changed independently." – my translation).
37 Zintzen 1979, 30 n. 71 ("whether QS's colouring and presentation in related scenes can be meaningfully identified as having been developed from Vergil's description." – my translation).
38 Noack 1892b, 795.
39 Duckworth 1936.
40 Buchheit 1963, 193–197.
41 E.g., Keydell 1963; cf. Keydell 1931, 1935b, 1939, 1941; 1954; 1961; 1965; 1966; 1968.
42 Erbse 1961; 1971.

going any further.[43] I stressed from the beginning, however, that "it makes little sense to limit the study to purely 'motif-parallels' or to the question of possible common sources; rather, an attempt should be made to take into account the poetic principles of these late authors as well and to cautiously ask not only the question of simple knowledge but also that of *interpretatio, imitatio,* and *aemulatio.*"[44] Moreover, I explicitly anticipated what recent research on Quintus has highlighted as a new approach, namely counter-concepts and reader responses: "furthermore, if the reception is different, one will have to ask whether this is really proof against the knowledge of the *Aeneid* or whether there may not even be a counter-concept here. Finally, the reader must not be left out of the picture. The question is therefore whether Quintus, when he alluded to the *Aeneid*, did so in such a way that a knowledgeable reader noticed the transposition and was able to interpret it in an obvious way"; reference was also made to the methodology and results of intertextuality research that draws on Genette's analysis.[45] And especially in the summary, I argued again that the question of a common source is unproductive, that Quintus must be granted an independent creative spirit, that some of the designs can be understood as counter-reception to the *Aeneid* (Sinon, Trojans, Greeks), and that the text can be read as a return to the Greek past in times of political powerlessness. With regard to a possible (implied) reaction of the audience, it was pointed out that an educated reader who was familiar with the *Aeneid* could appreciate the differences, but that an understanding of the *Posthomerica* would not be impossible without knowledge of the *Aeneid* as subtext.

As far as methodology was concerned, it became obvious that each individual case had to be examined anew. The proposal that Vergil and Quintus draw on *one* common source could be excluded quite clearly; it was always obvious that Quintus handles the material independently. However, no 'proof' could be provided to endorse the view that the *Aeneid* functioned as a subtext for the *Posthomerica*, recognisable to the recipient. This realisation led to the following conclusion: "There is still much to be done, and the more one learns about Quintus' techniques and aims, the more likely it will be to answer the question of the sources — with all due caution against a circle. So far, however, the theory of the one common source is not convincing; one may still demand a Vergilian specificity for Quintus, but the 'proof' that Quintus did not read or could not read the *Aeneid* has yet to be provided. One will not want to think that Quintus

---

[43] Gärtner 2005.
[44] Gärtner 2005, 11 (my translation).
[45] Gärtner 2005, 39 (my translation).

'depended' on Vergil, or think that Quintus 'developed' the *Posthomerica* by drawing on the *Aeneid*, or explain all the parallels discussed in this book from the *Aeneid*, or speak of deliberate allusions – here one has certainly overestimated the importance of the Βεργίλλιος as ἄλλος Ὅμηρος; but one cannot completely deny the poet of the *Posthomerica* the knowledge, the adoption and implementation of individual motifs or scenes, as well as a certain confrontation with the national epic of the Romans."[46] For me, further considerations on intertexuality in a stricter sense did not seem to be justified by scholarly caution. This was sometimes criticised[47] – an issue discussed in the next section.

James has argued once again for the possibility that Quintus referred to the *Aeneid* and talked of prejudice, but he did not provide any new methodological arguments.[48] Carvounis recently gave an objective overview of the much-discussed Aeolus scene (Quint. Smyrn. 14.474–487; Verg. *Aen.* 1.34–87) and referred to "undeniable echoes," which made it difficult for a reader of ancient or modern times not to think of the *Aeneid*.[49]

3.4 The Question of intertextuality: The *Aeneid* as a 'subtext'

It was D'Ippolito who pleaded for a differentiated approach to clarify the relationship between the texts. He rightly pointed to different levels in the relationship of an author to his source when it came to the adoption of expressions, content, and narrative style: he therefore distinguished between knowledge, use, and imitation. In his opinion, in the case of Quintus one should think of more than just knowledge.[50] Today, actually, one is rightly cautious about asserting 'knowledge.'[51]

More recently, Vergilian intertextuality in Quintus has been discussed anew, by Cuypers, Bär, and above all Maciver.[52] The concept and its application to ancient texts cannot be dealt with here in general terms, neither can the fun-

---

46 Gärtner 2005, 286–287 (my translation).
47 E.g., Maciver 2009, 150–151. Looking back after so many years, I still think that it was useful to put the parallels and lines of motifs together. But written today, my book would certainly look different.
48 James 2007.
49 Carvounis 2019, lxiii–lxv; cf. Buchheit 1963, 193–197; Gärtner 2005, 261–272.
50 D'Ippolito 1976; 1985; 1988.
51 Cf. Bär in this volume.
52 Cuypers 2005; Maciver 2011; 2012a; 2012b.

damental problems concerning the instances of the author and the reader.⁵³ However, since the different understanding of these terms is also important for our question, a brief *excursus* is included here.

On intertextuality, author, and reader
Contrary to how it was originally conceptualised by Julia Kristeva, who coined the term, here I apply a narrower approach to *intertextuality*, as is common practice in classical philology. Namely, not every text is related to every other text as part of the universal intertext, but one can assume an (intentional), usually marked reference of one text to its subtext.⁵⁴

As for the *author*, we will of course never know what the empirical author wanted and knew. Nevertheless, the 'author,' having been banned, if not declared dead, has rightly returned as an authority in literary research.⁵⁵ In our context, what is helpful, for example, is Hinds' following remark: "therefore, while conceding the fact that for us as critics the alluding poet is ultimately and necessarily a figure whom we ourselves read out from the text, let us continue to employ our enlarged version of 'allusion,' along with its intention-bearing author, as a discourse which is good to think with — which enables us to conceptualise and to handle certain kinds of intertextual transaction more economically and effectively than does any alternative."⁵⁶ Of the newer approaches, that by Jannidis seems particularly useful to me; it is based on an "author picture"⁵⁷ and on author functions.⁵⁸ Jannidis claims the following functions of the author concept to be useful, maybe

---

53 Still interesting in our field: Conte 1986; Hinds 1998.
54 Cf., e.g., Schmitz 2007, 77–85; Bendlin 2006; in our context cf., e.g., Bär 2009, 36–43.
55 Cf. Jannidis/Lauer/Martínez/Winko 1999; Spoerhase 2007 gives a fundamental overview of the different author concepts.
56 Hinds 1998, 50.
57 Cf. Jannidis 2002, 27, defined the term as follows: "Die Summe alles Wissens eines Lesers über einen realen Autor. Der Begriff Wissen ist hier sehr weit zu nehmen; er umfaßt alle Annahmen und Spekulationen. Zu diesem Wissen gehören auch die Erinnerung an die Lektüreerfahrung und die Rückschlüsse auf den Autor aufgrund seines Textes. Die Organisation dieses Autorwissens ist eine spannende Frage. Es ist offensichtlich personal organisiert und hat narrative und typologische Aspekte." ("The sum of a reader's complete knowledge about a real author. The term 'knowledge' is to be taken very broadly here; it encompasses all assumptions and speculations. This knowledge also includes memories of reading experience and conclusions drawn on the author from his text. The organisation of this 'author knowledge' is an interesting issue. Obviously, it is organised in personal terms and contains narrative and typological aspects." — my translation).
58 With "author function" Foucault had addressed the function assigned to an author in the projection of a reader which eventually had to lead to the parting from the author; e.g., in his presentation on "Was ist ein Autor?," delivered in 1969, quoted according to Foucault 1988. Today, the term is used with a different aim than Foucault's, namely for analysis of the application of author reference in literary theory and practice. This ranges from mental operations within author construction to consideration of the real author and his self-staging. In any case,

even ineluctable:[59] 1. Selection 2. Composition 3. Meaning 4. Insight 5. Innovation, i.e., cognitive processes attributed by the reader to the 'author.'[60]

When I write about 'Quintus' in this article, I am aware that this is an 'author image.' Of course, every reader creates their own author image. However, when it comes to literary reading, an outward perspective is preferable; this might seem impossible, but it is nevertheless indispensable when we deal with ancient texts.[61] And we certainly need to examine the strategies a text pursues in order to create a specific author image and, therefore, a certain interpretation. While I am not convinced of approaches that only focus on biography in general, there is no doubt that a real author of these texts exists and must be classified in time and space, otherwise all interpretations will be pointless.[62] And so for me, it remains important to bear in mind how the material outlined at the beginning, concerning the reception of the Latin language and literature in the Greek world, can be interpreted in different ways.

Of course, the *reader* is also central to our topic. Here too, it is important to clarify beforehand what we are talking about:[63] are we talking about interactionist models, where the interaction between reader and text is central? And in this case, do we think of an implicit reader (Iser), i.e., the reader inscribed in the text,[64] or a model reader (Eco) capable of contributing towards the updating of the text as the author intended, so that a text can be fully updated in its possible content, or an ideal reader who has all the skills, attitudes, experience, and knowledge to gain the maximum or the greatest value from reading a given text?[65] Or, are we talking in the end about the intended reader, who has a documented existence both inside and outside the text?

However, if we look at subjectivist models, we can obtain a different perspective, where the reader himself is seen to be central for generating meaning (Barthes, Derrida).[66] This approach is a convincing way to understand cultural practices, because, as readers, we actually have the greatest possible power over the text; we can interpret it as we wish, we do not even have to read it. But a complete privileging of the reader opens the door to arbitrary association; this seems problematic for a philological investigation of intertextuality in the strict sense — at least for me. Of course, the difficulty also lies in the philologist's self-understanding as a reader; if we base our interpretation primarily on 'our' reading, it becomes difficult to give this interpretation the weight it needs in scholarly discourse.

Depending on one's point of view, the question of the cultural conditionality of the recipients also has to be dealt with. This concerns not only the difficult question of the

---

it is the achievements attributed to an author, real or constructed. For an overview see Hoffmann/Langer 2007, 136–139.
59 For instance, Jannidis 1999, 378.
60 Cf. Jannidis 1999, 378–389; for an overview, cf. Hoffmann/Langer 2007, 136–139.
61 Cf. Jannidis 2002, 28–29.
62 Cf. Jannidis 1999, 385–386; for such interpretative strategies in general, cf. Winko 2002.
63 For the various reader models see Willand 2014; 2018.
64 Iser 1974.
65 Eco 1979.
66 E.g. Derrida 1976, 158; Barthes 1988, 172.

reader of the *Posthomerica* in antiquity and his/her actual familiarity with Latin literature, but above all ourselves. For us, the *Aeneid* is the central or one of the most central texts of Latin literature; we usually learn Latin first, then Greek, consequently the *Aeneid* is typically read before Homer, probably, in any case, before the *Posthomerica*, i.e., we are preformed to a degree which is often overlooked.

The importance to elucidate these aspects becomes clear when we look at some newer approaches.

In his important commentary, Bär convincingly characterised intertextuality in the *Posthomerica*: "Die Intertextualität des Quintus erweist sich vielmehr als *arte allusiva* in alexandrinischer Manier, welche dem *lector doctus* ein beständiges Rezeptionsangebot zur Verfügung stellt, das von Stelle zu Stelle genützt werden *kann*, aber nicht *muss*, während die *enarratio qua enarratio* als solche ihren Gesamtsinn nicht einbüßt. Dem Text wohnt somit das Potential inne, sowohl einem intellektuell anspruchsvollen, gebildeten Publikum [...] als auch einer breiteren, weniger gebildeten Rezipientensicht gerecht zu werden."[67] This, of course, does not allow us to draw any conclusions about the relationship with Vergil's *Aeneid*, just as Bär only referred to parallels here. Fratantuono tried to show how Quintus describes the aristeia and death of Penthesileia in book 1, by manipulating and reversing the plot of Vergil's *Aeneid* book 11 which is "recast in a complex homage."[68]

Cuypers and Maciver went further in their approach, stressing the deviations as markers of negotiations with the Latin text(s). Cuypers had pointed out: "We should therefore perhaps entertain the possibility that large discrepancies between Q[uintus] and V[ergil] in story matter, and that the scant of evidence for allusion, are not the result of ignorance but of a well-considered 'political' scheme to ignore the Romans' national epic and supplant it with a Greek account of the end of the Trojan War, viewed from the Greek perspective."[69] For Hadjittofi, it was not important whether Quintus knew the *Aeneid* in the original, from summaries or only the material; she was interested in the cultural politics in the *Posthomerica*. By comparing the depiction of Aeneas and Sinon in

---

[67] Cf. Bär 2009, 69 ("The intertextuality of Quintus proves to be rather an *arte allusiva* in the Alexandrian manner, which provides the *lector doctus* with a constant offer of reception that *can* be used from place to place, but does not *have to be*, while the *enarratio qua enarratio* as such does not lose its overall sense. The text thus has the potential to do justice both to an intellectually demanding, educated audience [...] and to a broader, less educated class of recipients." — my translation).

[68] Fratantuono 2016, 230. He did not go into detail about the methodological problems.

[69] Cuypers 2005, 607. I myself had also argued for the possibility of a counter-concept. For the reinforcement of the approach see below, 23–24.

the *Aeneid* and the *Posthomerica*, she wanted to prove Quintus' "revision of Roman literature and ideology" and to demonstrate "the need of Quintus' text to perform and redefine a Hellenic cultural identity against (and through) Rome."[70]

But it was above all Maciver who opposed "historicising parameters" and the emphasis on the author's intention, and based his approach on intertextuality and the role of the reader.[71] As the discussion above about the return of the 'author' has shown, the differences are not that great, at least as far as the first point is concerned. Maciver started from the following premise: "There is no evidence beyond any doubt to suggest that Quintus did *not* use the *Aeneid*."[72] By focusing on the reader's role, he concluded that Vergil served as a supplementary code model (alongside Homer) and as an exemplary model which feeds into our reading of the *Posthomerica*.[73] This might not convince every scholar, since on the one hand the proof of a reference — be it an allusion or a deliberate deviation — should be a prerequisite, and on the other hand we as readers might be too strongly shaped by reading the *Aeneid* to be able to transfer *our* image of the epic code to the reader of the 3rd century CE without further ado. Maciver emphasises that the interpretation presented is his own reading[74] illustrates vulnerability of this method, specifically the difficulty to determine the criteria that distinguish arbitrary associations from valid interpretations. He nevertheless seemed to presuppose such criteria when he discussed the many possible readings "within realistic boundaries of common sense."[75] It would have been interesting to know how we can set and, above all, justify these boundaries.

Maciver has certainly been one who "tends to pursue a productively maximalist approach to Quintus and the Latin question."[76] Therefore, it came as a

---

[70] Hadjittofi 2007, 365 and 378.
[71] In Maciver 2011, he interpreted Aeneas' words to Dido (*Aen.* 6.460–463) as a subtext for the words of Helen to Menelaus in the reconciliation scene (14.154–164) stressing the deviation. These allusions may not seem unconvincing. However, in my contribution (Gärtner 2013) I tried to show that an almost irresolvable network of relationships of various parallels can be revealed, so that the singled-out deviation from the *Aeneid* actually does not seem to be that striking, or that it is no longer possible to clarify what was a code model and what was an exemplary model in all these variants. In his monograph he also assumed the *Aeneid* as a subtext, for example, in the representation of Neoptolemus: Maciver 2012b, 171–192.
[72] Maciver 2011, 692. For the lack of reliability of such arguments cf. 1.
[73] Maciver 2011, 692.
[74] Maciver 2012b, 12: "my Quintus is only a reading." This approach was taken up by Scheijnen 2018, 31–32. For the necessity to differentiate the reader function see above.
[75] Maciver 2012b, 13.
[76] See Greensmith, this volume, 76 n. 3.

surprise that he presented a palinode at a conference in Vienna in 2017; he now believes "that Q.S. and Nonnus most likely *did not* allude to, or indeed even use in a broader sense, Latin epic."[77]

3.5 New approaches

The works in this volume break new ground because they are no longer necessarily focusing on whether or not Quintus had or had not read the *Aeneid*, or even seeking to prove or disprove this. Rather, the contributors start from the premise that there was a relationship because of the cultural context in which these texts were produced, acknowledging that the authors somehow knew the Latin works and used this knowledge in their own creative ways. The material mentioned earlier[78] is taken as the basis for the premise that "it is possible that the Greek poets of the Late Antiquity were indeed familiar with crucial works of Latin poetry such as Vergil's *Aeneid* and Ovid's *Metamorphoses*, be it in the original or in translation."[79]

In some of the contributions the emphasis is now no longer on the search for parallels but on the differences; in short, the lack of striking direct parallels is now seen as deliberate and systematic disregard for the Roman national epic. Thus, although Bär admits "we do not (and will never) know for sure whether Quintus read the *Aeneid*," he sets as his premise that "at least some contemporary readers will have perceived the *PH* through the prism of Vergil's Roman epic."[80] Bär convincingly shows, on the basis of a narratological analysis of the Sinon-Laocoon episode (12.252–585), that through such a reading the text can be interpreted as having been de-Romanised. He sees this demarcation, however, less in the political sphere than in the literary-cultural one. Greensmith argues in a similar manner; she presupposes familiarity with Latin literature and thus assumes a "more capacious, Greek-and-Latin form of 'intertextuality.'" Here, however, the author is again at the centre; Greensmith's main focus is not on the question of how the imperial Greek authors used Latin models, and why, but why *not*. She sees non-engagement as a direct and loaded choice.[81] In two passages (Aeneas' escape from Troy, *PH* 13.300–332; the *testudo*, *PH* 11.358–360) she shows how these can be read as an examination and rewriting of Vergil's

---

77 In a message from October 22, 2020. See now Maciver (forthcoming).
78 Cf. section 1 (above).
79 See the editors' Preface in this volume (p. 4).
80 Bär, this volume, 58.
81 Greensmith, this volume, 85 and 78.

representation. Scafoglio takes a similar approach to Triphiodorus, which presupposes that the author is familiar with Vergil; in the text Scafoglio identifies "a kind of silent dialogue with a text that is not a model in the usual meaning of the word, but rather an unavoidable interlocutor. This is why it is so hard to provide evidence to such an intertextual relationship that assumes an atypical and elusive form."[82] Helen Lovatt does not raise the question of dependence in her contribution. Rather, she compares Flavian epic with imperial Greek epic in terms of their complex intertextual tactics. Furthermore, she can impressively show a relationship between Ovid's Phaethon and that of Nonnus, through the complex framing and through the poetics of playfulness, temporality, childhood, and succession. It becomes clear that the view of the reader, who can undertake such a comparison, makes for a most interesting reading.

Kersten is cautious about the relationship of the Orphic *Argonautica* to Latin poetry and would like to point out that "a reading with an eye on the Latin epic tradition will lead to some more differentiated description of the text. [...] As an intermediate step, it seems sensible not to exclude the possibility that Ps-Orpheus was influenced by Roman literature."[83] Papaioannou considers that the innovative character of the pantomime contest between Maron and Silenus in Nonnus *D*. 19.136–286 is mainly inspired by Vergil's *Eclogue* 6. This is important because it would be an interlingual literary appropriation between genres, charged with metapoetic performance. Carvounis adds a new aspect by comparing a Latin and a Greek opening passage in Claudian, which show how a poet uses two different literary traditions to achieve a different effect, depending on the context and the audience of the work.

4 Summary

What remains after this overview? Each approach has a number of problems, all of which raise scepticism; in every case a 'but what if' seems to come up – for example, but what if a common source did or did not exist after all, or alternatively but what if knowledge of, e.g., the *Aeneid* was or was not that widespread. The 'ifs,' i.e., the necessary but very different premises are the reason why the question is still open and why many scholars did not want to commit them-

---

[82] Scafoglio, this volume, 104.
[83] Kersten, this volume, 125–126.

selves, even changed their minds or at least indicated that they knew these 'but what if' moments well.[84]

Let us look back to the questions raised at the beginning (pp. 9–10). I hope it has become clear that we have to differentiate: if we look at the external criteria (cf. 1.) we can state that poets and recipients alike could have had 'access' to Latin texts — but there is no clear conclusion to be drawn; Latin poetry did certainly not play a role in the Greek-speaking world that corresponds to the reception of Greek literature by the Romans. As it turns out, the materials are still evaluated in different ways today; therefore, sceptics may be reluctant to accept the interpretations which take this premise for granted, while others may read them as a convincing methodological development.

Looking at the internal criteria, the texts themselves (cf. 2.), 'knowledge' or even 'ignorance' cannot be 'proven' in general. 'Use' seems plausible in many cases, but has hardly been definitively 'proven' so far. The much-maligned *Quellenforschung* could not solve the question of the reception of Latin works in the Greek epics of the imperial era. The same can be said about an approach of intertextuality. The very fact that most of the overlaps occurred in themes such as the conquest of Troy, Paris' Judgement, the abduction of Helen, the defending of Helen, Hero and Leander, which were among the most frequently used and well-known themes of antiquity, reminds us to be cautious. And again, the premises are pivotal.

Approaches that place reader-response at the centre seem at first to circumvent the question 'what does the author allude to?,' but the author returns as a construct of the recipient. If we want to justify our interpretation, we cannot avoid setting certain parameters for the recipient and the author.

Finally, approaches that focus on differences are actually the most difficult, because they require the author and/or reader (however we define them) to be familiar with the Latin texts, even if there are no markers in the text (at least none that are convincing for all scholars), so that a certain subtext must be read along with the text. Under certain external and internal premises, however,

---

[84] Thus Lesky spoke out first against (Lesky 1957–58), later on in favour of (Lesky 1971) knowledge, and West (e.g., West 1964) did not want to commit himself; even with the strongest representative of the common source theory, Vian, one senses such doubts: e.g., Vian 1959, 47: "une conclusion est nécessairement subjective: on ne peut exclure une imitation de Virgile par Quintus; mais on peut tout aussi bien supposer un modèle commun hellénistique" ("A conclusion is necessarily subjective: an imitation of Vergil by Quintus cannot be excluded, but a common Hellenistic model can just as well be assumed." — my translation). Maciver was already mentioned above (pp. 22–23).

coherent interpretations can be presented here which make, e.g., the *Posthomerica* comprehensible as a critical reading of the *Aeneid*.

As mentioned above, this has been an overview setting out the advantages and disadvantages, as well as the respective dangers of different approaches. The justified consideration of the poetology of the later Greek poets in more recent times has shown how these texts subtly allow their readers to read along about a thousand years of literature. Whether and how Latin literature must or can be included will probably continue to be the subject of lively debate.

Bibliography

Adams, J.N. (2003), *Bilingualism and the Latin Language*, Cambridge.
Adams, J.N./Janse, M./Swain, S. (eds.) (2002), *Bilingualism in Ancient Society. Language Contact and the Written Text*, Oxford.
Bär, S. (2006), Review of Gärtner (2005), in: *Museum Helveticum* 63, 220–221.
Bär, S./Baumbach, M. (2015), "The Epic Cycle and Imperial Greek Epic", in: M. Fantuzzi/ C. Tsagalis (eds.), *The Greek Epic Cycle and its Ancient Reception. A Companion*, Cambridge, 604–622.
Bär, S. (2009), *Quintus Smyrnaeus, 'Posthomerica' 1. Die Wiedergeburt des Epos aus dem Geiste der Amazonomachie. Mit einem Kommentar zu den Versen 1-219*, Göttingen.
Barthes, R. (1988), "The Death of the Author", in: D. Lodge (ed.), *Modern Criticism and Theory: A Reader*, London, 172–195.
Baumbach, M./Bär, S. (eds. in collaboration with Dümmler, N.) (2007), *Quintus Smyrnaeus. Transforming Homer in Second Sophistic Epic*, Berlin/New York.
Bechert, J./Wildgen, W. (1991), *Einführung in die Sprachkontaktforschung*, Darmstadt.
Becker, P. (1913), "Vergil und Quintus", in: *Rheinisches Museum* 68, 68–90.
Bendlin, A. (2006), "Art. Intertextuality", in: *Brill's New Pauly*. First published online at http://dx.doi.org/10.1163/1574-9347_bnp_e525570 [Consulted on 07 Nov. 2020].
Braune, J. (1935), *Nonnos und Ovid*, Greifswald.
Buchheit, V. (1963), *Vergil über die Sendung Roms. Untersuchungen zum Bellum Poenicum und zur Aeneis*, Heidelberg.
Carvounis, K. (2019), *A Commentary on Quintus of Smyrna, Posthomerica 14*, Oxford.
Carvounis, K./Hunter, R. (2008), "Introduction", in: K. Carvounis/R. Hunter (eds.), *Signs of Life? Studies in Later Greek Poetry, Ramus* 37, 1–10
Conte, G.B. (1986), *The Rhetoric of Imitation. Genre and Poetic Memory in Virgil and Other Latin Poets*, tr. from the Italian, ed. and with a foreword by C. Segal, Ithaca/London.
Cribiore, R. (2003/4), "Latin Literacy in Egypt", in: *KODAI Journal of Ancient History* 13/14, 111–118.
Cribiore, R. (2007), "Higher Education in Early Byzantine Egypt", in: R.S. Bagnall (ed.), *Egypt in the Byzantine World 300-700*, Cambridge, 47–66.
Cuypers, M. (2005), Review of James, A.W./Lee, K., *A Commentary on Quintus of Smyrna, Posthomerica V* [...] 2000, in: *Mnemosyne* 58, 605–613.

D'Ippolito, G. (1976), *Trifiodoro e Vergilio: il proemio della "Presa di Ilio" e l'esordio del libro secondo dell' "Eneide"*, Palermo.

D'Ippolito, G. (1985), "Fortuna di Virgilio nella Grecia antica", in: *Enciclopedia Virgiliana* II, 801–804.

D'Ippolito, G. (1988), "Quinto Smirneo", in: *Enciclopedia Virgiliana* IV, 376–380.

Derrida, J. (1976), *Of Grammatology*, tr. G. Chakravorty Spivak, Baltimore.

Duckworth, G.E. (1936), "Foreshadowing and Suspense in the *Posthomerica* of Quintus of Smyrna", in: *American Journal of Philology* 57, 58–86.

Eco, U. (1979), *The Role of the Reader: Explorations in the Semiotics of Texts*, Bloomington, IN.

Erbse, H. (1961), Review of Vian (1959), in: *Byzantinische Zeitschrift* 54, 368–370.

Erbse, H. (1971), Review of Vian III (1969), in: *Gnomon* 43, 563–568.

Fisher, E.A. (1982), "Greek Translations of Latin Literature in the Fourth Century A.D.", in: *Yale Classical Studies* 27, 173–215.

Foucault, M. (1988), "Was ist ein Autor?", in: K. v. Hofer/A. Botond (eds.), *Michel Foucault. Schriften zur Literatur, aus dem Französischen*. Second Edition, Frankfurt a. M., 7–31.

Fratantuono, L. (2016), "The Penthesilead of Quintus Smyrnaeus. A Study in Epic Reversal", in: *Wiener Studien* 129, 207–231.

Gärtner, U. (2005), *Quintus Smyrnaeus und die Aeneis. Zur Nachwirkung Vergils in der griechischen Literatur der Kaiserzeit*, Munich.

Gärtner, U. (2013), "Πιερίδες, τί μοι ἁγνὸν ἐφωπλίσσασθε Μάρωνα; Das griechische Epos der Kaiserzeit und die Bezüge zur lateinischen Literatur", in: Schubert (2013a), 87–146.

Greensmith, E. (2018), "When Homer Quotes Callimachus. Allusive Poetics in the Proem of the *Posthomerica*", in: *Classical Quarterly* 68, 257–274.

Hadjitoffi, F. (2007), "*Res Romanae*: Cultural Politics in Quintus Smyrnaeus' *Posthomerica* and Nonnus' *Dionysiaca*", in: Baumbach/Bär/Dümmler (2007), 357–378.

Hahn, L. (1906), *Roms Sprache und der Hellenismus zur Zeit des Polybius*, Leipzig.

Hahn, L. (1907), *Zum Sprachenkampf im römischen Reich bis auf die Zeit Justinians*, Leipzig.

Hahn, L. (1912), "Zum Gebrauch der lateinischen Sprache in Konstantinopel", in: A. Dyroff (ed.), *Festgabe für M. v. Schanz*, Würzburg, 173–183.

Heinze, R. (1915), *Virgils epische Technik*. Third Edition, Leipzig/Berlin.

Heyne, C.G. (1832), *Publius Vergilius Maro. Varietate lectionis et perpetua adnotatione illustratus a C.G.H.*, Editio quarta. Curavit G.P.E. Wagner. Vol. IV. *Carmina minora. Quaestiones virgilianae et notitia literaria*, Leipzig/London.

Hidber, T. (2006), "Vom Umgang der Griechen mit lateinischer Sprache und Literatur", in: *Paideia* 61, 237–254.

Hinds, S. (1998), *Allusion and Intertext. Dynamics of Appropriation in Roman Poetry*, Cambridge.

Hoffmann, T./Langer, D. (2007), "Autor", in: T. Anz (ed.), *Handbuch Literaturwissenschaft. I: Gegenstände und Grundbegriffe*, Stuttgart, 131–170.

Irmscher, J. (1984), "Die Einheit der antiken Literatur im Bas-Empire", in: J. Harmatta (ed.), *Actes du VIIe congrès de la Fédération Internationale des Associations d'Études Classiques*, II, Budapest, 275–282.

Irmscher, J. (1985), "Vergil in der griechischen Antike", in: *Klio* 67, 281–285.

Irmscher, J. (1986), "Wechselwirkungen zwischen den beiden antiken Literaturen im ausgehenden Altertum", in: *Acta Classica Universitatis Scientiarum Debreceniensis* 22, 87–98.

Iser, W. (1974), *The Implied Reader: Patterns of Communication in Prose Fiction from Bunyan to Beckett*, Baltimore.

James, A.W. (2006), Review of Gärtner (2005), in: *Classical Review* 56, 328–329.
James, A.W. (2007), "Quintus of Smyrna and Virgil. A Matter of Prejudice", in: Baumbach/Bär/Dümmler (2007), 145–157.
Jannidis, F./Lauer, G./Martinez, M./Winko, S. (eds.) (1999), *Rückkehr des Autors. Zur Erneuerung eines umstrittenen Begriffs*, Tübingen.
Jannidis, F. (1999), "Der nützliche Autor. Möglichkeiten eines Begriffs zwischen Text und historischem Kontext", in: Jannidis/Lauer/Martinez/Winko (1999), 353–389.
Jannidis, F. (2002), "Autor, Autorbild und Autorintention", in: *Editio* 16, 26–35.
Jolowicz, D. (2021), *Latin Poetry in the Ancient Greek Novels*, Oxford.
Kehmptzow, F. (1891), *De Quinti Smyrnaei fontibus ac mythopoeia*, Diss. Kiel.
Keydell, R. (1931), "Die griechische Poesie der Kaiserzeit (bis 1929)", in: *Jahresbericht über die Fortschritte der klassischen Altertumswissenschaft* 230, 41–161.
Keydell, R. (1935a), "Die Dichter mit Namen Peisandros", in: *Hermes* 70, 301–311.
Keydell, R. (1935b), Review of Braune (1935), in: *Gnomon* 11, 597–605.
Keydell, R. (1939), "Triphiodoros", in: *Real Enzyclopaedie* VII A. 1, 178–181.
Keydell, R. (1941), "Die griechische Dichtung der Kaiserzeit. 1930–1939", in: *Jahresbericht über die Fortschritte der klassischen Altertumswissenschaft* 272, 1–71.
Keydell, R. (1954), "Quintus von Smyrna und Vergil", in: *Hermes* 82, 254–256.
Keydell, R. (1961), Review of Vian (1959), in: *Gnomon* 33, 278–284.
Keydell, R. (1963), "Quintus von Smyrna", in: *Real Enzyclopaedie* XXIV, 1271–1296.
Keydell, R. (1965), Review of Vian I (1963) and Kakridis (1962), in: *Gnomon* 37, 36–44.
Keydell, R. (1966), Review of D'Ippolito (1964), in: *Gnomon* 38, 25–29.
Keydell, R. (1968), Review of Vian II (1966), in: *Gnomon* 40, 571–575.
Keydell, R. (1975), "Peisandros 8.–10.", in: *Der Kleine Pauly*, IV, 588.
Knight, W.F.J. (1932a), "Iliupersides", in: *Classical Quarterly* 26, 178–189.
Knight, W.F.J. (1932b), "Vergil's Troy. Essays on the Second Book of the *Aeneid*", Oxford.
Köchly, A. (1853), *Quinti Smyrnaei Posthomericorum libri XIV. Relegit A.K.*, Leipzig.
Kroll, W. (1902), "Studien über die Komposition der *Aeneis*", in: *Jahrbücher für das classische Altertum (Fleckeisens Jahrbücher)* 27 Suppl., 135–169.
Leone, P. (1968), "La "Presa di Troia" di Trifiodoro", in: *Vichiana* 5, 59–108.
Leone, P. (1984), "Ancora sulla "Presa di Troia" di Trifiodoro", in: *Quaderni Urbinati di Civiltà Classica* 6, 5–15.
Lesky, A. (1971), *Geschichte der griechischen Literatur*. Third Edition, Bern/Munich [First Edition: 1957/8].
Lovatt, H. (2006), Review of Gärtner (2005), in: *Journal of Roman Studies* 96, 255–257.
Maas, P. (1935), Review of Braune (1935), in: *Byzantinische Zeitschrift* 35, 385–387.
Maciver, C.A. (2009), Review of Gärtner (2005), in: *Anzeiger für die Altertumswissenschaft* 62, 149–151.
Maciver, C.A. (2011), "Reading Helen's Excuses in Quintus Smyrnaeus' *Posthomerica*", in: *Classical Quarterly* 61, 690–703.
Maciver, C.A. (2012a), "Representative Bees in Quintus Smyrnaeus' *Posthomerica*", in: *Classical Philology* 107, 53–69.
Maciver, C.A. (2012b), *Quintus Smyrnaeus' Posthomerica. Engaging Homer in Late Antiquity*, Leiden/Boston.
Maciver, C.A. (forthcoming), "Homer without Vergil (and Ovid): *Erwartungshorizont* and Late Antique Greek Epic", Turnhout.

Most, G. (2016), "The Rise and Fall of Quellenforschung", in: A. Blair/A. Goeing (eds.), *For the Sake of Learning. Essays in Honor of A. Grafton*, Leiden/Boston, 922–954.

Myers-Scotton, C. (1993), *Duelling Languages. Grammatical Structure in Codeswitching*, Oxford.

Nesselrath, H.-G. (2013), "Latein in der griechischen Bildung? Eine Spurensuche vom 2. Jh. v. Chr. bis zum Ende des 3. Jh. n. Chr.", in: Schubert (2013a), 281–319.

Noack, F. (1892), Review of Kehmptzow (1891), in: *Göttingischen Gelehrten Anzeigen (GGA)* 20, 769–812.

Norden, E. (1901), "Vergils Äneis im Lichte ihrer Zeit", in: *Neue Jahrbücher für das klassische Altertum* 4, 313–334.

Reichmann, V. (1943), *Römische Literatur in griechischer Übersetzung*, Leipzig.

Rochette, B. (1990), "Les traductions grecques de l'Énéide sur papyrus. Une contribution à l'étude du bilinguisme gréco-romain au Bas-Empire", in: *Les Études Classiques* 58, 333–346.

Rochette, B. (1993), "La diversité linguistique dans l'antiquité classique. Le témoignage des auteurs de l'époque d'Auguste et du Ier siècle de notre ère", in: L. Isebaert (ed.), *Miscellanea linguistica graeco-latina*, Namur, 219–237.

Rochette, B. (1994), "Traducteurs et traductions dans l'Égypte gréco-romaine", in: *Chronique d'Egypte* 69, 313–322.

Rochette, B. (1995a), "Grecs et Latins face aux langues étrangères. Contribution à l'étude de la diversité linguistique dans l'antiquité classique", in: *Revue Belge de Philologie et d'Histoire* 73, 5–16.

Rochette, B. (1995b), "Du grec au latin et du latin au grec. Les problèmes de la traduction dans l'antiquité gréco-latine", in: *Latomus* 54, 245–261.

Rochette, B. (1997), *Le latin dans le monde grec. Recherches sur la diffusion de la langue et des lettres latines dans les provinces hellénophones de l'Empire romain*, Brussels.

Rochette, B. (2006), Review of Gärtner (2005), in: *L'Antiquité Classique* 75, 327–329.

Rochette, B. (2008), Review of Gärtner (2005), in: *Latomus* 67, 245–249.

Scheijnen, T. (2018), *Quintus of Smyrna's Posthomerica. A Study of Heroic Characterization and Heroism*, Leiden/Boston.

Schmitt, R. (1983), "Die Sprachverhältnisse in den östlichen Provinzen des Römischen Reiches", in: *Aufstieg und Niedergang der römischen Welt* II.29.2, 554–586.

Schubert, P. (ed.) (2013a), *Les grecs héritiers des romains*, Vandœuvres, Geneva.

Schubert, P. (2013b), "L'apport des papyrus grecs et latins d'Égypte Romaine", in: Schubert (2013a), 243–279.

Schmitz, T. (2007), *Modern Literary Theory and Ancient Texts*, Malden/Oxford/Carlton.

Spoerhase, C. (2007), *Autorschaft und Interpretation. Methodische Grundlagen einer philologischen Hermeneutik*, Berlin/New York.

Szabat, E. (2015), "Late Antiquity and the Transmission of Educational Ideals and Methods", in: W.M. Bloomer (ed.), *A Companion to Ancient Education*, Malden, 267–278.

Tilg, S. (2010), *Chariton of Aphrodisias and the Invention of the Greek Love Novel*, Oxford.

Vian, F. (1959), *Recherches sur les Posthomerica de Quintus de Smyrne*, Paris.

Vian, F. (1963-9), *Quintus de Smyrne. La suite d'Homère*. Texte établi et traduit par F. Vian. Tome I. Livres I–IV, 1963; Tome II. Livres V–IX, 1966; Tome III. Livres X–XIV, 1969, Paris.

Wenskus, O. (2001), Review of Rochette (1997), in: *Gnomon* 73, 70–72.

West, M.L. (1964), Review of Vian I (1963), in: *Classical Review* 14, 257–259.

Whitmarsh, T. (2010), "Thinking Local", in: T. Whitmarsh (ed.), *Local Knowledge and Microidentities in the Imperial Greek World*, Cambridge, 1–16.
Willand, M. (2014), *Lesermodelle und Lesertheorien. Historische und systematische Perspektiven*, Berlin.
Willand, M. (2018), "Der Leser als/im Kontext interpretativer Zuschreibungen", in: U. Tischer/ A. Forst/U. Gärtner (eds.), *Text, Kontext, Kontextualisierung. Moderne Kontextkonzepte und antike Literatur*, Hildesheim/Zurich/New York, 81–100.
Winko, S. (2002), "Autor-Funktionen. Zur argumentativen Verwendung von Autorkonzepten in der gegenwärtigen literaturwissenschaftlichen Praxis", in: D. Detering (ed.), *Autorschaft. Positionen und Revisionen*, Stuttgart, 334–354.
Zintzen, C. (1979), *Die Laokoonepisode bei Vergil*, Wiesbaden.

Katerina Carvounis
The Poet as Sailor: Claudian between the Greek and Latin Traditions

Abstract: This paper focuses on the bilingual poet Claudian and the connection between sailing and poetry that he develops at the opening of his Greek *Gigantomachia* and in the preface to his Latin mythological epic *De Raptu Proserpinae* 1. It is argued that allusion to Hesiod's sea journey to Chalcis underscores the poet's confidence in the Greek *Gigantomachia* as he is heading to a poetic competition, whereas the imagery of the first sailor boldly distancing himself from the shore in the preface to *De Raptu Proserpinae* 1 is set within the context of programmatic statements and poetic development in Latin literature. This study aims to highlight Claudian's readiness to use the Greek and Latin literary traditions to different effect depending on context and audience, and to illustrate the poet's movement and flexibility between the two traditions.

Keywords: Claudian; Greek *Gigantomachia*; prefaces; seafaring imagery and poetry.

Discussions of the influence of Latin literature on later Greek poetry in the imperial period and Late Antiquity often focus on general trends that are based on evidence from a wider literary-historical context.[1] The few statements made by Greek-speaking authors on their familiarity with Latin must be assessed in their own context and with caution,[2] and claims by Roman authors implying that there were some, at least, Greeks who read Latin[3] can arguably be taken to point to exceptions rather than the rule. Evidence for the systematic teaching of Latin in the East before the fourth century is scanty, and surviving translations and glossaries for (parts of) Vergil's *Aeneid* on contemporary material (mainly 4th–

---

[1] For a recent, informed overview of some parameters involved in the debate see Gärtner 2013, 87–139.
[2] See, for example, the statements by Plutarch (*Dem.* 2.2–4) and Libanius (*Epist.* 1004, 1036) from different periods and different parts of the empire: for a recent discussion see Carvounis 2019, lviii–lix.
[3] See, for example, Aulus Gellius' description of learned Greeks as *homines amoeni et nostras quoque litteras haut incuriose docti* (Aul. Gell. 19.9.7) and Pliny's reference to Greeks who learnt Latin and read his hendecasyllables (Pl. *Epist.* 7.4): see Hose 1994, 78–79.

6th centuries) mostly offer literal renderings of the Latin text.[4] Given this uncertain context, scholars have been reluctant to explore further the influence of Latin texts upon later Greek literature. Moreover, it is difficult to establish linguistic echoes between Latin models and later Greek texts, and the argument that shared points may derive from earlier, now lost, Greek sources cannot be overlooked.

On the other hand, the information that Vergil had been translated into Greek in the reign of Claudius (first century CE) and again — probably — in the third century CE,[5] as well as the evidence of the so-called 'bilingual papyri' mentioned above, can be taken as indications that there was interest in reading Vergil's poetry in translation and in learning Latin from his poetry. Even if the few surviving statements made by authors on familiarity with Latin point to exceptions, it remains important that such exceptions did exist and that specific works of Greek literature that are scrutinised in terms of their relationship to Latin literature have stood out precisely because they are exceptional in some respect(s). Quintus' *Posthomerica* and Nonnus' *Dionysiaca* are two such works, and their engagement with Vergil's *Aeneid* and Ovid's *Metamorphoses* respectively can be further studied alongside that of their earlier Greek models.

This chapter focuses on Claudian as an example of a poet versed in both languages: apart from his numerous extant works in Latin, there also survive, and are attributed to him, several epigrams in Greek and two fragments from a *Gigantomachia*.[6] The Suda provides later testimony that the poet Claudian who lived at the time of Arcadius and Honorius was an Alexandrian: Suda κ 1707 Κλαυδιανός, Ἀλεξανδρεύς, ἐποποιὸς νεώτερος· γέγονεν ἐπὶ τῶν χρόνων Ἀρκαδίου καὶ Ὀνωρίου τῶν βασιλέων. Some information about his life and works at the end of the fourth century can be gauged from Claudian's own writings (but

---

[4] See Schubert 2013 for a clear discussion of this evidence.
[5] See Sen. *Dial.* 11.8.2, 11.11.5 for Polybius' translation of Vergil under Claudius; Suda α 3867 (with Swain 1991).
[6] For a detailed discussion of the MSS containing this *Gigantomachia* and for points of textual criticism see Livrea 2000, 416–417. For a detailed discussion of, and commentary on, Claudian's Greek epigrams see Weise 2013. I am grateful to Dr. Stefan Weise who kindly sent me an electronic copy of his (unpublished) doctoral thesis entitled *Die griechischen Gedichte Claudians* (Martin–Luther–Universität Halle–Wittenberg, 2013), which includes a thorough study of these epigrams and of Claudian's Greek *Gigantomachia*. I received the thesis after I had completed the penultimate draft for the present paper, and was subsequently able only to include references to relevant parts of the thesis.

not without uncertainties):⁷ on the basis of the prologue to his Greek *Giganto-machia*, where the poet refers to a performance before the people of Alexandria (see section 1, below), it is generally assumed that he performed in his native city before moving to Rome. Evidence linking him to Egypt and Alexandria in particular include his references to the Nile as *nostro... Nilo* (*Carm. min.* 19.3) and to "our common land" (*commune solum, Carm. min.* 12.56) when addressing a man from Egypt, as well as to Alexander the Great as founder of the fatherland (*conditor hic patriae, Carm. min.* 22.20), which is understood to be Alexandria.⁸ From Claudian's surviving works in Latin, his first composition for a Roman audience is taken to be the panegyric written for the consulship of Olybrius and Probinus in 395.⁹ He describes in a letter to Probinus how during the latter's consulship he accomplished the move from composing in Greek to composing in Latin:

> *Romanos bibimus primum te consule fontes*
> *et Latiae cessit Graia Thalia togae.*
>
> *Carm. min.* 41.13–14

When you were consul, I first drank from the Roman fountains
and my Greek Thalia put on the Latin toga. (tr. Ware 2004, 190)¹⁰

This is the year when the emperor Theodosius I died and was succeeded in the West by his (still very) young son Honorius (b. 384). In his subsequent career Claudian composed panegyrics celebrating the leading general Stilicho, who was an important figure in the West until his execution in 408.¹¹ Claudian's last

---

7 In what follows, I adopt the *opinio communis* on Claudian's origin as outlined most recently in Coombe 2018, 7–8. For a different view that questions Claudian's eastern origins see Christiansen 1997 and Christiansen/Christiansen 2009; see Mulligan 2007 for a detailed reply to Christiansen 1997 to confirm that Claudian's origin from the eastern empire remains "the best supported conclusion" (p. 307).
8 Coombe 2018, 7. For a brief overview of literary culture in Alexandria see Agosti 2014. See also Cameron 1970a, 4–6, where he argues that "Alexandria was no longer the only city in Egypt with either the schools or the literary traditions to turn out a poet" (p. 5).
9 Coombe 2018, 7.
10 For a discussion of Claudian's use of Thalia see Ware 2004, 189–191; see also Hinds 2013, 172 and Gualandri 2013, 116.
11 See Gruzelier 1993, xvii–xx, for a succinct and clear overview of Claudian's biographical information and his historical context; see also Guipponi-Gineste 2000, 8 (with n. 2) on what (little) is known about Claudian and his move from Alexandria to Italy. For a more detailed discussion see the seminal work by Cameron 1970a; some of his earlier points are revisited in Cameron 2000.

political work was a panegyric on the sixth consulship of Honorius in 404; he is believed to have died before the second consulship of Stilicho in 405, since this would have merited a poem.[12]

Claudian is not alone in composing in a language other than his native one at the end of the fourth century; Ammianus, known as the 'last Roman historian' and originating from the eastern part of the empire, may be another parallel from Late Antiquity.[13] An important inscription from a statue that was placed in the Forum of Trajan at the request of Arcadius and Honorius survives as external evidence for Claudian's literary activity,[14] and the following lines indicate that he was recognised in his time as a high-quality poet, who was thought to combine the best of both literary worlds represented by Vergil and Homer:

> Εἰν ἑνὶ Βιργιλίοιο νόον | καὶ Μοῦσαν Ὁμήρου |
> Κλαυδιανὸν Ῥώμη καὶ | βασιλῆς ἔθεσαν.
>
> Rome and her emperors set up Claudian: In one man, the mind of Vergil and the Muse of Homer. (tr. Coombe 2018, 2)[15]

---

12 Coombe 2018, 9.
13 Cameron 1970a, 316–320; see also Mulligan 2007, 286. On Greek-speaking poets and the Latin language cf. also, more recently, Cameron 2016, 23–25. On Statius as a "precedent" for Claudian's "mediation of the dialogue" between the Greek and Latin traditions see Parkes 2015, 473; cf. also Kaufmann 2015, 487.
14 [Cl(audii)] Claudiani v(iri) c(larissimi). | [Cla]udio Claudiano v(iro) c(larissimo), tri|[bu]no et notario, inter ceteras | [de]centes artes prae[g]loriosissimo | [po]etarum, licet ad memoriam sem | piternam carmina ab eodem | scripta sufficiant, adtamen | testimonii gratia ob iudicii sui | [f]idem, dd. nn. Arcadius et Honorius | [fe]licissimi et doctissimi | imperatores senatu petente | statuam in foro divi Traiani | erigi collocarique iusserunt. ("Of Claudius Claudianus v.c. To Claudius Claudianus v.c., tribune and notary, among other fitting skills the most outstanding of poets, although the poems written by this man provide eternal remembrance, yet to bear witness to his loyalty and his discretion, our lords Arcadius and Honorius, most blessed and learned emperors, by the request of the senate, ordered a statue to be erected and positioned in the forum of the divine Trajan"; tr. Coombe 2018, 1–2). See Christiansen/Christiansen 2009, 142–144 (see n. 7, above), for the view that these lines "are to be interpreted as allegorical references to Claudian's poems. The poem exhibiting the mind of Vergil would apply to the recently delivered political masterpiece on the consulship of Probinus and Olybrius. The poem exhibiting the Muse of Homer would suitably apply to the great mythological poem on the abduction of Proserpina. At this time, Claudian was being honoured as the poet he had been up to this point."
15 On this bilingual dedication see also Hinds 2013, 173. The association of Homer and Vergil is also found in the proem of Dracontius' *De raptu Helenae* (*Romul.* 8): see Pohl 2019, 154–156, for a relevant discussion.

The Poet as Sailor: Claudian between the Greek and Latin Traditions — 35

In a volume exploring possible influence of the Latin literary tradition upon later Greek literature, the choice to focus on Claudian may need further justification, for a poet composing in both languages is by default immersed into both the Greek and Latin literary traditions (and it seems more likely that this happened in that order in Claudian's case). The aim here, then, is not to examine whether one author may have been influenced by another; the question I would rather like to pursue within the scope of this volume explores how a poet composing in Greek and Latin uses the two literary traditions to different effect, depending on the context and audience of the work in question. For the main part of this chapter I shall focus on two opening passages by Claudian, which draw on the widespread analogy between sailor and poet, namely the preface to his Latin mythological epic *De Raptu Proserpinae* and the opening to his fragmentary Greek *Gigantomachia*.[16]

The practice of appending an independent preface to poetic works in Late Antiquity is common in both traditions. More than half of the books in Claudian's major hexameter poems in Latin have brief verse prefaces in elegiacs attached to them.[17] The development of formal prefaces in late antique hexameter poems has been connected with the voice of the poet that is evident in epic proems and in dedications or programmatic verses at the opening of poetic collections; as Gruzelier notes, by Statius' time, *topoi* common in later prefaces, such as the author's perceived modesty and compliments to the addressees, have already appeared.[18] On the Greek side of the tradition there is a strong tendency between the fourth and sixth centuries to compose a simple preface before an elevated and more complex composition, such as an encomium or ecphrasis; these prefaces were normally in iambics, which were more accessible than the hexameters of the main poem that followed,[19] but in Claudian's Greek *Giganto-*

---

16 Felgentreu 1999, 165: "Er beginnt seine griechische Gigantomachie als 'Eponaut' (ἐγὼ δέ τε δεινὸς ἀοιδός / μουσοπόλος ναύτης Ἑλικωνίδι νηὶ πιθήσας / ἰθύνω πρὸς ἄεθλα; c. gr. 1, 13–15), und in der *praefatio* zum rapt. Pros. kommt er auf dasselbe Bild zurück." See also Onorato 2008, 19; Weise 2013, II.66–69.
17 Harrison 2017, 236.
18 Gruzelier 1993, 79. For prefaces as a post-Augustan development see Harrison 2017, 236–238. On prefaces in the late antique Latin tradition see Sivan 1992 and (on Ausonius in particular) Scafoglio 2018.
19 An example often cited to illustrate this point comes from the prologue to a fourth-century funerary oration (*epicedion*) for a professor from Berytus, which has survived on papyrus (P. Berol. 10559B: *GDRK* 30A.31–32): καὶ νῦ]ν ἰά[μ]βων κωμικῶν πεπαυμέν[ος] / [ἡρῴ' ἔπη τ]ὸ λοιπὸν εἰσκυκλήσομ[αι. ("And now I have made an end of Comedy's iambics: for the rest, I shall wheel on to the stage my Heroic verse"; tr. Page 1942). See Agosti 2001, 223; Bajoni 2001, 111 (n. 9), who points to the important work by Cameron 1970b on iambic prologues.

machia, which will be discussed below, the preface is in hexameters like the rest of the poem. My purpose here in comparing this preface to that of Claudian's *De Raptu Proserpinae* 1 is to illustrate the poet's versatility as he draws on different models from the Greek and Latin traditions when using the imagery of the poet as sailor in different contexts.

1 The Preface to Claudian's Greek *Gigantomachia*

The Greek *Gigantomachia* opens with the poet contemplating a situation when he sailed in rough seas and the wind went quiet and the waves were lulled after he prayed to the sea-gods. The sailor recognised in this sudden change the work of a god and rejoiced, and his perception of divine intervention constitutes the link with a parallel drawn with the poet's own present experience as he seeks the help of Apollo, god of song and poetry, when he is about to embark upon his poetic journey that will culminate in prizes for his song. These are the first fifteen verses of a poem that otherwise describes a fight between gods and giants; when considered in the larger context, the divine power suggested in these opening verses prefigures the main plot of the poem, as the gods will be called to establish order in the cosmic battle against the giants.[20]

Let us then turn to the opening lines of Claudian's Greek *Gigantomachia*, which elaborate on this parallel between poet and sailor:[21]

εἴ ποτέ μοι κυανῶπιν ἐπιπλώοντι θάλασσαν
καὶ φρεσὶ θαμβήσαντι κυκώμενα βένθεα πόντου
εὔξασθαι μακάρεσσιν ἐσήλυθεν εἰναλίοισι,
φωνῆς δὲ πταμένης ἀνεμοτρεφὲς ἔσβετο κῦμα,
λώφησεν δ' ἀνέμοιο βοή, γήθησε δὲ ναύτης   5
ὀσσόμενος μεγάλοιο θεοῦ παρεοῦσαν ἀρωγήν·
ὣς † καὶ νῦν †, Δήλιε, † (σὺ γὰρ θεὸς ἔπλευ ἀοιδῆς) †
εὔξομαι αὐδήεντα κατὰ πλόον εὐεπιάων.
ἵλαθι καί μευ ἄκουσον, ἐπεὶ σέθεν εὐμενέοντος
παυρότερον δέος ἐστὶν ἐπ' ἐλπίσι λωιτέρῃσιν.   10
ὡς γὰρ δὴ πέλαγος μέγ' Ἀλεξάνδροιο πόληος
πάντοθεν ἐκτέταται, τάδε μυρία κύματα λαῶν

---

20 Coombe 2018, 106.
21 The text printed here is from Livrea 2000 with specific departures from Hall's 1985 Teubner edition briefly raised below. For stylistic features in Claudian's Greek fragmentary poem and their relationship to the Nonnian style in particular see Whitby 1994, 126–128 (with nn. on pp. 151–153).

ὄρνυτ' ἐπ' ἀλλήλοισιν, ἐγὼ δέ τε δεινὸς ἀοιδός
μουσοπόλος ναύτης Ἑλικωνίδι νηὶ πιθήσας
ἰθύνω πρὸς ἄεθλα, φέρω δ' ἔπι φόρτον ἀοιδήν.   15
                                            Gk *Gig.* 1–15

If ever it happened to me, as I sailed over the dark blue sea and was astonished at the seething sea depths, to pray to the blessed sea-gods, once my voice had flown, the wave, swollen by the wind, was lulled and the noise of the wind abated; then the sailor rejoiced, as he perceived the helpful presence of the great god. So now, too, Delian one — for you are the god of song — I pray for a vocal sea-journey endowed with eloquence.[22] Be propitious and listen to me, for if you are well disposed, fear is reduced on top of higher hopes. For as the great sea of Alexander's city extends from every side, these countless waves of people press upon each other, and I, a skilful singer,[23] a sailor trusting in the Heliconian ship and serving the Muses, am heading to the prizes and carry a song as freight. (my translation).

Despite textual difficulties in the middle of the passage,[24] the imagery conveyed in this prologue seems clear: the sailor is already out on the open sea (1–2) and prays to the sea-gods (3); when he discerns the wind going quiet and the waves being lulled (4–5), he recognises the presence of the divine and rejoices (5–6). The poet then turns to Apollo, god of poetry and song (7), as he is about to embark on a journey in eloquence (εὐεπιάων, 8) before countless people (12) in the city of Alexandria (Ἀλεξάνδροιο πόληος, 11). The poet is openly identified with a sailor (ἀοιδός... ναύτης, 14) and claims to be serving the Muses (μουσοπόλος, 14) on a Heliconian ship (Ἑλικωνίδι νηί, 14) as he intends to win prizes (ἄεθλα, 15) with his song (ἀοιδήν, 15).

From an early stage in the ancient literary tradition, seafaring imagery is linked with, and used as an analogy for, poetic activity; Pindar offers relevant examples: P. *N.* 3.26–28 (θυμέ, τίνα πρὸς ἀλλοδαπάν / ἄκραν ἐμὸν πλόον παρα-

---

[22] Hall prints εὐδιόωντα (participle of εὐδιάω, "to be fair or calm") for the MSS' αὐδήεντα.
[23] Cf. Hall's app. cr. (*ad loc.*): δειλὸς Ludwich: δεινὸς codd. The apparent contradiction between δεινὸς ἀοιδός and the δέος inherent in the dangerous undertaking account for the emendation δειλός (printed in Hall's Teubner edition). The phrase δεινός τ' αἰδοῖός τε (θ 21), however, supports the manuscripts' δεινός and Claudian here underscores his skill rather than his fear.
[24] See Livrea 2000, 431. In verse 7 Hall prints Ludwich's Διδυμαῖε (δή με codd.). See Livrea 2000, 428: ὥς L P, Köchly: ὡς M / δή με ω, unde Δήλιε *recte restituit Buecheler, at metrum laborat*: δὴ Φοῖβε Birt Zamora: Διδυμαῖε Ludwich Hall: Διδυμεῦ σε olim Ludwich / σὺ γὰρ θεὸς L Ludwich Birt Hall Zamora: σὺ γὰρ δὴ θεὸς M P: ὥς καὶ νῦν σέ, σὺ γὰρ δή μοι θεὸς Köchly: ὡς καὶ νῦν δὴ ἐγώ, σύ τε γὰρ θεὸς Schenkl: καὶ νῦν, Δήλιε, σοὶ (δὴ γὰρ θεὸς... Buecheler, *at totam sententiam ineptissimam laborare censet Livrea, qui* ὡς νῦν, Δήλι' ἄναξ, ὅς δὴ θεὸς ἔπλευ ἀοιδοῦ *fere temptaverit* / ἀοιδῆς P, at η ft. e corr., an ἀοιδοῦ voluit?).

μείβεαι; "my spirit, to which foreign headland do you turn my sailing?"), *Pyth.* 11.39–40 (ἤ με τις ἄνεμος ἔξω πλόου / ἔβαλεν, ὡς ὅτ' ἄκατον ἐνναλίαν; "or did some wind cast me away, like a small boat on the sea?").[25] This analogy assumes further metapoetic nuances in the Latin tradition, where the sailor's journey in the open sea is taken to illustrate the poet's ambitious endeavours (see section 2, below). In the preface to Claudian's Greek *Gigantomachia*, however, the sailor is already from the outset in the high seas;[26] the emphasis here is not on the sailor's journey outward, but rather on "prizes" (ἄεθλα, 15) and "waves of people" (μυρία κύματα λαῶν, 12; cf. ἀνεμοτρεφὲς... κῦμα, 4)[27] that constitute important additions to this imagery and suggest a competitive context.[28]

Such contexts for poetic performances have been established through archaeological excavations in Alexandria (with the Kom el-Dikka auditorium in particular),[29] while games and poetic contests are attested on contemporary papyrus fragments.[30] Such contests and performances are also represented in later Greek epic: in the funeral games for the dead Achilles in *Posthomerica* 4 Quintus departs from the Homeric models as he adds Nestor's uncontested victory in a performance of words (4.128–170),[31] and the first narrative of funeral games in Nonnus' *Dionysiaca* 19 includes a poetic competition between Erechtheus and Oeagrus, where the latter is proclaimed winner.[32] Both in Nestor's performance and in the competition between Erechtheus and Oeagrus attention

---

25 See Rosen 1990, 113 (n. 47), who also includes Theognis 969–970 (νηῦς ἅθ' ἑκὰς διέχω, "like a ship I stand apart") and Alcman *PMG* 1.94–5, where the Chorus-leader is likened to a ship's captain (τ[ῶι] κυβερνᾶται δὲ χρὴ / κ[ἢ]ν νᾶϊ μάλιστ' ἀκούην, "even on a ship it is necessary especially to give heed to the helmsman"); note, however, the apparatus criticus in Hutchinson 2001, 7 (on *PMGF* 1.95): "μάλιστ' ἀκούην (μαλιστακούεν) non legendum est."
26 As Weise 2013, II.67, also points out.
27 For the "waves of people" see *Il.* 2.144 κινήθη δ' ἀγορὴ φὴ κύματα μακρὰ θαλάσσης. From the epic tradition Livrea 2000 *ad loc.* compares further images of crowds in similar terms: *Il.* 4.422–427: ὡς δ' ὅτ' ἐν αἰγιαλῷ πολυηχέϊ κῦμα θαλάσσης / ὄρνυτ' ἐπασσύτερον Ζεφύρου ὕπο κινήσαντος / ... ὣς τότ' ἐπασσύτεραι Δαναῶν κίνοντο φάλαγγες; A.R. 4.214–215: ἐς δ' ἀγορὴν ἀγέροντ' ἐνὶ τεύχεσιν, ὅσσα τε πόντου / κύματα χειμερίοιο κορύσσεται ἐξ ἀνέμοιο; Triph. 109: λαῶν ὀρνυμένων ὅμαδον καὶ κῦμα φυγόντες; Nonn. *Par.* 4.147: στεινομένων νεφεληδὸν ἐπήτριμα κύματα λαῶν.
28 Cameron 1970a, 26 on the reference to a prize as an indication "that the poem was recited at a contest."
29 See Agosti 2006, 40; Agosti 2012, 377–378. On poetry and Alexandria in the Late Antiquity see Cameron 2016, 3–4.
30 See Rea 1996, 2, for references in the papyri to poetic competition. For games involving poetic and musical contests see Remijsen 2015.
31 On Nestor's performance see Appel 1993, 66–75 and Carvounis 2022.
32 On the poetic competition in *Dionysiaca* 19 see Carvounis/Papaioannou 2022.

is drawn to the reaction of the audience as they praise the winner (*Posthomerica* 4.171–172; *Dionysiaca* 19.106–115).

While Claudian's elaboration of the 'poet as sailor' *topos* in his Greek *Gigantomachia* points to the performative context of the poem, the final lines of this analogy and the poet's open identification as a "sailor serving the Muses" (μουσοπόλος ναύτης)[33] and trusting "in the Heliconian ship" (Ἑλικωνίδι νηί) recall Hesiod's self-referential statements at the opening of the *Theogony*, where the Heliconian Muses taught him how to sing (*Theog.* 1–35), and, especially, in the Hesiodic sphragis in the *Works and Days* (*Op.* 646 ff., esp. lines 654–662). Hesiod describes there the only sea-journey he ever undertook to travel from Aulis to Chalcis, where he successfully participated in funeral games.[34]

> Εὖτ' ἂν ἐπ' ἐμπορίην τρέψας ἀεσίφρονα θυμὸν
> βούληαι [δὲ] χρέα τε προφυγεῖν καὶ λιμὸν ἀτερπέα,
> δείξω δή τοι μέτρα πολυφλοίσβοιο θαλάσσης,
> οὔτε τι ναυτιλίης σεσοφισμένος οὔτε τι νηῶν.
> οὐ γάρ πώ ποτε νηὶ [γ'] ἐπέπλων εὐρέα πόντον,   650
> εἰ μὴ ἐς Εὔβοιαν ἐξ Αὐλίδος, ᾗ ποτ' Ἀχαιοὶ
> μείναντες χειμῶνα πολὺν σὺν λαὸν ἄγειραν
> Ἑλλάδος ἐξ ἱερῆς Τροίην ἐς καλλιγύναικα.
> ἔνθα δ' ἐγὼν ἐπ' ἄεθλα δαΐφρονος Ἀμφιδάμαντος
> Χαλκίδα [τ'] εἰσεπέρησα· τὰ δὲ προπεφραδμένα πολλὰ   655
> ἄεθλ' ἔθεσαν παῖδες μεγαλήτορες· ἔνθα μέ φημι
> ὕμνῳ νικήσαντα φέρειν τρίποδ' ὠτώεντα.
> τὸν μὲν ἐγὼ Μούσῃσ' Ἑλικωνιάδεσσ' ἀνέθηκα
> ἔνθα με τὸ πρῶτον λιγυρῆς ἐπέβησαν ἀοιδῆς.
> τόσσον τοι νηῶν γε πεπείρημαι πολυγόμφων·   660
> ἀλλὰ καὶ ὣς ἐρέω Ζηνὸς νόον αἰγιόχοιο·
> Μοῦσαι γάρ μ' ἐδίδαξαν ἀθέσφατον ὕμνον ἀείδειν.
>   *Op.* 646–662

If you turn your foolish spirit to commerce and decide to flee debts and joyless hunger, I shall show you the measures of the much-roaring sea, I who have no expertise at all in either seafaring or boats. For never yet did I sail the broad sea in a boat, except to Euboea from Aulis, where once the Achaeans, waiting through the winter, gathered together a

---

33 For μουσοπόλος in the later poetic tradition note Opp. *Hal.* 1.680 (μουσοπόλων ἔργων), Nonn. *D.* 45.185 (μουσοπόλος Πάν), GDRK (*laudes Theonis gymnasiarchi*) in *P.Oxy.* 7.1015, lines 1–6.
34 Weise 2013, II.29 and II.53–54, makes an interesting point about Claudian's techniques of *imitatio cum variatio* and *oppositio in imitando* in the first line of his *Gigantomachia* (εἴ ποτέ μοι κυανῶπιν ἐπιπλώοντι θάλασσαν) with respect to Hes. *Op.* 650 (οὐ γάρ πώ ποτε νηί γ' ἐπέπλων εὐρέα πόντον).

great host to sail from holy Greece to Troy with its beautiful women. There I myself crossed over into Chalcis for the games of valorous Amphidamas – that great-hearted man's sons had announced and established many prizes – and there, I declare, I gained victory with a hymn, and carried off a tripod with handles. This I dedicated to the Heliconian Muses, where they first set me upon the path of clear-sounding song. This is as much experience of many-bolted ships as I have acquired; yet even so I shall speak forth the mind of aegis-holding Zeus, for the Muses taught me to sing an inconceivable hymn. (tr. Most 2006).

Although Hesiod announces that he will unravel "the measures of the much-roaring sea" (*Op.* 648), he claims limited first-hand experience of seafaring, since the voyage he cites – from Aulis to Chalcis – was very brief and he thus indirectly gives credit, once again, to the Muses.[35] The mention of Aulis as his starting-point has been taken as an allusion to the Trojan War (*Op.* 651–653), with Hesiod's use of the epithets ἱερή and καλλιγύναιξ (acc. -κα) for the nouns Ἑλλάς and Τροίη (respectively) apparently inverting the Homeric use of these epithets for the same nouns (e.g., Ἑλλάδα καλλιγύναικα, *Il.* 2.683; Ἴλιον ἱρήν, *Il.* 4.416).[36] This has been interpreted as a hint of an implicit competition between Hesiod and the Homeric tradition,[37] highlighting the poetological significance of verses 650–659 as a self-conscious "declarative program" about poetry.[38] The motivation for Hesiod's journey from Aulis is explained with a piece of 'autobiographical' information: he states that he participated in the funeral games for Amphidamas and that he composed a poetic work (ὕμνος) to celebrate his victory in these games;[39] this work earned him a tripod (τρίπους ὠτώεις) as a prize (*Op.* 654–657), which he dedicated to the Heliconian Muses at the place where they first taught him how to sing (*Op.* 658–659).[40] It is precisely because the Muses inspired him that Hesiod claims, in conclusion, that he can

---

35 See Rosen 1990, 101–102.
36 See Canevaro 2015, 130–132 (with further bibliography), for this allusion.
37 See Nagy 1982, I.66 and Rosen 1990, 99–100. See Steiner 2005, 349, on the scholia to this passage anticipating this reading by Nagy and Rosen, as they cite a variant to verse 657 where Hesiod announces his victory over Homer (see Nagy 2009, 304). See Bassino 2019, 5–7, for *Op.* 648–662 and the tradition of Hesiod's contest with Homer.
38 Rosen 1990, 100.
39 West 1978, 321 (on *Op.* 657: ὕμνῳ), where he notes that "the word is not yet specialised in the sense 'hymn' but may be used equally of narrative and didactic poetry." He also adds (*loc. cit.*) that "[t]he poem Hesiod recited may have been the *Theogony*, or a version of it."
40 West 1978, 322 (on *Op.* 659). This tripod that Hesiod dedicated to the Muses on Helicon was still visible at the time of Pausanias (9.31.3), who describes it as the oldest of the dedications on display: Hunter 2006, 19.

read the mind of Zeus, as he puts it, that is, the wind and weather that govern seafaring and are, in turn, governed by Zeus.[41]

Hesiod credited the Muses with the extraordinary inspiration (*Theog.* 30–34) that allowed him to describe the beginning of the world and the subsequent struggles of Zeus and the Olympians in the *Theogony*, and he honoured these same Muses in the *Works and Days* (*Op.* 658: ἐγὼ Μούσησ' Ἑλικωνιάδεσσ' ἀνέθηκα) in the context of his victory in the games for Amphidamas (*Op.* 654: ἄεθλα... Ἀμφιδάμαντος). Both the imagery and verbal resonances in verses 14–15 of Claudian's preface show him heading towards prizes (15: ἰθύνω πρὸς ἄεθλα) as another Hesiod, a servant of the Muses trusting in Helicon's timber (14: μουσοπόλος ναύτης Ἑλικωνίδι νηὶ πιθήσας). In bringing to the foreground Hesiod's elaborate "self-referential statement of poetics"[42] from the *Works and Days* and in engaging with what may be seen as the earliest poetological imagery of seafaring in Greek literature, Claudian underscores his confidence as he prepares to perform and sing about the struggles of Zeus and the Olympians against the Giants and, like Hesiod, claim victory in a competitive context.

2 Claudian's preface to *De Raptu Proserpinae* 1

The first two books of Claudian's mythological epic *De Raptu Proserpinae* both open with prefaces in elegiacs. Here is the preface to *De Raptu Proserpinae* 1 (verses 1–12):[43]

> *Inventa secuit primus qui nave profundum*
>   *et rudibus remis sollicitavit aquas,*
> *qui, dubiis ausus committere flatibus alnum,*
>   *quas natura negat, praebuit arte vias,*
> *tranquillis primum trepidus se credidit undis*   5
>   *litora securo tramite summa legens;*
> *mox longos temptare sinus et linquere terras*
>   *et leni coepit pandere vela Noto;*
> *ast ubi paulatim praeceps audacia crevit*
>   *cordaque languentem dedidicere metum,*   10

---

41 West 1978, 322 (on *Op.* 661).
42 Tsagalis 2006, 103, where the poetological reading put forward by Nagy 1982 and expanded by Rosen 1990 (see n. 38 above) is further discussed.
43 Text by Charlet 1991/2020.

> *iam vagus irrumpit pelagus caelumque secutus*
> *Aegaeas hiemes Ioniumque domat.*
>
>   *DRP praef.* 1–12

He who first cut the deep with the ship he had invented and disturbed the waters with rough-hewn oars, who dared to commit his vessel of alder-wood to the unreliable blasts and made available by his art ways which nature denies, at first trusted himself trembling to the calm waves, coasting along the edge of the shores on a safe course; soon he began to try out vast bays, to leave the land and spread his sails to the mild south wind; but when, little by little, his impetuous boldness grew and his heart forgot sluggish fear, roving now far and wide he burst upon open water, and, following the sky, mastered Aegean storms and the Ionian Sea. (tr. Gruzelier 1993).

In the Latin tradition, the analogy between seafaring and the composition of poetry comes to the foreground in the Augustan period in particular,[44] and Vergil's address to Maecenas in *Georgics* 2.39–46 has been taken to offer a metapoetic comment on the poet's engagement with his subject matter and choice of genre:[45]

> *tuque ades inceptumque una decurre laborem,*
> *o decus, o famae merito pars maxima nostrae,*   40
> *Maecenas, pelagoque volans da vela patenti.*
> *non ego cuncta meis amplecti versibus opto,*
> *non, mihi si linguae centum sint oraque centum,*
> *ferrea vox. ades et primi lege litoris oram;*
> *in manibus terrae. non hic te carmine ficto*   45
> *atque per ambages et longa exorsa tenebo.*
>   *G.* 2.39–46

And you, Maecenas, my pride, my justest title to fame, come and traverse with me the toilsome course I have essayed, and spread your sails to speed over an open sea. Not mine the wish to embrace all the theme within my verse, not though I had a hundred tongues, a hundred mouths, and a voice of iron! Draw nigh, and skirt the near shoreline–the land is close at hand. Not here will I detain with songs of fancy, amid rambling paths and lengthy preludes. (tr. Fairclough/Gould 1990).[46]

Vergil invites Maecenas first to set sail with him for the open sea (41); however, after referring to the exhaustiveness of his subject (42–44), he invites his ad-

---

[44] Minissale 1975–1976, 496.
[45] On seafaring as analogy for poetry from Pindar to the Latin poets see Wimmel 1960, 227–231.
[46] On Vergil's use of the 'many-mouths' motif in these verses see Gowers 2005, 172; for its Iliadic model see the *Excursus* (below).

dressee to stay close to the shoreline (44–45), promising to avoid fiction, digressions, and long introductory material. Mynors has interpreted this move as indicative first of the expanse of Vergil's proposed subject and then of his choice to avoid technicalities.[47] Thomas, by contrast, takes the reference to the open sea in verse 41 to indicate that Vergil regards the poem "as a large-scale, even epic, project,"[48] and has argued for the *Georgics* as a poem of transition between the *Eclogues* and the *Aeneid*.[49] The speech that Phoebus addresses to the poet in the first part of Propertius 3.3 corroborates this interpretation:[50] not unlike Callimachus in his *Aetia* (fr. 2.1–2 Pfeiffer), the poet dreamt that he was on Mount Helicon preparing to compose epic poetry, when Apollo advised him to write elegy instead, a shorter and more familiar genre:[51] in deploying imagery from sailing, the god of poetry points to the poet's small boat (*cumba*, 3.3.22)[52] and asks him to remain in the safety of the shallow waters by keeping one oar in the water and the other in the sand, and thus to find safety near the shore rather than put himself in danger by sailing out in the open sea:[53]

> *cur tua praescriptos evecta est pagina gyros?*
> *Non est ingenii cumba gravanda tui.*
> *alter remus aquas alter tibi radat harenas,*
> *tutus eris: medio maxima turba mari est.*
> Prop. 3.3.21–24

Why has your page veered from the prescribed orbit? The little bark of your genius must not be burdened with a heavy load. With one oar skimming the waters, the other scraping the sand, you will be safe: out in mid-sea occur the roughest storms. (tr. Goold 1990).

---

47 See †Mynors 1990, 105 (*ad* 41), on Vergil's "two different, but not inconsistent, points," indicating first that this is a large subject and "we will hoist full sail" and then that "it is expert, factual work and we will not launch on a sea of technicalities, but will make sure that we can stop when we wish to (45–6, 4.117)."
48 Thomas 1988, 163 (*ad* 41–5). See also Thomas 1998, 2, where he takes the passage discussed here (*G.* 2.39–46) as suggesting "a poem of epic proportions."
49 Thomas 1988, 1–3; Thomas 1999, 111–112.
50 Thomas 1999, 111–112.
51 Propertius shows himself unwilling to sail in the open sea again in Prop. 3.9.3–4 (and 3.9.35–36): cf. Heyworth/Morwood 2011, 184 (and 191, 274), and Wimmel 1960, 231, who notes the echo between Prop. 3.9.35 and Verg. *G.* 2.42 (*non ego*...). For the suggestion of "generic ascent" in Prop. 3.9 and Verg. *G.* 2.39–46 see the discussion in Wallis 2018, 70.
52 See Heyworth/Morwood 2011, 119 (*ad* 21–24 *cumba*).
53 See Wimmel 1960, 230–231. See also Hor. *C.* 4.15.1–4, where it is Phoebus, again, who advises the poet against setting out to the Tyrrhenian Sea with small sails (4.15.3–4: *ne parva Tyrrhenum per aequor / vela darem*), in a line that echoes Verg. *G.* 2.41 (*pelagoque volans da vela patenti*).

The idea that only expert crews venture to go out in the open sea away from the coast is described at length in the first simile in book 6 of Statius' *Thebaid* in a passage that has no obvious programmatic function (6.23–24: *at cum experta cohors, tunc pontum irrumpere fretae / longius ereptasque oculis non quaerere terras*).[54] At the end of the third century CE, however, Nemesianus opens his *Cynegetica* with an exhaustive list of mythological topics that have already been covered in poetry, and he uses this sailing imagery in an openly programmatic way for the new paths he will define with his own poetry on hunting:[55]

> *talique placet dare lintea curae,*
> *dum non magna ratis, vicinis sueta moveri*
> *litoribus tutosque sinus percurrere remis,*
> *nunc primum dat vela Notis portusque fideles*
> *linquit et Hadriacas audet temptare procellas.*
>
> Cynegetica 58–62[56]

> For such a task it is our resolve to set sail, while our little barque, wont to coast by the neighbouring shore and run across safe bays with the oar, now first spreads its canvas to southern winds, and, leaving the trusty havens, dares to try the Adriatic storms. (tr. Duff/Duff 1935).

From Vergil and Propertius to Nemesianus and Claudian, the contrast between the safety of the coast and the dangers of the open sea is used in programmatic statements to describe the poet's choice of genre or subject. What is distinctive, however, with Claudian's *praefatio* is that he combines this programmatic analogy of the poet as a courageous sailor who distances himself from the coast with the boldness of the first sailor, for the main character in the *praefatio* both tries the sea in the first place and gradually moves away from the shore. In the literary tradition, while negative sentiment is often directed against the first ship (Argo) and the changes it brought to mankind,[57] the bravery and toughness of

---

54 Translation by Shackleton Bailey 2003, 329: "[B]ut when their crews are trained, then confidently they break far into the main nor does their gaze seek the lost land."
55 See Minissale 1975–76, 497, where reference is made to Nemesianus' *Cynegetica* 58–64 as the closest precedent to the *praefatio* of *De Raptu Proserpinae* 1. See also Charlet 1991/2020, 5.
56 The text is from Jakobi 2014.
57 For negative sentiment expressed against the Argo cf. Ov. *Am.* 2.11.1–2. Neptune in Valerius' *Argonautica* foresees the banes that Argo has devised for "unhappy nations" (Val. Fl. 1.648–649) and Statius' Thetis dwells on the negative repercussions of seafaring (Stat. *Achill.* 1.61–65). Cf. also Prop. 1.17.13–14, Stat. *Silv.* 3.2.61–64. See Nisbet/Hubbard 1970, 49 (*ad* Hor. *C.* 1.3.12: *primus*); Charlet 1991/2020, 4–5. On the Greek side of the tradition see Eur. *Medea* 1–5,

the first sailor are also a *topos* in references to sailing.⁵⁸ Claudian's preface likewise states from the outset the boldness of the first sailor who dared (*ausus*, 3) commit his ship to the winds and overcome nature with his skill. He then describes how this confidence gradually gained in strength:⁵⁹ although at first trembling (*trepidus*, 5) and trusting himself to calm waves (*tranquillis... undis*, 5), the sailor then spread his sails to the mild south wind (*leni... Noto*, 8) and ended up mastering Aegean storms (*Aegaeas hiemes*, 12). From staying close to the coastline, he began (*coepit*, 8) to distance himself from the land and by the end is roving far and wide (*vagus inrumpit pelagus*, 11). The emphasis here is both on beginnings (*inventa... nave*, 1; *primus... primum*, 1, 5; *rudibus remis*, 2) and on the sailor's daring (*ausus*, 3; *audacia crevit*, 9), innovation (*arte*, 4), and achievements (*dedidicere metum*, 10; *vagus inrumpit pelagus*, 11; *hiemes... domat*, 12).

Whereas the narrators in *Georgics* 2.39–46 and Propertius 3.3.21–24 remain close to the shore and to their familiar literary genre, the sailor's ambitions in the preface to *De Raptu Proserpinae* 1 are not restrained. Claudian's readers are left to draw out for themselves the second part of the analogy between sailor and poet.⁶⁰ Minissale's article drew attention to Claudian's subtle colouring of the sailor,⁶¹ and scholars subsequently engaged with the poetological significance of this particular imagery here: on one level, the sailor's move has been seen to reflect the poet's progression from shorter compositions of occasional poetry to long mythological epic;⁶² on another level, the analogy in this preface can be seen as a statement pointing to the poet's move between languages, for, as Felgentreu has put it, the Greek from Alexandria has successfully dared to master Latin poetry and considers himself now ready to write a Latin epic.⁶³

---

where the Nurse reviews Medea's situation in Corinth and wishes that the Argo had never gone to Colchis.
58 Cf. Hor. *C.* 1.3.9–12: *illi robur et aes triplex / circa pectus erat, qui fragilem truci / conmisit pelago ratem / primi* ("oak and triple bronze was around his breast who first entrusted a fragile ship to the fierce sea"; tr. Ware 2004, 184); Sen. *Med.* 301–304: *audax nimium qui freta primus / rate tam fragili perfida rupit / terrasque suas post terga videns / animam levibus credidit auris* ("Too venturesome the man who in frail barque first cleft the treacherous seas and, with one last look behind him at the well-known shore, trusted his life to the fickle winds"; tr. Ware 2004, 184).
59 Note the sequence *primus... mox... iam* and the force of *paulatim*.
60 As Gruzelier 1993, 81, puts it: "Interestingly, there is no explanation of the metaphor at the end of the preface making direct reference to the poet himself."
61 Minissale 1975–6, 498.
62 Gruzelier 1993, 81. See also Harrison 2017, 241; Formisano 2017, 221; Felgentreu 1999, 165.
63 Felgentreu 1999, 167: "Der Grieche aus Alexandria hat es erfolgreich gewagt, die lateinische Poesie zu meistern, und er hält sich jetzt für reif genug, ein lateinisches Epos zu schreiben."

According to this reading, then, the safety of the shore initially sought after by the trembling sailor stands for composition in Greek, to which Claudian is presumably accustomed, but his triumphant sailing in the open sea shows him gradually gaining confidence in Latin hexameters too.[64]

The reference to both the Aegean and the Ionian Sea might be hinting at a move between the two worlds,[65] but the programmatic placement of this *praefatio* and the parallel passages with shared imagery that were mentioned earlier rather point to a generic ascent. Elsewhere in his longer poems Claudian deploys varied imagery to elaborate on his own poetic development: not far from the imagery of the sailor going out in the open sea there is that of a young eagle that is tested before it becomes Jupiter's bird, like the poet about to face the emperor (*III. Cons. Hon., praefatio*), while in other works he is represented as an accomplished singer, either Orpheus himself (*De Raptu Proserpinae 2, praefatio*) or, in a dream, a singer of the Typhonomachy before the gods (*VI. Cons. Hon., praefatio*).[66]

As Charlet notes, it is not easy to draw correspondences between the sailor's gradual move from the shores to the open sea (*primum*, 5; *mox*, 7; *ast ubi*, 9) and Claudian's own poetic production.[67] Given the programmatic status of this *praefatio* and the overwhelming confidence it adumbrates, as it refers specifically to the first sailor who dares not only to set sail, but also to distance himself from the shore, it seems plausible to read it along the lines of previous similar statements in the tradition of literary progression, where epic is regarded as the

---

[64] In both cases the 'poet as sailor' metaphor as expressed in this preface has been used to point to an earlier chronology for the composition of *De Raptu Proserpinae*, setting it closer to Claudian's arrival to Rome from Alexandria (at around 395 CE). For attempts to connect this preface with the poet's own circumstances see, e.g., Harrison 2017, 242, for "some autobiographical colour" inherent in the allusions to the Ionian and the Aegean seas, and Gruzelier 1993, xvii, on the "purely personal nature of th[is] first preface, without any reference to a patron or audience," which may help place *De Raptu Proserpinae* 1 "before Claudian achieved extensive senatorial patronage in 395"; *contra* Onorato 2008, 13, who underlines that it is rare for Claudian to include the dedicatee's name in the first preface.

[65] See Hinds 2013, 179, for the suggestion that Claudian may be moving along a "horizontal" axis in addition to a "vertical" one. However, as Charlet 1991/2020, 84, points out, the Aegean is often associated with the Ionian Sea in descriptions of ships sailing and of tempests, as, for instance, in Stat. *Achill*. 1.35 (*Ionium Aegaeumque*) and Stat. *Silv*. 15.157 (*Ionium Aegaeo miscet mare*) respectively.

[66] See Ware 2004, 185–186; see also Coombe 2018, 1, for further instances of Claudian's self-presentation in his works.

[67] Charlet 1991/2020, xx–xxii (with further bibliography).

crowning literary achievement. The final lines of Vergil's *Georgics*, which identify the poet, convey this sense of progression:

> *illo Vergilium me tempore dulcis alebat*
> *Parthenope studiis florentem ignobilis oti,*
> *carmina qui lusi pastorum audaxque iuventa,*
> *Tityre, te patulae cecini sub tegmine fagi.*[68]
>
>   G. 4.563–566

> In those days I, Virgil, was nursed by sweet Parthenope, and rejoiced in the arts of inglorious ease – I who toyed with shepherds' songs, and, in youth's boldness, sang of you, Tityrus, under the canopy of a spreading beech. (tr. Fairclough/Goold 1999). [69]

Claudian thus inscribes himself within the Vergilian tradition of literary progression and this "symbolic ship of poetry," as Harrison puts it, "represents a transition... to traditional mythological narrative, marking an upward progression through the hexameter genres in the manner of Vergil."[70] The combination in this *praefatio* of the boldness of the first sailor and his gradual distancing from the coast, which culminates in a confident sense of triumph, draws attention to Claudian's own achievement, as there is a clear sense from the outset of *De Raptu Proserpinae* 1 that this is something new, different and extraordinary in his poetic corpus.[71]

In the Latin *praefatio*, then, Claudian makes no mention of prizes and competition; the poet elaborates on a familiar theme from the earlier Latin tradition and describes the first sailor's brave movement away from the shore, pointing to the poet's literary progression as he moves to the higher mythological epic. By contrast, in the opening verses of the Greek *Gigantomachia*, Claudian's emphasis is on prizes, performance, victory and the Muses, and the allusion to the Hesiodic *sphragis*, which reminds the reader of Hesiod's confidence gained from the earlier success of the *Theogony*, underscores Claudian's own confidence for the imminent poetic competition.

---

68 See Harrison 2017, 241–242, where he draws attention to Statius' *praefatio* to his *Silvae* 1 with "upward moves of Homer and Vergil from the parodic *Batrachomyomachia* and *Culex* to their serious poems" (p. 242). On Vergil's "literary career" see Hardie/Moore 2010, 1–16 (esp. 4–5).
69 On Vergil's depiction here as a pastoral poet both in the sense that he is a poet who describes musical shepherds within his works and in the sense that he is himself a musical shepherd see Hunter 2006, 126–127.
70 Harrison 2017, 251.
71 As Formisano 2017, 221, argues, Claudian uses the theme of displacement to underline his *novitas*.

This juxtaposition of Claudian's different elaborations of the 'poet as sailor' analogy exhibits his command of both languages and both literary traditions before different audiences. This is what one would expect from a Greek-speaking and Greek-educated poet who was as prolific in Latin and as successful in Rome as Claudian was; yet it remains a point worth recalling in face of hesitation often displayed in scholarly discussions of Latin influence on later Greek poetry, for Claudian may be exceptional but surely not unique. It is hoped, therefore, that in further discussions of notable divergences between later Greek poets and their possible Latin models this brief illustration of Claudian's engagement with the two traditions may encourage us to look for subtle versatility and creative adaptation on the part of the later poets without necessarily assuming lack of familiarity with Latin models.

Excursus

This sort of versatility is, of course, readily accepted between authors composing in the same language. In opening the catalogue of Dionysus' allies in *Dionysiaca* 13, Nonnus turns to the Muses for help and claims that he cannot sing about all the tribes gathered by the god even if he had ten tongues and ten mouths, and that he will confine himself to mentioning only the leaders, calling for Homer as his helper just as sailors call for Poseidon:

> οὐ γὰρ ἐγὼ τόσα φῦλα δέκα γλώσσῃσιν ἀείσω
> οὐδὲ δέκα στομάτεσσι χέων χαλκόθροον ἠχώ,
> ὁππόσα Βάκχος ἄγειρε δορυσσόος. Ἀλλὰ λιγαίνων
> ἡγεμόνας καὶ Ὅμηρον ἀοσσητῆρα καλέσσω,   50
> εὐεπίης ὅλον ὅρμον, ἐπεὶ πλωτῆρες ἀλῆται
> πλαγκτοσύνης καλέουσιν ἀρηγόνα Κυανοχαίτην.
>
>   D. 13.47–52

For I could not tell so many peoples with ten tongues, not if I had ten mouths pouring a voice of brass, all those which Bacchos gathered for his spear-chasing. Yet I will loudly name their leaders, and I will call to my aid Homer, the one great harbour of language undefiled, since mariners lost astray call on Seabluehair to save them from their wandering ways. (tr. Rouse 1940).

The obvious model for this passage is the beginning of the catalogue of ships in *Iliad* 2, and Nonnus openly names Homer here as his helper: after the Iliadic narrator has appealed to the all-knowing Muses (*Il.* 2.484–485), he claims that even with ten tongues and ten mouths, an unbreakable voice, and a heart of bronze, he could not name the crowds, but that he will list the captains and the ships:

> πληθὺν δ' οὐκ ἂν ἐγὼ μυθήσομαι οὐδ' ὀνομήνω,
> οὐδ' εἴ μοι δέκα μὲν γλῶσσαι, δέκα δὲ στόματ' εἶεν,
> φωνὴ δ' ἄρρηκτος, χάλκεον δέ μοι ἦτορ ἐνείη,
> εἰ μὴ Ὀλυμπιάδες Μοῦσαι Διὸς αἰγιόχοιο
> θυγατέρες μνησαίαθ' ὅσοι ὑπὸ Ἴλιον ἦλθον·
> ἀρχοὺς αὖ νηῶν ἐρέω νῆάς τε προπάσας.
>
> *Il.* 2.488–493

But the multitude I could not tell nor name, not even if ten tongues were mine and ten mouths and a voice unwearying, and the heart within me were of bronze, unless the Muses of Olympus, daughters of Zeus who bears the aegis, call to my mind all those who came beneath Ilios. Now will I tell the leaders of the ships and all the ships. (tr. Murray/Wyatt 1999).

It has long been noted that the lines that follow the reference to Homer in the Nonnian passage mentioned above seem to be inspired by Claudian's preface to his Greek *Gigantomachia*.[72] In both passages, eloquence and sailing are included in the same metaphor (εὐεπίης ὅλον ὅρμον, *D.* 13.51; cf. εὔξομαι αὐδήεντα κατὰ πλόον εὐεπιάων, Gk *Gig. pr.* 8);[73] moreover, the narrator on each occasion calls for help on either Homer (in Nonnus' case: Ὅμηρον ἀοσσητῆρα, *D.* 13.50) or Apollo (in the case of Claudian: Gk *Gig. pr.* 7), just as sailors in the open seas pray to the sea-gods (ἀρηγόνα Κυανοχαίτην, *D.* 13.52; cf. μακάρεσσιν... εἰναλίοισι, Gk *Gig. pr.* 3, ἀρωγήν, Gk *Gig. pr.* 6).

As Cariou points out, this comparison with the sailors underlines the poet's own difficulty in his task and his attempt to secure the reader's goodwill.[74] The Hesiodic intertext in Claudian's preface, which, as we saw earlier, added a confident tone to the poet's imminent performance in a poetic competition, is absent from Nonnus' appeal to the Muses in this catalogue of Dionysus' allies in *Dionysiaca* 13;[75] for Nonnus, who composes his long mythological epic without

---

[72] Keydell 1973, 24, noted in Vian 2003, 214–215 (on *D.* 13.51–52) and Weise 2013, II.72. See also Cameron 1970a, 11, on the argument that Nonnus may have been familiar with Claudian's Latin work.
[73] On εὐεπίη in the context of inspiration in later Greek poetry cf. (e.g.) the anonymous encomium of Marcellus of Side in *AP* 7.158.7: εἵνεκεν εὐεπίης, τήν οἱ πόρε Φοῖβος Ἀπόλλων, Christod. *AP* 2.415: πνείων εὐεπίης Βεργίλλιος· Livrea 2000, 435.
[74] Cariou 2014, 55.
[75] For the combination of the 'many-mouths' motif and the metaphor of sailing as poetry cf. also Verg. *G.* 2.39–45 (cited above).

hinting that he is performing in a competition, it is upon Homer that he calls for assistance.[76]

Bibliography

Agosti, G. (2001), "Late Antique Iambics and *iambikè idéa*", in: A. Cavarzere/A. Aloni/A. Barchiesi (eds.), *Iambic Ideas. Essays on a Poetic Tradition from Archaic Greece to the Late Roman Empire*, Lanham/Boulder/New York/Oxford, 219–255.
Agosti, G. (2006), "La voce dei libri. Dimensione performativa dell'epica greca tardoantica", in: E. Amato/A. Roduit/M. Steinrück (eds.), *Approches de la troisième sophistique. Hommages à Jacques Schamp*, Brussels, 35–62.
Agosti, G. (2012), "Greek Poetry", in: S.F. Johnson (ed.), *The Oxford Handbook of Late Antiquity*, Oxford, 361–404.
Agosti, G. (2014), "Greek Poetry in Late Antique Alexandria: Between Culture and Religion", in: L.A. Guichard/J.A. García Alonso/M.P. de Hoz (eds.), *The Alexandrian Tradition. Interactions between Science, Religion and Literature*, Bern, 287–311.
Appel, W. (1993), *Mimesis i Kainotes. Kwestia oryginalności literackiej Kwintusa ze Smyrny na przykładzie IV pieśni "Posthomerica"*, Toruń.
Bajoni, M.G. (2001), "La retorica della memoria: a proposito degli epicedi di P.Berol. Inv. 10559 / 10558 e della 'Commemoratio Professorum Burdigalensium' di Ausonio", in: *Hermes* 129, 110–117.
Bassino, P. (2019), *The Certamen Homeri et Hesiodi. A Commentary*, Berlin.
Cameron, A. (1970a), *Claudian. Poetry and Propaganda at the Court of Honorius*, Oxford.
Cameron, A. (1970b), "*Pap. Ant.* III. 115 and the Iambic Prologue in Late Greek Poetry", in: *Classical Quarterly* 20, 119–129.
Cameron, A. (2000), "Claudian Revisited", in: F.E. Consolino (ed.), *Letteratura e propaganda nell'occidente latino da Augusto ai regni Romano-Barbarici*, Rome, 127–144.
Cameron, A. (2016), *Wandering Poets and Other Essays on Late Greek Literature and Philosophy*, Oxford.
Canevaro, L.-G. (2015), *Hesiod's Works & Days: How to Teach Self-Sufficiency*, Oxford.
Cariou, M. (2014), "Le *topos* de l'ineffable dans les catalogues poétiques", *Revue de Philologie, de Littérature et d'Histoire Anciennes* 88.2, 27–58.
Carvounis, K. (2019), *A Commentary on Quintus of Smyrna, Posthomerica 14*, Oxford.

---

[76] For Nonnus' relationship to Homer as "emulation and rivalry" see Hopkinson 1994, 9–14. Versions of this paper were presented in the FIEC panel in London (2019), which was the starting-point for this volume, and in an interdisciplinary workshop on Late Antique language and culture entitled "From Athens to Constantinople" at the University of Vienna (2019): I would like to thank the audiences in both these settings for their questions and suggestions, which helped me revise this paper. I would also like to thank Sophia Papaioannou, Giampiero Scafoglio, and Mary Whitby, who read an earlier draft of the paper and gave constructive feedback and help with the bibliography. I alone, of course, am responsible for remaining infelicities.

Carvounis, K. (2022), "Poetry, Performance, and Quintus' *Posthomerica*", in: S. Bär/E. Greensmith/L. Ozbek (eds.), *Writing Homer under Rome: Quintus of Smyrna in and beyond the Second Sophistic*, Edinburgh, 38–56.

Carvounis, K./Papaioannou, S. (2022), "Rivalling Song Contests and Alternative Typhonomachies in Ovid and Nonnus: Revisiting the Issue of Latin Influence on Greek Poetry in Late Antiquity", in: B. Verhelst/T. Scheijnen (eds.), *Greek and Latin Poetry of Late Antiquity. Form, Tradition, and Context*, Cambridge, 13–30.

Charlet, J.-L. (1991/2020), *Claudien. Œuvres. Tome I. Le Rapt de Proserpine*, Paris.

Christiansen, P.G. (1997), "Claudian: a Greek or a Latin?", in: *Scholia* 6, 79–95.

Christiansen, P.G./Christiansen, D. (2009), "Claudian: The Last Great Pagan Poet", in: *L'Antiquité Classique* 78, 133–144.

Coombe, C. (2018), *Claudian the Poet*, Cambridge.

Duff, J.W./Duff, A.M. (1935), *Minor Latin Poets*, Cambridge, MA.

Fairclough, H.R./Goold, G.P. (1999), *Vergil. Eclogues, Georgics, Aeneid 1–6. Vol. 1*. Revised Edition, Cambridge, MA.

Felgentreu, F. (1999), *Claudians praefationes. Bedingungen, Beschreibungen und Wirkungen einer poetischen Kleinform*, Stuttgart/Leipzig.

Formisano, M. (2017), "Displacing Tradition: A New-Allegorical Reading of Ausonius, Claudian, and Rutilius Namatianus", in: J. Elsner/J.H. Lobato (eds.), *The Poetics of Late Latin Literature*, Oxford/New York, 207–235.

Gärtner, U. (2013), "Πιερίδες τί μοι ἁγνὸν ἐφωπλίσσασθε Μάρωνα; Das griechische Epos der Kaiserzeit und die Bezüge zur lateinischen Literatur", in: P. Schubert/P. Ducrey/P. Derron (eds.), *Les Grecs héritiers des Romains*, Vandœuvres, Geneva, 87–139.

Goold, G.P. (1990), *Propertius. Elegies*, Cambridge, MA.

Gowers, E. (2005), "Virgil's Sibyl and the 'Many Mouths' Cliché (*Aen.* 6.625–7)", in: *Classical Quarterly* 55, 170–182.

Gualandri, I. (2013), "Claudian, from Easterner to Westerner", *Talanta* 45, 115–129.

Guipponi-Gineste, M.-F. (2010), *Claudien: poète du monde à la court d'Occident*, Paris.

Gruzelier, C. (1993), *Claudian. De Raptu Proserpinae*, Oxford.

Hall, J.B. (1985), *Claudii Claudiani carmina*, Leipzig.

Hardie, P./Moore, H. (2010), "Literary Careers — Classical Models and Their Receptions", in: P. Hardie/H. Moore (eds.), *Classical Literary Careers and their Reception*, Cambridge, 1–16.

Harrison, S. (2017), "Metapoetics in the Prefaces of Claudian's *De Raptu Proserpinae*", in: J. Elsner/J.H. Lobato (eds.), *The Poetics of Late Latin Literature*, Oxford/New York, 236–251.

Heyworth, S.J./Morwood, J.H.W. (2011), *A Commentary on Propertius, Book 3*. Oxford.

Hinds, S. (2013), "Claudianism in the *De Raptu Proserpinae*", in T.D. Papanghelis/S.J. Harrison/S. Frangoulidis (eds.), *Generic Interfaces in Latin Literature. Encounters, Interactions and Transformations*, Berlin/Boston, 169–192.

Hopkinson, N. (1994), "Nonnus and Homer", in: N. Hopkinson (ed.), *Studies in the Dionysiaca of Nonnus*, Cambridge, 9–42.

Hose, M. (1994), "Die römische Liebeselegie und die griechische Literatur: Überlegungen zu POxy 3723", in: *Philologus* 138, 67–82.

Hunter, R. (2006), *The Shadow of Callimachus. Studies in the Reception of Hellenistic Poetry at Rome*, Cambridge.

Hutchinson, G.O. (2001), *Greek Lyric Poetry. A Commentary on Selected Larger Pieces. Alcman, Stesichorus, Sappho, Alcaeus, Ibycus, Anacreon, Simonides, Bacchylides, Pindar, Sophocles, Euripides*, Oxford.

Jakobi, R. (2014), *Nemesianus, Cynegetica. Edition und Kommentar*, Berlin/Boston.
Kaufmann, H. (2015), "Papinius Noster: Statius in Roman Late Antiquity", in W.J. Dominik/C.E. Newlands/K. Gervais (eds.), *Brill's Companion to Statius*, Leiden, 481–496.
Keydell, R. (1973), Review of W. Peek, *Kritische und erklärende Beiträge zu den Dionysiaka des Nonnos*, in: *Gnomon* 45, 23–26.
Livrea, E. (2000), "La *Gigantomachia* greca di Claudiano. Tradizione manoscritta e critica testuale", in: *Maia* 52, 415–437.
Miller, F.J. (1917), *Seneca. Tragedies*, Cambridge, MA.
Minissale, F. (1975–1976), "Il poeta e la nave: Claud. *rapt. Pros.* I.1–14", in: *Helikon* 15–16, 496–499.
Most, G.W. (2006), *Hesiod. Theogony, Works and Days, Testimonia*, Cambridge, MA/ London.
Mulligan, B. (2007), "The Poet from Egypt. Reconsidering Claudian's Eastern Origin", in: *Philologus* 151, 285–310.
Murray, A.T./Wyatt, W.F. (1999), *Homer. Iliad. Books 1–12*. Revised edition, Cambridge, MA/ London.
Mynors, R.A.B. (ed.) (1990), *Virgil. Georgics*, Oxford.
Nagy, G. (1982), "Hesiod", in: T.J. Luce (ed.), *Ancient Writers: Greece and Rome*, New York, I.43–73.
Nagy, G. (2009), "Hesiod and the Ancient Biographical Traditions", in: F. Montanari/ A. Rengakos/C. Tsagalis (eds.), *Brill's Companion to Hesiod*, Leiden, 271–311.
Nisbet, R.G.M./Hubbard, M. (1970), *A Commentary on Horace: Odes 1*, Oxford.
Onorato, M. (2008), *Claudio Claudiano. De Raptu Proserpinae*, Naples.
Page, D.L. (1942), *Greek Literary Papyri*, Cambridge, MA.
Parkes, R. (2015), "Reading Statius through a Biographical Lens", in: W.J. Dominik/C.E. Newlands/K. Gervais (eds.), *Brill's Companion to Statius*, Leiden, 463–480.
Pohl, K. (2019), *Dracontius: De Raptu Helenae*, Stuttgart.
Rea, J.R. (1996), "4352. Hexameter Verses", in: *The Oxyrhynchus Papyri* 63, 1–17.
Remijsen, S. (2015), *The End of Athletics in Late Antiquity. Greek Culture in the Roman World*, Cambridge.
Rosen, R.M. (1990), "Poetry and Sailing in Hesiod's *Works and Days*", in: *Classical Antiquity* 9, 99–113.
Rouse, W.H.D. (1940), *Nonnos. Dionysiaca* (3 vols.), Cambridge, MA.
Scafoglio, G. (2018), "La poesia come colloquio: il caso di Ausonio", in: B. Bonhomme/ A. Cerbo/ J. Rieu (eds.), *La poésie comme entretien/La poesia come colloquio*, Paris, 19–43.
Schubert, P. (2013), "L'apport des papyrus grecs et latins d'Égypte romaine", in: P. Schubert/ P. Ducrey/P. Derron (eds.), *Les Grecs héritiers des Romains*, Vandœuvres, Geneva, 243–271.
Shackleton Bailey, D.R. (2003), *Statius. Thebaid, Books 1–7* (2 vols.), Cambridge, MA.
Sivan, H. (1992), "The Dedicatory Presentation in Late Antiquity: The Example of Ausonius", in: *Illinois Classical Studies* 17, 83–101.
Steiner, D. (2005), "Nautical Matters: Hesiod's Nautilia and Ibycus Fragment 282 *PMG*", in: *Classical Philology* 100, 347–355.
Swain, S. (1991), "Arrian the Epic Poet", in: *Journal of Hellenic Studies* 111, 211–214.
Thomas, R.F. (1988), *Virgil. Georgics. Volume 1. Books I–II*, Cambridge.
Thomas, R.F. (1999), *Reading Virgil and his Texts. Studies in Intertextuality*, Ann Arbor.

Tsagalis, C. (2006), "Poet and Audience: from Homer to Hesiod", in: F. Montanari/A. Rengakos (eds.), *La poésie épique grecque: métamorphoses d'un genre littéraire*, Vandœuvres, Geneva, 79–130.

Vian, F. (2003), *Nonnos de Panopolis. Les Dionysiaques. Tome V. Chants XI–XIII*, Paris.

Wallis, J. (2018), *Introspection and Engagement in Propertius. A Study of Book 3*, Cambridge.

Ware, C. (2004), "Claudian: the Epic Poet in the Prefaces", in: M. Gale (ed.), *Latin Epic and Didactic Poetry*, Swansea, 181–201.

Weise, S. (2013), *Die griechischen Gedicht Claudians. (2 Teile)*, PhD Dissertation, Martin-Luther-Universität Halle Wittenberg.

West, M.L. (1978), *Hesiod. Works & Days*, Oxford.

Whitby, M. (1994), "From Moschus to Nonnus: the Evolution of the Nonnian Style", in: N. Hopkinson (ed.), *Studies in the Dionysiaca of Nonnus*, Cambridge, 99–155.

Wimmel, W. (1960), *Kallimachos in Rom. Die Nachfolge seines Apologetischen Dichtens in der Augusteerzeit*, Wiesbaden.

Silvio Bär
Sinon and Laocoon in Quintus of Smyrna's *Posthomerica*: A Rewriting and De-Romanisation of Vergil's *Aeneid*?

Abstract: This chapter compares the episodes of Sinon and Laocoon in Quintus of Smyrna's *Posthomerica* and Vergil's *Aeneid*. Unlike most previous research, the comparison does not look at the two scenes from the angle of source criticism, but from a narratological perspective. It is argued that Quintus to a large degree removes the specific *Romanitas* from the famous Vergilian scene and thus redrafts the final days of Troy in a new, cleaned-up, and seemingly more objective manner. By doing so, Quintus raises a claim for Greek authority in literary and cultural terms, communicated through a Homeric voice with corresponding weight.

Keywords: Quintus of Smyrna (*Posthomerica*); Vergil (*Aeneid*); *quaestio Latina*; Sinon; Laocoon; Second Sophistic.

1 Introduction

The *Posthomerica* (*PH*) by Quintus of Smyrna is a Greek epic about the final days of the city of Troy, written during the time of the Second Sophistic, probably in the third (or perhaps late second) century CE.[1] For a long time, scholarship on the *PH* was dominated by the *quaestio Latina*, that is, the question of whether Quintus had access to Latin epics such as Ovid's *Metamorphoses* and, in particular, Vergil's *Aeneid*, and whether he used these texts as sources for the composition of his own epic. In the twentieth century, this question was a matter of major dispute between Rudolf Keydell and Francis Vian — the former arguing in favour of Latin influence on the *PH*, the latter arguing against it.[2] The latest

---

[1] On Quintus the poet and the dating of the *PH* see James/Lee 2000, 1–9; James 2004, xvii–xxi; Baumbach/Bär 2007, 1–8; Bär 2009, 11–23; Maciver 2012a, 1–6; Scheijnen 2018, 1–4. The textual editions used in this chapter are by Vian 1963–9 for the *PH* and Mynors 1969 for the *Aeneid*. Translations are my own.
[2] See Keydell 1949/50; Keydell 1954; Keydell 1961, 279–282; Vian 1959, 95–101; Vian 1963, xxxiv. On the further history of the debate see Gärtner 2005, 30–37 (with detailed further references); James 2007, 145–149.

comprehensive study on this topic was that by Ursula Gärtner from 2005, who examined all passages in the *PH* where a potential parallel to the *Aeneid* could be suspected. Yet, the final statement in her conclusion is fairly cautious: "It cannot be entirely denied that the poet of the *Posthomerica* may have had knowledge of, and adopted or transformed, single motifs or scenes from the Roman national epic, and that he may have dealt with [the *Aeneid*] at a certain level" (Gärtner 2005, 287).[3] Likewise, Alan W. James, whose chapter from 2007 was written independently of Gärtner's study, solely discusses issues relating to direct vs indirect influence and dependence, although he laudably attempts to dismantle "prejudice concerning Quintus' general quality as a poet, which has led too many to discount originality in his use of sources" (James 2007, 149).

The main problem with all existing studies on the *quaestio Latina* is that they (explicitly or implicitly) follow a positivistic idea of source criticism, according to which similarities between two texts must be explained either as the result of direct dependence (the Keydell model) or as the result of a lost common source (the Vian model). It seems evident that such a unidirectional approach is hugely outdated and that there is no need for ample justification to reject it. Therefore, a different approach is taken in this chapter. The insight that Vergil's *Aeneid* was known and read in the Roman East during the second and third centuries CE is taken as a tenet to claim that a contemporary reader was likely to have read the *PH* through the prism of Vergil's national epic. Based on these premises, the episodes of Sinon and Laocoon are analysed, two characters who stand at the beginning of the events that lead to the fall of Troy and who were part of the epic tradition from the archaic Greek period onwards. Methodologically, a narratological approach is chosen (narratological approaches to the *PH* having as of yet remained vastly underexploited). It is demonstrated that the Posthomeric[4] version is characterised by a number of contrasts and inversions as compared to the Vergilian account, and it is argued that Quintus to a large degree removes the specific *Romanitas* from this famous Vergilian scene and in so doing raises a claim for Greek authority in literary and cultural terms, a claim communicated through a Homeric voice with corresponding weight.

---

3 My translation; German original: "Kenntnis aber sowie Übernahme und Umsetzung einzelner Motive oder Szenen wie auch eine gewisse Auseinandersetzung mit dem Nationalepos der Römer wird man dem Dichter der Posthomerica nicht gänzlich absprechen können."
4 The term 'Posthomeric' is used in this chapter solely to refer to Quintus' *PH*.

2 *Romanitas* and Vergil in the Second Sophistic

Issues relating to Greek identity and self-consciousness in the Second Sophistic, to "being Greek under Rome,"[5] have been much debated. For several decades, a major focus has been on how the sophists and their public declamations should be understood in relation to the Roman Empire and its power. Traditionally, there have been two schools of explanation. One argues that mastery and performance of Greek rhetoric was a first step (maybe even a necessary requirement) for Greeks towards a career in the Roman administration on a supraregional level (the career model).[6] Another school claims essentially the opposite, namely, that the obsession with the language and the culture of a bygone past provided the Greeks with a mental escape from (or even active resistance to) the realities of Roman supremacy (the escapist model).[7] In the event, however, probably neither the first nor the second school is entirely right or wrong – and indeed, models of combining both approaches have been suggested more recently.[8] As Lieve Van Hoof aptly puts it, "Greek literature under the Roman Empire was an extremely powerful locus for taking a stance on contemporary issues, allowing people both to construct their own [...] identity, and to negotiate (with those in) power" (Van Hoof 2010, 215).

In this context, the question also arises as to what the position of the Latin language was in the Greek homeland under the rule of the Roman Empire.[9] The overall scope of proficiency and reading habits may be difficult to assess in the details, but it can be said with a fair amount of certainty that knowledge of Latin was a requirement for Greeks to make a career in the Roman administration, and that Vergil's *Aeneid* was a major school text that was used to teach and

---

[5] The phrase "being Greek under Rome" stems from the title of a collected volume by Goldhill 2001.
[6] See, e.g., Bowersock 1969; Schmitz 1997; Puech 2002.
[7] See, e.g., Bowie 1970; Swain 1996; Whitmarsh 2001.
[8] See, e.g., Eshleman 2012, who proposes a novel way of understanding identity construction in the Second Sophistic. However, the fact that there is not one straightforward model does not entail the necessity to deny the existence of the Second Sophistic and its cultural primacy, as Tim Whitmarsh does in the introduction to his collection of essays from 2013, claiming that the Second Sophistic was "a modern fantasy projected back on to the ancient world" (Whitmarsh 2013, 3). This distorted view is the result of a misreading of Erwin Rohde's use of the term in *Der griechische Roman und seine Vorläufer* (Rohde 1914, 318–321).
[9] On this topic see especially the studies by Woolf 1994; Rochette 1997 (with a comprehensive bibliography); Adams 2003; Gärtner 2005, 13–22 (with 13 [n. 4] for further references); Hidber 2006; Gärtner 2013, 93–94 (with 93–94 [n. 20] for further references).

learn Latin.¹⁰ It is also known that Greek translations of the *Aeneid* existed in the second and third centuries CE.¹¹ We can conclude from such evidence that Vergil's national epic must have been read (or listened to on the occasion of recitals?) by an audience that was wider than the small group of those Greeks who needed knowledge of Latin for their professional career.

Therefore, to put it bluntly, from a reader-response perspective the *quaestio Latina* as such is futile, and both the Keydell model and the Vian model must be dismissed. We do not (and will never) know for sure whether Quintus read the *Aeneid* (and, if he did, whether he used the Latin original or a Greek translation) and/or whether he thought of the *Aeneid* when he composed the *PH*. However, as the *PH* was supposed to appeal to the intellectual elite of its time, the πεπαιδευμένοι (while it could also be appreciated by the general public, οἱ πολλοί),¹² we can say with a high degree of probability that at least some contemporary readers will have perceived the *PH* through the prism of Vergil's Roman epic and that therefore a de-Romanising interpretation of the *Aeneid* is a likely approach taken by a Greek reader of that time.

3 The Sinon and Laocoon episodes in the *Aeneid* and the *PH* compared

The stories of Sinon and Laocoon (S&L) stand at the beginning of the dramatic chain of events that lead to the fall of Troy, and they constitute the hinge between the preparations for the sack of Troy and the city's actual, final destruction. Both characters are first attested in the *Iliupersis* by Arctinus of Miletus (see test. 2 *EpGF* [p. 62]). Like all other poems from the Epic Cycle, the *Iliupersis* is for the most part lost, and therefore, the question of whether or not Vergil and, even more so, Quintus used it as a source is impossible to answer.¹³ However, the simple fact is that both figures were traditional, transtextual characters inherited by a centuries-old stream of reception, and that they themselves were

---

10 See Fisher 1982, 183–189; Irmscher 1985; Rochette 1997, 165–210; Gärtner 2005, 14–16 (with further references); Hidber 2006, 242–243; Gärtner 2013, 95–98 (with further references).
11 See Reichmann 1943; Baldwin 1976; Baldwin 1982, 81–82; Fisher 1982, especially 176; Hidber 2006, 249–250. Vergil's works remained known in the Roman East as late as the sixth century (see Baldwin 1982).
12 See Bär 2009, 85–91.
13 On Vergil and the Epic Cycle see Kopff 1981; Gärtner 2015. On Quintus and the Epic Cycle see Bär/Baumbach 2015, 606–614; Scafoglio 2022.

embedded in an even richer and more complex traditional narrative about the fall of Troy, a narrative which "was a topic common to all the periods and genres of Greek literature known" to both authors (Horsfall 2008, xix).[14]

In the *Aeneid*, the episode constitutes the first part of Aeneas' intradiegetic narration of the fall of Troy at Dido's court in book 2:[15]

> **A: 13–39:** In a compressed narrative, Aeneas mentions the building of the Horse and its function, the Greek heroes entering the belly of the Horse,[16] the departure of the Greek fleet, and the first disagreements among the Trojans as to whether or not the Horse should be admitted into the city.
>
> **B: 40–56:** First appearance of Laocoon. Laocoon warns against the Horse and speculates about several possible forms of ruse (direct speech: 42–49). He hurls a spear at the Horse, but by divine destiny, the ambush is not revealed.
>
> **C: 57–198:** The appearance of Sinon, almost all of which is taken up by his extended false speech (direct speech: 69–72, 77–104, 108–144, 154–194), interrupted by a few comments by Aeneas and by Priam's reassurance to grant Sinon asylum (direct speech: 148–151). Sinon introduces himself as a relative of Palamedes who was bullied by Ulixes because he publicly called for Palamedes' rehabilitation. When Apollo demanded a human sacrifice prior to the departure of the Greeks, the seer Calchas (influenced by Ulixes) disclosed that Sinon should be chosen, but Sinon was able to escape and hide until the Greeks set sail. The Horse, in turn, was built in order to make amends for the theft of Minerva's Palladium by Ulixes and Diomedes.[17] Calchas gave instructions to build the Horse higher than the walls of Troy so that it could not unfold its protective function for the Trojans, but Sinon tricks the Trojans into destroying their city walls in order to admit the Horse.
>
> **B': 199–231:** Second appearance of Laocoon. Laocoon and his two sons are killed by two giant snakes which approach them coming from the isle of Tenedos (extended description of the snakes and of the agony of Laocoon and his sons). Subsequently, the snakes seek shelter at the feet of Minerva's statue, which the Trojans misunderstand as a punishment by Minerva for Laocoon's sacrilege against the Horse.

---

14 See Gärtner 2005, 133–160, on the existing textual sources about the fall of Troy before Quintus. On Arctinus' *Iliupersis* see Finglass 2015 (with further references). On Laocoon before Vergil see Zintzen 1979, 18–24; Horsfall 2008, 77–82 (with ample further references); Nesselrath 2009; Most 2010, 326–329. On Laocoon in the *PH* see also Zintzen 1979, 27–48; Gärtner 2009.

15 For the details of the scene and its structure see the commentaries by Austin 1964, 27–116; Horsfall 2008, 45–221; Binder 2019, vol. 3, 96–126.

16 I use the term "Greek(s)" for the sake of convenience despite the terminological inaccuracy. Quintus calls them Ἀχαιοί, Ἀργεῖοι, and Δαναοί by turns, following Homeric practice. In the *Aeneid*, they are sometimes called *Graii*, sometimes *Achivi*, but the most common term is *Danai* ("the name used most often by Vergil for the Greeks, and least often by Homer" according to Austin 1964, 29; see also Horsfall 2006, 101).

17 The Palladium was a talisman-like image of Pallas Athene that should guarantee the protection of Troy. Its theft was a prerequisite for the city to be sacked (see Horsfall 2008, 162–163; Binder 2019, vol. 3, 117; see also n. 27 below).

A': 232–249: In another compressed narrative, Aeneas recounts the destruction of the city walls, the fetching of the Horse, and Cassandra's warnings, which are ignored.

The rest of book 2 is taken up by Aeneas' narration of the fall of Troy, the encounter with his mother Venus, the loss of his wife Creusa, and the flight from Troy. In the *PH*, in turn, the S&L episode constitutes the second half of book 12 (the first part of the book is occupied by a debate about the further course of action and the subsequent construction of the Horse, followed by an in-text proem in which the author stages himself as a Homeric figure, and a catalogue of the Greek warriors who enter the Horse):[18]

A: 353–388: The Trojans find the Horse and Sinon on the beach. First they interrogate Sinon, but then they torture him cruelly. Sinon, however, insists on his version of the story: he claims that the Greeks have set sail and left the Horse behind in order to avoid Athene's wrath, and that he had been chosen as a human sacrifice, but was able to escape (direct speech: 375–386).

B: 389–417: First appearance and first punishment of Laocoon. There is disagreement among the Trojans as to whether or not Sinon should be trusted. Laocoon, who is among those who distrust Sinon, warns against the Horse and is struck blind by Athene as punishment (extended description of the process of his going blind).

A': 418–443: The Trojans misunderstand Laocoon's blindness as a punishment for his sacrilege against Athene (the sacrilege being his warning). They feel remorse about having mistreated Sinon and admit the Horse into the city.

B': 444–480: Second appearance and second punishment of Laocoon. As Laocoon continues to warn the Trojans against the Horse, Athene sends two giant snakes coming from the isle of Kalydna which kill Laocoon's sons (but not Laocoon). All other Trojans flee in panic and watch the scene from afar.

C: 480–499: The narrator reports about a cenotaph that the Trojans erected for Laocoon's two sons, and how it was lamented by Laocoon and his wife.

B'': 500–524: Appearance of *omina*. Numerous fateful *omina* appear that warn the Trojans against the Horse, but the Trojans are blind to them (unlike Laocoon, who was able to recognise the truth despite his blindness).

B''': 525–585: Appearance of Cassandra. Cassandra warns the Trojans against the Horse (direct speech: 540–551), but is only met with scorn and mockery (direct speech of an unnamed Trojan: 553–561). She attempts to destroy the Horse with fire and an axe, but is prevented from doing so.

Several detailed source-critical comparisons of the two episodes exist, and there is no need to provide excerpts or summaries of them here.[19] On the other hand,

---

18 For the details of the scene and its structure see the commentaries by Vian 1969, 102–111, 218–224; Campbell 1981, 115–194; James 2004, 331–333.
19 See especially Kehmptzow 1891, 68–69; Noack 1892, 785–787, 795–800; Becker 1913, 80–86; Heinze 1915, 64–71; Kleinknecht 1944; Vian 1959, 55–71, 95–101; Vian 1969, 78–84; Zintzen

the main differences in the overarching narrative composition and, along with them, the implications of the wider picture have hardly been considered. The total length of both S&L episodes is equal (*Aeneid*: 237 lines; *PH*: 233 lines), and thus the Posthomeric version calls for a comparison with its Vergilian counterpart. However, there are fundamental differences in focalisation. The Vergilian account is part of Aeneas' intradiegetic narration at Dido's court; Aeneas is thus a secondary narrator with a subjective perspective. His point of view is that of a Trojan; it is limited, non-total, and retrospective — and thus prone to distortion. This limitation is obvious at the beginning where Aeneas compresses the events leading up to the S&L episode into a total of 27 lines, and his specific focalisation becomes apparent when he comments that "we *reckoned* that they'd left and were on their way to Mycenae on a [good] wind" (*Aen.* 2.25: *nos abiisse rati et vento petiisse Mycenas*). In contrast, the corresponding Posthomeric account occupies as much as half of book 12, including a detailed debate about the envisaged course of action (12.1–103), an equally thorough description of the construction process of the Horse (12.104–156), instructions to the Greek warriors and Sinon (12.217–305), and a catalogue of the heroes who enter the Horse (12.314–352). In other words, the primary narrator of the *PH* supplements those pieces of information that the Trojan Aeneas as a secondary narrator did not have in sufficient detail. The principal difference between the two versions thus lies not mainly in the contrast between a Trojan and a Greek perspective, but primarily in the difference between a homodiegetic (and thus limited) and a heterodiegetic (and hence omniscient) narrator. The voice of the Posthomeric account can be tied back to the preceding in-text proem in which the author stages himself as a Homeric figure with a Hesiodic and a Callimachean touch (*PH* 12.306–313; interrupted by the catalogue of the heroes in the Horse, *PH* 12.314–352). This is the only passage in the entire *PH* where Quintus makes an explicitly authorial first-person intervention. In doing so, he also evokes the homodiegetic voice of his anti-model, Vergil's *Aeneid* book 2, and at the same time virtually claims Homeric authority for his own version.

A comparison of the actual content of the S&L episodes further reveals two major differences, namely, a difference in narrative speed (viz., compression vs extension) and a difference in narrative sequence (viz., the arrangement of the narrative units). Let us consider narrative speed first. The total length of both S&L episodes is, as said, equal; yet, in the Vergilian version, the Sinon episode is in the centre, and its major part is occupied by Sinon's false speech — report-

---

1979, 27–48; Campbell 1981, 115–194; Gärtner 2005, 161–226 (with detailed further references); James 2007, 149–150, 153–157.

ed in direct speech by Aeneas in a total of 110 lines (69–72, 77–104, 108–144, 154–194) — whereas Sinon's speech in the *PH* is restricted to 12 lines (375–386). In contrast, the Posthomeric narrator provides his reader with a detailed and graphic description of Sinon's torture (*PH* 12.363–373),[20] which is something that the Vergilian account lacks completely. In fact, Aeneas only mentions that Sinon had "his hands tied behind his back" (*Aen.* 2.57: *manus* [...] *post terga revinctum*) when he was taken before Priam, but that afterwards "we granted him his life and pitied him" (*Aen.* 2.145: *vitam damus et miserescimus*) and that "Priam ordered the bonds to be taken off" (*Aen.* 2.146–147: *levari / vincla iubet Priamus*). Many scholars have pointed out that the Vergilian Sinon is treated surprisingly kindly by the Trojans, whereas the Trojans in the Posthomeric version mistreat him with atrocious cruelty; and that Vergil puts all his emphasis on the deviousness and falsehood of Sinon and his tongue, while Quintus highlights Sinon's integrity and perseverance, but does not equip him with rhetorical skills.[21] It has even been suggested that the "endurance under torture" by the Posthomeric Sinon be read as "an exhibition of Stoic qualities" (Maciver 2012a, 109).[22] True though this may be, the main point here too lies in the different narratorial focalisation. It appears that the primary narrator of the *PH* supplements those pieces of information that the secondary narrator of the *Aeneid* may have suppressed. Sinon's torture — cruel as it is — is motivated by the Trojans' desire for absolute certainty about the truth (in antiquity, torture was a common means to find the truth in legal contexts, and by the time of Quintus, not only slaves, but also free men could be subjected to it).[23] In turn, Aeneas' remark that they "pitied" Sinon (*Aen.* 2.145: *miserescimus*) may be re-read, from the Posthomeric perspective, as a subtle allusion to torture. In other words, the Posthomeric account makes the reader re-interpret Aeneas' account in a new light; Quintus exposes in his narration what the Vergilian Aeneas may be hiding.[24]

---

[20] The visual senses are also of great importance in the *PH* elsewhere: see Ozbek 2007; Argyrouli 2017; Kauffman 2019.

[21] See, e.g., Heinze 1915, 65–66; Campbell 1981, 119–121; Clausen 1987, 35; Gärtner 2005, 189–191; Hadjittofi 2007, 365–370; Binder 2019, vol. 3, 105. On Vergil's Sinon see Manuwald 1985; further references as provided by Horsfall 2008, 93–95; Binder 2019, vol. 3, 106.

[22] Maciver (*eo loco*) refers to the narratorial comment at *PH* 12.387–388 to support this interpretation: ὣς φάτο κερδοσύνῃσι καὶ οὐ κάμεν ἄλγεσι θυμόν· / ἀνδρὸς γὰρ κρατεροῖο κακὴν ὑποτλῆναι ἀνάγκην. ("Such was his cunning speech, and he did not languish in his mind: For, [it is a sign] of a strong man to endure gruesome violence"). See also Maciver 2007, 273 (n. 63).

[23] See, e.g., Harries 1999, 122–134.

[24] Binder's claim that "the motivation for the torture is unclear" is misguided, and calling the Trojans "warmhearted" is exaggerated ("die Motivation der Folter ist unklar"; "die warmher-

The Posthomeric narrator adds information where Aeneas has omitted it — and vice versa. The fact that the speech by the Posthomeric Sinon is considerably shorter than that of his Vergilian counterpart cannot only be interpreted as a way of transforming a double-tongued liar into an upright Stoic, but what we can see here is again (narratologically speaking) an inversion of compression and extension. The concision of Sinon's speech has been interpreted differently, and there has been disagreement as to whether Sinon should be imagined as having been silent in the beginning or whether his brief speech is a repetition of what he already said under torture.[25] However, this question distracts from the actual point, namely, that Sinon's speech is in parts unintelligible by and of itself and that it leaves several textual gaps (*Leerstellen*). Let us look at the full speech:

> Ἀργεῖοι μὲν νηυσὶν ὑπὲρ πόντοιο φέβονται   375
> μακρῷ ἀκηδήσαντες ἐπὶ πτολέμῳ καὶ ἀνίῃ.
> Κάλχαντος δ' ἰότητι δαΐφρονι Τριτογενείῃ
> ἵππον ἐτεκτήναντο, θεῆς χόλον ὄφρ' ἀλέωνται
> πάγχυ κοτεσσαμένης Τρώων ὕπερ. ἀμφὶ δὲ νόστου
> ἐννεσίη<ς> Ὀδυσῆος ἐμοὶ μενέαινον ὄλεθρον,   380
> ὄφρα με δηώσωσι δυσηχέος ἄγχι θαλάσσης
> δαίμοσιν εἰναλίοις. ἐμὲ δ' οὐ λάθον, ἀλλ' ἀλεγεινὰς
> σπονδάς τ' οὐλοχύτας τε μάλ' ἐσσυμένως ὑπαλύξας
> ἀθανάτων βουλῇσι παραὶ ποσὶ κάππεσον ἵππου.
> οἱ δὲ καὶ οὐκ ἐθέλοντες ἀναγκαίῃ μ' ἐλίποντο   385
> ἀζόμενοι μεγάλοιο Διὸς κρατερόφρονα κούρην.
>
> *PH* 12.375–386

> The Argives have fled across the sea in their ships,
> having been worn out by the long war and the distress.
> By Calchas' instruction, for the war-minded Tritogeneia [= Athene]
> they timbered the Horse, so as to avoid the goddess' wrath,
> who was very angry on behalf of the Trojans. For the sake of their return,
> on Odysseus' advice, they concocted my doom,
> to slaughter me at the ill-sounding sea
> to the deities of the ocean. Yet [the plan] did not escape me, but

---

zigen Trojaner"; Binder 2019, vol. 3, 105). After all, Aeneas mentions that Sinon is being mocked in the beginning (*Aen.* 2.63–64: *Troiana iuventus / circumfusa ruit certantque inludere capto*, "the Trojan youth comes forward in a crowd and they compete [with each other] in mocking the captive").

25 See Becker 1913, 82 ("spricht [...] nicht eher, als bis seine Standhaftigkeit gebrochen ist") vs Heinze 1915, 66 ("[seine Festigkeit,] die ihn trotz aller Qualen auf seiner Aussage beharren läßt") and Gärtner 2005, 182 ("was er schon die ganze Zeit unter der Folter behauptete").

> I escaped from the pain-inflicting libations and the barley offerings at once,
> and by the will of the immortals I threw myself down at the feet of the Horse.
> And so they were forced to leave me behind although they didn't want to,
> respecting the stouthearted daughter of the great Zeus.

Essentially, there are three textual gaps opened here. First, why does Sinon state that the Horse was built "by Calchas' instruction" (*PH* 12.377), when it is Odysseus who recommends its construction (12.25–45), and Calchas only supports and reinforces Odysseus' decision (12.51–65)? Secondly, the nature of Athene's wrath "on behalf of the Trojans" (12.379) remains unexplained. Thirdly, Sinon mentioning Odysseus as the driving force behind his purported sacrifice is not entirely congruent with Odysseus' instructions at the beginning of book 12 that the chosen decoy should "pretend to have escaped the haughty violence of the Achaeans" (*PH* 12.35–36: ὑποκρίναιτο βίην ὑπέροπλον Ἀχαιῶν / [...] ὑπαλύξαι): why does Sinon add this piece of information about Odysseus that does not seem to have any additional value? There has been ample discussion about how far these (seeming) inconsistencies may be the result of Quintus having combined pieces from different sources.²⁶ However, they make perfect sense when Sinon's speech is regarded as a compression of its extensive Vergilian counterpart. There, it is Calchas who initiates the construction of the Horse (*Aen.* 2.182–188); and the reason for Minerva's anger is explained at great length, namely, because of the theft of the Palladium (2.163–171, 183–184) – which is part of the horizon of expectation of the Posthomeric reader because it is mentioned in the internal prolepsis in book 10, when Hera and the Four Seasons discuss the forthcoming events (*PH* 10.353–360).²⁷ Similarly, Odysseus as the driving force behind Sinon's sacrifice becomes clear through the Vergilian account too, where Ulixes is said to have played a major role in making Calchas choose Sinon for the invidious task (2.97–100, 128–129). Thus, the purported inconsistencies in Sinon's speech turn out to be deliberate textual gaps that invite the reader to read the Posthomeric account of the S&L episode against that of the *Aeneid*.

That the Posthomeric Sinon should be read through the prism of his Vergilian counterpart is alluded to again in book 14 when the feasting Greeks single him out as a particularly brave hero (14.105–111). There he is called Σίνωνα περικλυτόν by the primary narrator: "the widely renowned Sinon" (14.107). The adjective περικλυτός is also used in the *Dichterweihe* in book 12 where the narra-

---

26 See the extensive discussion by Gärtner 2005, 182–188, with ample further references.
27 On these lines see Vian 1969, 208–209 (nn. 8–13); James 2004, 321; Tsomis 2018, 196–198; Greensmith 2020, 303.

tor recounts having tended to "the widely renowned sheep," which is an allusion both to Hesiod's *Dichterweihe* (*Theog.* 22–28) and to Callimachus' dream about this Hesiodic passage (*Aet.* 1 fr. 2.1–2 Pfeiffer).[28] In a similar vein, by applying the adjective περικλυτός to qualify Sinon, the Greeks do not only sing the praise of his heroic deed, but they also (implicitly) provide an Alexandrian footnote that can be read as an allusion to the Vergilian account of Sinon's fame in literary history.[29]

Let us proceed to the other main compositional difference, the difference in narrative sequence. Richard Heinze, in his epoch-making study *Vergils epische Technik*, stated that Quintus' depiction of the fall of Troy "consist[ed] of loose episodes [...] which could be decreased or increased or rearranged without affecting the composition," whereas Vergil, in contrast, had "successfully overcome the episodic effect that clings to such actions" (Heinze 1915, 444–445).[30] Some scholars even went so far as to reproach Quintus for his alleged clumsiness in handling his sources,[31] whereas Vergil's composition of the S&L episode has repeatedly been praised for its circular structure.[32] Leaving aside the fact that there is nothing inherently superior in a circular composition, the accusation of a lack of coherence and structure does not do justice to Quintus' composition. Rather, the Posthomeric version can be analyzed as a double dovetailing: the Sinon episode (*PH* 12.353–388) is followed by Laocoon's first appearance and his first punishment (12.389–417); this scheme is repeated by a zooming back to Sinon (12.418–443), which then leads to Laocoon's second appearance and his second punishment (12.444–480).[33] Thereafter, Laocoon's second punishment is mirrored twice. First, the faithful *omina* that unsuccessfully warn the Trojans against the Horse invert the motif of the blind Laocoon who can see the truth despite his blindness (12.500–524), whereas the Trojans are blind to the *omina* despite their intact visual sense. Secondly, Cassandra reinforces Laoco-

---

28 See Bär 2007, 45–51; Maciver 2012a, 34–38; Greensmith 2018, 272–273.
29 Along those lines see also Carvounis 2019, 73. Further see also Hadjittofi 2007, 369.
30 Translation: Heinze 1993, 353. German original: "[Im übrigen hat Vergil mehrfach] das Episodische, das solchen Handlungen anhaftet, glücklich überwunden. In Episoden aufgelöst ist [z.B. die Iliupersis bei Quintus und Tryphiodor:] wir haben eine Fülle von Einzelereignissen vor uns, die beliebig verringert oder vermehrt oder umgestellt werden können, ohne daß dies Einfluß auf die Komposition hätte."
31 See, e.g., Heinze 1915, 66 (n. 1); Keydell 1931, 76; Gärtner 2005, 182, 213, 218.
32 See, e.g., Anderson 1969, 32; La Penna 2005, 328–332; Horsfall 2008, xv–xvi.
33 A similar analysis is provided by Gärtner 2005, 218.

on's warnings, but remains equally unsuccessful (12.525–585).³⁴ With regard to Cassandra, it may be noted that the Posthomeric account again constitutes an inversion of compression and extension, as Quintus gives Cassandra and her warnings considerably more room than Vergil does (12.245–246).

The *PH* and the *Aeneid* have in common that they distribute the appearance of Laocoon on two scenes. However, there are numerous differences in detail;³⁵ and there is one major difference and one major addition in the *PH*: for one, only Laocoon's sons, but not Laocoon himself, are killed (12.447–463), and, for another, the blinding of Laocoon (12.399–415) is added in the Posthomeric account (or, to be more precise, the blinding replaces Laocoon's death).³⁶ The Posthomeric narration contains several metapoetic signposts that suggest an authoritative claim for objectivity as compared to the subjective narration of Aeneas in the *Aeneid*. First, in the Vergilian account, the killing of Laocoon and his sons is (like the rest of the intradiegetic narration) recounted by, and thus focalised through, Aeneas. In the *PH*, on the other hand, we have a typical case of embedded focalisation: the killing of Laocoon's son is told by the primary narrator, but focalised through the Trojans, who all flee and watch the gruesome scene from afar: "and terrible flight overcame the Trojans when they saw the dreadful monsters in the city" (*PH* 12.463–464: κακὴ δ' ἐπενίσετο φύζα / Τρῶας, ὅτ' εἰσενόησαν ἀνὰ πτόλιν αἰνὰ πέλωρα).³⁷ By making the entire population of Troy his eyewitnesses, the Posthomeric narrator challenges the eyewitness perspective by a single individual (Aeneas) projected in the *Aeneid*, and hence, indirectly, the uncontested value of the Vergilian account of this event.

Secondly, the snakes are identified as descendants of Typhon, a creature that, according to Hesiod (*Theog.* 304–325), procreated numerous monsters together with Echidna.³⁸ Typhon is mentioned on two further occasions in the *PH*: at 5.485, Ajax's suicide is compared to Typhon's slaughter by Zeus, and at 6.260–262 (in the ecphrasis of Eurypylus' shield), he is mentioned as the father

---

34 On the similarity of the roles of Laocoon and Cassandra as they both warn unsuccessfully see Zintzen 1979, 40–41; Campbell 1981, 177–178; Clausen 2002, 67; Gärtner 2005, 221–225.
35 See Vian 1959, 64–68; Zintzen 1979, 32–39; Gärtner 2005, 195–197, 205–218.
36 On the different traditions as to who is killed (Laocoon and one of his two sons; both sons, but not Laocoon; all three) see Vian 1959, 66; Vian 1969, 81 (n. 3), 221 (n. 6); James 2004, 332. On the blinding of Laocoon see van Krevelen 1964, 179; Vian 1969, 105–106, James 2004, 331; James 2007, 155–157; Ozbek 2007, 179–183.
37 Embedded focalisation, typically expressed via *verba videndi*, is very common in the *PH*; see Argyrouli 2017.
38 The tradition of the two snakes being the offspring of Typhon is not attested elsewhere and may well be Quintus' invention.

of the hellhound Cerberus.[39] Thus, the reference to Typhon at 12.452 does not only "illustrate the menacing nature of the two snakes" (Bärtschi 2019, 329 [n. 299]),[40] but it also (first and foremost) inscribes the two snakes and their story into the context of the *PH* as a whole and — via the implied reference to Hesiod — also into the wider context of Greek literary history. Additionally, the triple reference to the giant Typhon in the *PH* also harks back to the Gigantomachic element that plays a dominant role in the *Aeneid*.[41] That way, the primary narrator adds authority to his version as compared to that of Vergil's Aeneas. The same goes, *mutatis mutandis*, for the third point to be addressed here: the report about the cenotaph which the Trojans erect for Laocoon's two sons and which Laocoon and his wife beweep (*PH* 12.480–499).[42] At the beginning of this digression, the primary narrator notes that "their tomb is still visible" (*PH* 12.480–481: τῶν δ' ἔτι σῆμα / φαίνεθ'). Through this remark, he anchors his version of the story in his own reality by suggesting that what happened in the Homeric past can still be verified now in the present.[43]

These metapoetic signposts, admittedly, do not establish a direct connection to the Vergilian account of the S&L episode, but they add authority and credibility to the primary narration of the *PH*. Thus, they invite the reader of the *PH* to juxtapose this high degree of authority with the subjective and limited narratorial perspective of the version from the *Aeneid*. Moreover, here too it must be recalled again that the S&L episode follows right after the in-text proem in which the author stages himself as a *Homerus novus* (*PH*. 12.306–313). By unveiling his identity as a Homeric figure, Quintus claims corresponding authority in his role as a poet — a poet who was inspired and nobilitated by none else than the Muses from Mount Helicon. This, in turn, entails that the following description of the fall of Troy, beginning with the S&L episode, comes with an enhanced claim for authority too: Quintus claims Homeric authority for his own version of the events and thus implicitly downgrades the analogous account by Vergil.

---

39 See also Bärtschi 2019, 328–329.
40 My translation. German original: "[Die Bezeichnung des Verwandtschaftsverhältnisses] illustriert [an dieser Stelle] die Bedrohlichkeit der beiden Schlangen [...]."
41 See Hardie 1986, 85–156 on the Gigantomachy in the *Aeneid*.
42 This detail of the story too is unattested elsewhere and may likewise be Quintus' own invention.
43 A similar interpretation is offered by Tomasso 2010, 120–121. As Tomasso (*eo loco*) rightly observes, such anchoring signposts can be found in the Homeric epics too, e.g., the mention of Patroclus' tomb at *Il.* 24.16.

4 Conclusion: Re-writing and de-Romanising the *Aeneid* in the Second Sophistic?

In his commentary on *PH* 12, Malcolm Campbell comments on the *quaestio Latina* in relation to the S&L episode as follows (Campbell 1981, 117–118):

> It may be said at once that direct imitation is out of the question, unless Q[uintus] had a remarkably stubborn temperament – so stubborn that, having scanned what V[ergil] had to say on the building of the Horse, on Sinon, on Laocoon, on the introduction of the Horse, he promptly forgot or ignored almost every memorable detail and instead contented himself with reflecting, not always with precision, and sometimes in a spirit of blatant contradiction, the underlying structure, preferring to go elsewhere for a large variety of key elements in the saga.

On a literal level, this statement hardly deserves further attention. However, on a meta-level (which most certainly is not the level of comprehension intended by the author), it hits the nail on its head: for, indeed, the differences between Vergil's account of the S&L story and Quintus' treatment of the same episode are striking, both on the level of detail and with regard to its narrative embedding and narratorial focalisation. Based on the insight that a contemporary reader would, in all likelihood, almost automatically have read the *PH* from the backdrop of the *Aeneid*, these differences must be understood as significant. Martine P. Cuypers was the first to suggest the hypothesis of a potential unwriting or silencing of the *Aeneid* by Quintus (Cuypers 2005, 607):

> We should [...] entertain the possibility that the large discrepancies between Q[uintus] and Vergil in story matter, and the scant evidence for allusion, are not the result of ignorance but of a well-considered 'political' scheme to ignore the Romans' national epic and supplant it with a Greek account of the end of the Trojan war, viewed from the Greek perspective.

With regard to the Posthomeric Sinon, Fotini Hadjittofi has suggested a similar approach (Hadjittofi 2007, 366, 368):

> [Quintus] wanted to efface that very antipathetic picture of Greekness that defined the Roman version of this myth. [...] Quintus' handling of the story of Sinon proves to be a systematic un-doing of the Vergilian version. [...] If Quintus is indeed making a specific textual reference to the *Aeneid*, the effect he is creating is one of contrast; this is no longer just literary *imitatio* or *aemulatio*, but, rather, a case of politically motivated 'renegade' reading and re-writing.

Further, in a more recent study, Lee Fratantuono has taken a similar (yet unpolitical) stance in relation to the story of the Amazon queen Penthesileia in *PH* 1.

Fratantuono suggests that this narrative be read as a reversal of the episode of the Amazon-like heroine Camilla in *Aeneid* 11, whereby *PH* 1 constitutes "a complex hommage [...] that highlights numerous aspects of its poetic commentary on the troubled heroine Camilla" (Fratantuono 2016, 230–231).

The *PH* is a sequel to the *Iliad* as well as a prequel to the *Odyssey*; hence, the implied author of the *PH* must be read as a Homeric figure in an almost pseudepigraphic sense.[44] Under these premises, ignoring, unwriting or silencing the *Aeneid* (or anything Roman, for that matter) appears to be a logical measure for such an author. However, the Roman allusions in the *PH* should not too easily be neglected — although there are few of them in absolute numbers. For one, there are two well-known Roman anachronisms: first, the allusion to beast fights and/or gladiatorial combats in a simile at 6.531–536; and, secondly, Calchas' prophecy of Aeneas' destiny as the founder of Rome after the fall of Troy at 13.336–341.[45] For another, two passages in the *PH* resemble their Vergilian counterpart to such an extent that it seems hard not to regard them as direct signs of *Romanitas*: first, the description of the typically Roman *testudo* technique at 11.358–375 (cf. *Aen.* 9.503–524), and, secondly, the poppy simile at *PH* 4.423–429, which has a strikingly Vergilian colouring (*Aen.* 9.434–437).[46] All these passages should not be dismissed as casual traces or even slips of a seemingly careless poet, but, rather, as subtle (but deliberate) signposts of *Romanitas* that remind the reader of the *PH*'s broader cultural context and its anchoring in imperial Rome. They allow the reader to understand the *PH* as a Greek epic under Rome despite its decidedly Homeric character.[47]

As illustrated above, the relation between Greece and Rome in the Second Sophistic was a complex one and therefore neither the career model nor the escapist model can do justice to the intricate realities of the time. In the Second

---

44 The direct continuity from the *Iliad* to the *PH* is emphasised by the absence of a Muse invocation at the beginning, while the connection to the *Odyssey* is highlighted by a reference to the proem of the *Odyssey* at *PH* 14.630–631. On the metapoetics of the *PH* see Bär 2007; Bär 2009, 69–78; Maciver 2012a, 27–38. On the emphatic lack of a beginning and a closure, see Gärtner 2017.
45 See Vian 1963, viii–ix; James/Lee 2000; Cantilena 2001, 55–56; James 2004, xviii–xix; Gärtner 2005, 24; Tomasso 2010, 127–139, 146–157; Bärtschi, forthcoming.
46 On the *testudo* see Keydell 1954; James 2004, 326; James 2007, 151–152; Tomasso 2010, 140–146; Greensmith (this volume). On the poppy simile see James 2004, 292; James 2007, 152 (oddly, the parallel is not mentioned by Gärtner 2005). See also Bärtschi, forthcoming.
47 Along similar lines see also Tomasso 2010, 158: "I prefer to see the backgrounding of Rome as part of the overall narrative strategy of the *Posthomerica* to link the present more closely with the past." Further see also Avlamis 2019 and Greensmith (this volume).

Sophistic, Greek literature was a powerful, important and much-used means of constructing and negotiating Greek identity and self-consciousness under Rome from various perspectives. Therefore, unlike Cuypers and Hadjittofi, I do not believe that the *PH* should primarily be understood as a text with a political, anti-Roman sense of mission. Rather, the overall message is that of Greek authority in literary and cultural terms, communicated through a Homeric voice with corresponding weight.[48] The Posthomeric version of the S&L episode, with its salient contrasts, inversions, and (at times also) contradictions as compared to Vergil's *Aeneid*, ties in with this message. It is logical that the Trojan Aeneas should portray his own kin in a positive light, but that does not mean that the primary narrator of the *PH* automatically sends a political correction through his shift of perspective and focalisation. The Trojans who torture Sinon are not cruel proto-Romans, nor is the brave Sinon who endures all the pains a Greek Stoic *avant la lettre*.[49] In fact, neither Sinon nor Laocoon are exclusively positive figures in the *PH*: Sinon, despite his much-praised bravery, is closely associated with Odysseus; yet the Posthomeric Odysseus is a highly ambivalent figure who displays clear traits of the villainous liar as inherited from the First Sophistic.[50] Laocoon, in turn, is presented as an ambivalent character through the focalisation of his wife who "bewailed the delusion of her husband [inflicted] by his folly" (*PH* 12.487–488: ἔστενε δ' ἄτην / ἀνέρος ἀφραδίῃ). On the other hand, Rome and the Roman Empire are positively connotated in the *PH* via the phrase ἱερὸν ἄστυ, which is used on several occasions to denote the city of Troy, and on one occasion to denote the city of Rome, by Calchas in his prophecy (*PH* 13.338).[51] By calling Rome a ἱερὸν ἄστυ just like Troy, Calchas evokes the idea

---

[48] I have argued elsewhere that the *PH* can (and should) be read as a response to the widespread revisionist tendencies against Homer in the Second Sophistic (Bär 2010; see already Baumbach/Bär 2007, 8–15, and Bär 2009, 85–91). This view has been challenged by Maciver 2012a, 17–18, and Maciver 2012b. A middle position with a different angle is taken by Avlamis 2019.
[49] It has also been suggested that the Vergilian Sinon be read as an anti-Greek figure: see Stahl 1999, 257–267.
[50] See especially the verbal contest between Odysseus and Ajax at *PH* 5.180–316, where Odysseus resorts to a blatant lie in order to be awarded Achilles' armour (see Bär 2010, 297–310). The Vergilian Sinon with his rhetorical skills is a virtual copy of Ulixes (see, e.g., Highet 1972, 247–248; for further references see Horsfall 2008, 93–95).
[51] The phrase ἱερὸν ἄστυ is used five times by the primary narrator (at 2.242; 3.216; 3.284; 12.351; 13.558) and once by a secondary narrator (at 5.191, by the Greater Ajax) as a reference to Troy. Furthermore, it is used once by Odysseus with reference to Tenedos (at 12.235).

that Troy will live eternally through Rome despite its fall.[52] Thus, Quintus is not an anti-Roman author in a political sense, and he even occasionally reminds his readers of the real-life context of his Homeric epic.[53] Yet, with his own account of the S&L episode, Quintus removes the specific *Romanitas* from its famous Vergilian counterpart, and he redrafts the final days of Troy in a new, cleaned-up, and—so it seems—more objective manner. By rewriting and de-Romanising parts of the *Aeneid*, Quintus claims literary authority for his own version with the help of his Homeric voice.[54]

Bibliography

Adams, J.N. (2003), *Bilingualism and the Latin Language*, Cambridge.
Anderson, W.S. (1969), *The Art of the Aeneid*, Englewood Cliffs.
Argyrouli, E. (2017), *Embedded Focalization and Visuality in Quintus Smyrnaeus' Posthomerica*, Amsterdam (unpublished MA thesis).
Austin, R.G. (1964), *P. Vergili Maronis Aeneidos liber secundus*, Oxford.
Avlamis, P. (2019), "Contextualizing Quintus: The Fall of Troy and the Cultural Uses of the Paradoxical Cityscape in *Posthomerica* 13", in: *Transactions of the American Philological Association* 149, 149–208.
Baldwin, B. (1976), "Vergilius Graecus", in: *American Journal of Philology* 97, 361–368.
Baldwin, B. (1982), "Vergil in Byzantium", in: *Antike und Abendland* 28, 81–93.
Bär, S. (2007), "Quintus Smyrnaeus und die Tradition des epischen Musenanrufs", in: Baumbach/Bär/Dümmler (2007), 29–64.
Bär, S. (2009), *Quintus Smyrnaeus. »Posthomerica« 1. Die Wiedergeburt des Epos aus dem Geiste der Amazonomachie. Mit einem Kommentar zu den Versen 1–219*, Göttingen.
Bär, S. (2010), "Quintus of Smyrna and the Second Sophistic", in: *Harvard Studies in Classical Philology* 105, 287–316.
Bär, S./Baumbach, M. (2015), "The Epic Cycle and Imperial Greek Epic", in: Fantuzzi/Tsagalis (2015), 604–622.
Bärtschi, A. (2019), *Titanen, Giganten und Riesen im antiken Epos: Eine literaturtheoretische Neuinterpretation*, Heidelberg.

---

[52] I disagree with Hadjittofi's interpretation that the parallelism of Troy and Rome via this phrase should be "suggestive of a Rome that is not eternal, but just as ephemeral as her predecessor" (Hadjittofi 2007, 364). On the widespread idea of Rome as a second Troy see, e.g., Henry 1989, 43–65.
[53] See also Greensmith (this volume) on the idea of reconciling the Roman and the Homeric contexts using the *Odyssey* as an aetiological bridge.
[54] I offer my thanks to Emma Greensmith and to the three editors of this volume for their most valuable feedback on a first version of this chapter. Furthermore, I also warmly thank Emma for her proficient copy-editing.

Bärtschi, A. (forthcoming), *"Testudo ad portas!* A Narratological Deconstruction of Anachronisms".
Baumbach, M./Bär, S. (eds. in collaboration with Dümmler, N.) (2007), *Quintus Smyrnaeus. Transforming Homer in Second Sophistic Epic*, Berlin/New York.
Baumbach, M./Bär, S. (2007), "An Introduction to Quintus Smyrnaeus' *Posthomerica*", in: Baumbach/Bär/Dümmler (2007), 1–26.
Becker, P. (1913), "Vergil und Quintus", in: *Rheinisches Museum* 68, 68–90.
Binder, G. (2019), *P. Vergilius Maro: Aeneis. Ein Kommentar*, 3 vols., Trier.
Bowersock, G.W. (1969), *Greek Sophists in the Roman Empire*, Oxford.
Bowie, E.L. (1970), "Greeks and their Past in the Second Sophistic", in: *Past and Present* 46, 3–41.
Campbell, M. (1981), *A Commentary on Quintus Smyrnaeus Posthomerica XII*, Leiden.
Cantilena, M. (2001), "Cronologia e tecnica compositiva dei Posthomerica di Quinto Smirneo", in: F. Montanari/S. Pittaluga (eds.), *Posthomerica: Tradizioni omeriche dall'Antichità al Rinascimento*, Genoa, 51–70.
Carvounis, K. (2019), *A Commentary on Quintus of Smyrna, Posthomerica 14*, Oxford.
Clausen, W.V. (1987), *Virgil's Aeneid and the Tradition of Hellenistic Poetry*, Berkeley/Los Angeles/London.
Clausen, W.V. (2002), *Virgil's Aeneid: Decorum, Allusion, and Ideology*, Munich/Leipzig.
Cuypers, M.P. (2005), Review of James/Lee (2000), in: *Mnemosyne* 58, 605–614.
Eshleman, K. (2012), *The Social World of Intellectuals in the Roman Empire: Sophists, Philosophers, and Christians*, Cambridge.
Fantuzzi, M./Tsagalis, C. (2015), *The Greek Epic Cycle and its Ancient Reception: A Companion*, Cambridge.
Finglass, P.J. (2015), "Iliou persis", in: Fantuzzi/Tsagalis (2015), 344–354.
Fisher, E.E. (1982), "Greek Translations of Latin Literature in the Fourth Century A.D.", in: *Yale Classical Studies* 27, 173–215.
Fratantuono, L. (2016), "The Penthesilead of Quintus Smyrnaeus: A Study in Epic Reversal", in: *Wiener Studien* 129, 207–231.
Gall, D./Wolkenhauer, A. (eds.) (2009), *Laokoon in Literatur und Kunst*, Berlin/New York.
Gärtner, U. (2005), *Quintus Smyrnaeus und die Aeneis: Zur Nachwirkung Vergils in der griechischen Literatur der Kaiserzeit*, Munich.
Gärtner, U. (2009), "Laokoon bei Quintus Smyrnaeus", in: Gall/Wolkenhauer (2009), 127–145.
Gärtner, U. (2013), "Πιερίδες, τί μοι ἁγνὸν ἐφωπλίσσασθε Μάρωνα; Das griechische Epos der Kaiserzeit und die Bezüge zur lateinischen Literatur", in: P. Schubert/P. Derron (eds.), *Les grecs héritiers des Romains*, Vandœuvres/Geneva, 87–146.
Gärtner, U. (2015), "Virgil and the Epic Cycle", in: Fantuzzi/Tsagalis (2015), 543–564.
Gärtner, U. (2017), "Ohne Anfang und Ende? Die *Posthomerica* des Quintus Smyrnaeus als ›Intertext‹", in: C. Schmitz/J. Telg genannt Kortmann/A. Jöne (eds.), *Anfänge und Enden: Narrative Potentiale des antiken und nachantiken Epos*, Heidelberg, 313–338.
Goldhill, S. (ed.) (2001), *Being Greek Under Rome: Cultural Identity, the Second Sophistic and the Development of Empire*, Cambridge.
Greensmith, E. (2018), "When Homer Quotes Callimachus: Allusive Poetics in the Proem of the *Posthomerica*", in: *Classical Quarterly* 68, 257–274.
Greensmith, E. (2020), *The Resurrection of Homer in Imperial Greek Epic: Quintus Smyrnaeus' Posthomerica and the Poetics of Impersonation*, Cambridge.
Hadjittofi, F. (2007), "*Res Romanae*: Cultural Politics in Quintus Smyrnaeus' *Posthomerica* and Nonnus' *Dionysiaca*", in: Baumbach/Bär/Dümmler (2007), 357–378.

Hardie, P.R. (1986), *Virgil's Aeneid: Cosmos and Imperium*, Oxford.
Harries, J. (1999), *Law and Empire in Late Antiquity*, Cambridge.
Heinze, R. (1915), *Vergils epische Technik*. Third Revised Edition, Leipzig/Berlin.
Heinze, R. (1993), *Vergil's Epic Technique*, tr. H. Harvey/D. Harvey/F. Robertson, Berkeley/Los Angeles.
Henry, E. (1989), *The Vigour of Prophecy: A Study of Virgil's Aeneid*, Bristol.
Hidber, T. (2006), "Vom Umgang der Griechen mit lateinischer Sprache und Literatur", in: *Paideia* 61, 237–254.
Highet, G. (1972), *The Speeches in Vergil's Aeneid*, Princeton.
Holzberg, N. (2006), *Vergil: Der Dichter und sein Werk*, Munich.
Horsfall, N. (2006), *Virgil, Aeneid 3: A Commentary*, Leiden/Boston.
Horsfall, N. (2008), *Virgil, Aeneid 2: A Commentary*, Leiden/Boston.
Irmscher, J. (1985), "Vergil in der griechischen Antike", in: *Klio* 67, 281–285.
James, A.W. (2004), *Quintus of Smyrna. The Trojan Epic. Posthomerica*, Baltimore.
James, A.W. (2007), "Quintus of Smyrna and Vergil – A Matter of Prejudice", in: Baumbach/Bär/Dümmler (2007), 145–157.
James, A.W./Lee, K. (2000), *A Commentary on Quintus of Smyrna, Posthomerica V*, Leiden/Boston/Cologne.
Kauffman, N. (2019), "Slaughter and Spectacle in Quintus Smyrnaeus *Posthomerica*", in: *Classical Quarterly* 68, 634–648.
Kehmptzow, F. (1891), *De Quinti Smyrnaei fontibus ac mythopoeia*, Kiel.
Keydell, R. (1931), "Die griechische Poesie der Kaiserzeit (bis 1929)", in: *Jahresbericht über die Fortschritte der klassischen Altertumswissenschaft* 230, 41–161.
Keydell, R. (1949/50), "Seneca und Cicero bei Quintus von Smyrna", in: *Würzburger Jahrbücher für die Altertumswissenschaft* 4, 81–88.
Keydell, R. (1954), "Quintus von Smyrna und Vergil", in: *Hermes* 82, 254–256.
Keydell, R. (1961), Review of Vian (1959), in: *Gnomon* 33, 278–284.
Kleinknecht, H. (1944), "Laokoon", in: *Hermes* 79, 66–111.
Kopff, E.C. (1981), "Vergil and the Cyclic Epics", in: *Aufstieg und Niedergang der römischen Welt* II.31.2, 919–947.
La Penna, A. (2005), *L'impossibile giustificazione della storia. Un'interpretazione di Virgilio*, Rome/Bari.
Maciver, C.A. (2007), "Returning to the Mountain of *Arete*: Reading Ecphrasis, Constructing Ethics in Quintus Smyrnaeus' *Posthomerica*", in: Baumbach/Bär/Dümmler (2007), 259–284.
Maciver, C.A. (2012a), *Quintus Smyrnaeus' Posthomerica: Engaging Homer in Late Antiquity*, Leiden/Boston.
Maciver, C.A. (2012b), "Flyte of Odysseus: Allusion and the *Hoplōn Krisis* in Quintus Smyrnaeus *Posthomerica* 5", in: *American Journal of Philology* 133, 601–628.
Manuwald, B. (1985), "*Improvisi aderunt*: Zur Sinon-Szene in Vergils *Aeneis* (2,57–198)", in: *Hermes* 113, 183–208.
Most, G.W. (2010), "Laocoons", in: J. Farrell/M.C.J. Putnam (eds.), *A Companion to Vergil's Aeneid and Its Tradition*, Malden/Oxford/Chichester, 325–340.
Mynors, R.A.B. (1969), *P. Vergili Maronis Opera*, Oxford.
Nesselrath, H.-G (2009), "Laokoon in der griechischen Literatur bis zur Zeit Vergils", in: Gall/Wolkenhauer (2009), 1–13.
Noack, F. (1892), Review of Kehmptzow (1891), in: *Göttingische Gelehrte Anzeigen* 20, 769–812.

Ozbek, L. (2007), "Ripresa della tradizione e innovazione compositiva: la medicina nei *Posthomerica* di Quinto Smirneo", in: Baumbach/Bär/Dümmler (2007), 159–183.
Puech, B. (2002), *Orateurs et sophistes grecs dans les inscriptions d'époque impériale*, Paris.
Reichmann, V. (1943), *Römische Literatur in griechischer Übersetzung*, Leipzig.
Rochette, B. (1997), *Le latin dans le monde grec: Recherches sur la diffusion de la langue et des lettres latines dans les provinces hellénophones de l'Empire romain*, Brussels.
Rohde, E. (1914), *Der griechische Roman und seine Vorläufer*. Third Revised Edition, Wiesbaden.
Scafoglio, G. (2022), "Quintus and the Epic Cycle", in: S. Bär/E. Greensmith/L. Ozbek (eds.), *Quintus of Smyrna's Posthomerica: Writing Homer Under Rome*, Edinburgh, 298–318.
Scheijnen, T. (2018), *Quintus of Smyrna's Posthomerica. A Study of Heroic Characterization and Heroism*, Leiden/Boston.
Schmitz, T. (1997), *Bildung und Macht: Zur sozialen und politischen Funktion der zweiten Sophistik in der griechischen Welt der Kaiserzeit*, Munich.
Stahl, H.-P. (1999), "Griechenhetze in Vergils *Aeneis*: Roms Rache für Troja", in: G. Vogt-Spira/B. Rommel (eds.), *Rezeption und Identität: Die kulturelle Auseinandersetzung Roms mit Griechenland als europäisches Paradigma*, Stuttgart, 249–273.
Swain, S. (1996), *Hellenism and Empire: Language, Classicism, and Power in the Greek World AD 50–250*, Oxford.
Tomasso, V. (2010), *"Cast in Later Grecian Mould": Quintus of Smyrna's Reception of Homer in the Posthomerica*, PhD Dissertation, Stanford University. Available online at: https://purl.stanford.edu/hn098nn5393.
Tsomis, G.P. (2018), *Quintus Smyrnaeus: Originalität und Rezeption im zehnten Buch der Posthomerica*, Trier.
Van Hoof, L. (2010), "Greek Rhetoric and the Later Roman Empire. The Bubble of the 'Third Sophistic'", in: *Antiquité Tardive* 18, 211–224.
Van Krevelen, D.A. (1964), "Quintus Smyrnaeus und die Medizin", in: *Janus* 51, 178–183.
Vian, F. (1959), *Recherches sur les Posthomerica de Quintus de Smyrne*, Paris.
Vian, F. (1963-9), *Quintus de Smyrne. La suite d'Homère*. Tome I. Livres I–IV, 1963; Tome II. Livres V–IX, 1966; Tome III. Livres X–XIV, 1969, Paris.
Whitmarsh, T. (2001), *Greek Literature and the Roman Empire: The Politics of Imitation*, Oxford.
Whitmarsh, T. (2013), *Beyond the Second Sophistic. Adventures in Greek Postclassicism*, Berkeley/Los Angeles/London.
Woolf, G. (1994), "Becoming Roman, Staying Greek: Culture, Identity and the Civiziling Process in the Roman East", in: *Proceedings of the Cambridge Philological Society* 40, 116–143.
Zintzen, C. (1979), *Die Laokoonepisode bei Vergil*, Wiesbaden.

Emma Greensmith
Odysseus the Roman: Imperial Temporality and the *Posthomerica*

Abstract: This chapter offers a reformulation of the *quaestio Latina* for Quintus of Smyrna's *Posthomerica*, centred on the contentious issue of the poem's level of engagement with Vergil's *Aeneid*. Using a re-reading of two key passages of potential Vergilian intertextuality — Calchas' prophecy about the future glory of Rome (*PH* 13.333–399), and the invention of the *testudo* battle formation (*PH* 11.358–396) — I argue that Quintus' silence with regard to the *Aeneid* is a sign of deliberate distancing, which sheds light on the broader cultural poetics of his work. By delicately evoking in these episodes not Vergil's *Aeneid* but rather Homer's *Odyssey*, Quintus, I suggest, co-opts features of Vergilian epic and re-absorbs them into a Homeric dominant model. Through this process, Greek and Roman poetics, plots, and aetiologies are combined and synchronised, in a positive statement of Quintus' position as a Homerising poet composing under Roman rule.

Keywords: Quintus/*Posthomerica*; Vergil/*Aeneid*; anachronism; intertextuality; temporality; empire.

> *Language failed me very often, but then, the substitute was silence, but not violence.*
> Elie Wiesel

> *To be honest, I hate silence.*
> Chuck Palahniuk

1 Introduction: 'Who speaks'?

The question of Quintus' engagement with Latin literature — and particularly, the influence of Vergil's *Aeneid* — is one which will not fall silent.[1] The strategies of finding an answer, as for most imperial Greek epic, have tended to fall into two opposing camps — either hard-core *Quellenforschung* (the hunt for

---
[1] The text of Quintus throughout is that of Vian (1963–9); and translations are adapted from Hopkinson 2018. Text and translations of the *Iliad* are taken from Murray/Wyatt 1999; of the *Odyssey* from Murray/Dimock 1998; and of the *Aeneid* from Fairclough/Goold 1999.

definitive parallels and "allusions")[2] or self-abnegating reader-reception (we cannot know for sure what Quintus knew, so "our Quintus must always be a reading").[3] Needless to say, neither camp has emerged victorious. Difficulty in both cases arises not only from the obvious and perennial problems with searching for intertextual equivalences between different languages, but also, in imperial literature more specifically, from the fact that in the Greek and Latin poems which cover the same themes, divergences seem to outweigh similarities. This situation has led many scholars to conclude that these Greek poets either did not know the Latin material at all; knew it insufficiently closely to make detailed use of it — a possibility apparently 'corroborated' by the existence of a number of Greek translations of canonical Latin works from the 3rd and 4th centuries –[4]; or relied on now-unknown Alexandrian material to construct their narratives: the durable adage of the 'lost Hellenistic source' still exerts a very strong hold in this field.

So, if *Quellenforschung* "is not dead, but moribund"[5] for most assessments of classical literary interactions, then a quirk arises in the case of the *Posthomerica* that not only does this approach still hold sway in a surprising number of scholarly quarters, but also that it is driven by a very specific attitude to the work as a poetic text. Ursula Gärtner's *Quintus Smyrnaeus und die Aeneis* (2005) illustrates the situation. Gärtner systematically examines some 75 parallel passages of Quintus and Vergil's epics and tests them for possible correspondences (largely single motifs: images, descriptions, character actions, and speech). For the large majority (63 cases) her verdict concerning direct influence is either uncertain or negative.[6] Gärtner also reminds us of some rather more conclusive judgements of Quintus' achievements as a poet. She ends by imploring her readers to free themselves from the long-standing dichotomy in which Vergil is

---

[2] I use the German term *Quellenforschung* non-pejoratively, to refer to the process of source-criticism, due to the traction which the term continues to have in Anglophone scholarship to refer to a particular mode of reading (see Most 2016 as discussed below for one stark illustration).

[3] Quotation adapted from Maciver 2012a, 12. Maciver in practice tends to pursue a productively maximalist approach to Quintus and the Latin question (see particularly Maciver 2011). In recent years Maciver seems to have changed his viewpoint on the matter; see Gärtner, this volume, p. 23 (with n. 77), and Preface, n. 5 (on p. 3).

[4] See especially Fisher 1982, who shows that many of these are dated to the 4th century.

[5] Most 2016, 933.

[6] For earlier studies of Quintus and Vergil see Tychsen 1807, Köchly 1850, and Heinze 1915, 63–81 respectively. Keydell, in a series of publications – 1931, 1954, 1961, and 1963 – offers a positive reading of direct dependence of Quintus on Vergil. His arguments were strongly contested by Vian 1959.

brilliant, and Quintus is "a poor poet"[7] "whose epic is like a shark's stomach, full of undigested material."[8]

Such pessimistic views of the *Posthomerica*'s poetic merits show above all how the Latin debate for this epic most particularly has been hampered not only by historical unknowns, but also by inherent assumptions about intertextuality and aesthetic quality. Silencing Latin influences has meant silencing Quintus, used as further evidence for his lack of originality or critical precision.[9] Reversing the situation — appreciating more fully Quintus' poetic capabilities and capacious allusive range — can and must lead to a reformulation of the Latin question for this epic and its agenda.

In many ways this process is already well underway. The revival of the *Posthomerica* as a text worth reading 'in its own right' is evidenced by the flurry of output on the poem in the past decades, with more soon to come.[10] A far cry from the critical position even thirty years ago, when Christian Habicht could declare with confidence that in imperial Greece "poetry was dead,"[11] verse is recognised as a living medium of expression in the imperial Greek world, and Quintus is taking his place as a major witness to the literary and cultural concerns driving his period at large. In terms of the Latin question too, as this volume's preface makes clear, a number of initiatives have already sought to reinvigorate the exploration of later Greek literature alongside Latin works, and to open up a dialogue between the two traditions. Taking our cue from such projects, and from this volume's starting-premise — that "it is possible that the Greek poets of the Late Antiquity were indeed familiar with crucial works of Latin poetry such as Vergil's *Aeneid* and Ovid's *Metamorphoses*, be it in the original or in translation, and that this familiarity was used in individual, crea-

---

7 Gärtner takes this quotation from Keydell 1931, 75, and Bethe 1910, 327.
8 Gärtner 2005, 286. For the shark image she borrows from a letter by Robert Musil to Johannes v. Allesch dated 15.3.1931. See also the discussion by James 2006, 329.
9 Thus James 2007, 414 summarises that "the success with which [Quintus] imitated the language and style of the Homeric epics encouraged the opinion that he lacked sufficient originality to do more than simply reproduce the material from the sources" — i.e., *had* he known Vergil as well as he does Homer, he would have used him directly and non-adaptively.
10 To take just some examples from the past ten years alone: at the time of writing this chapter there has been an international conference on Quintus (Zurich, 2006) and an international workshop (Cambridge, 2016); two major edited volumes (Baumbach/Bär/Dümmler 2007; Bär/Ozbek/Greensmith 2022) and a number of monographs and commentaries (most recently Scheijnen 2018, Carvounis 2019, and Greensmith 2020).
11 Habicht 1985. See further discussion in Bowie 1989.

tive ways" —[12] we should now pursue with confidence a model of intertextuality, in which imperial Greek poets engage with a range of models, inventively and often covertly, involving not only the 'quotation' of lines or borrowed material, but also the ideological and aesthetic transportation of one set of literary signs, symbols, and even whole cultural systems onto another. We can, in other words, move on: from asking not (just) whether our imperial Greek authors used Latin models, but how they used them, and why... or why *not*.

It is now rightly being perceived that this question of 'why not' is just as important: that *non*-engagement with Latin sources on the part of imperial Greek poets does not necessarily bespeak incompetence or ignorance, but can be read as a directed and loaded choice. In the case of Quintus specifically, as an author intent on re-writing Homeric epic for a Greek readership living under Roman rule in the 3rd century (and we shall return to this central issue of Homer later), the refusal to acknowledge the *Aeneid* — as the foundational text of Roman imperial glory — becomes significant, on a political as well as literary plain. As Simon Goldhill has recently argued, to a Greek reader familiar with the *Aeneid* in any form or medium, and aware of its role in Roman literary culture, a lack of reference to the *Aeneid* would itself be significant — "as a ghostly echo of distinctiveness if not as a strategy of cultural independence."[13] Fotini Hadjittofi has closely analysed such moments of "emphatic silence" in Quintus' treatment of the *Aeneid*, which she reads as reflective of a "certain distance" from Roman ideology that Greek authors of the Second Sophistic could maintain; a contestation and re-negotiation of Roman and Greek identities which is distinctly *of its time*.[14] And Silvio Bär's chapter in this volume further reveals the successful results that such an approach can yield: considering the Sinon and Laocoon episodes of the *Posthomerica* as a "re-writing and de-Romanization of Vergil's

---

12 See Preface to this volume, p. 4. That this premise is not only sensible, but correct, is surely corroborated by the evidence for widespread bilingualism in the imperial Greek period: see recently Adams 2003; Adams/Janse/Swain 2002, and Mullen/Elder 2019. As for the idea that the existence of Greek translations of Latin works suggests that Greeks could not read the original, one wonders what a historian of the future would make of any modern Classicist's Latin and Greek abilities should they discover the hordes of Penguin translations and Loebs in every library, office, and personal collection...
13 Goldhill, forthcoming. See also the earlier and instructive comments along these lines by Cuypers 2005, 607, as discussed and quoted in Bär's chapter in this volume.
14 Hadjittofi 2007, quotations from p. 360. Hadjittofi contraposes this "accentuated... Hellenism of the Second Sophistic" to the "prevalence of cultural pluralism" more demonstrative of Late Antiquity, as is revealed (she argues) in the different treatments of Roman material of Quintus in the 3rd century and Nonnus in the 5th.

Aeneid," he reveals how Quintus' interaction with Vergil can take the form of a bold turning away from his obvious Latin model, as Quintus removes the Roman-ness from these two famous Vergilian scenes and redrafts the sack of Troy in a new, "cleaned-up" fashion.

This chapter in one respect makes a further contribution to this style of reading. However, it also takes it in a different direction. Acknowledging that Quintus makes full and creative use of 'weaponised silence' in relation to the *Aeneid*, and largely removes Vergil's poem from his narrative, I want to consider what takes its place. If the silence speaks, then what sounds do we hear instead? Taking as my starting point the most fundamental paradox of the *Posthomerica* — that Quintus both implicitly claims Homeric identity and engages subtly with his imperial context — I shall read two key passages of Vergilian (dis)engagement as a self-conscious commentary on the poem's anachronistic technique: Calchas' prophecy about the future glory of Rome (*PH* 13.333–349), and the invention of the *testudo* battle formation (*PH* 11.358–396). By evoking in these episodes systematically and pointedly not Vergil's *Aeneid* but rather Homer's *Odyssey*, Quintus co-opts symbolic Vergilian imagery and motifs and turns them (back) into Homeric tropes. Rome's foundational poem is thus deconstructed to become a pre-Roman, yet fully imperial, Greek epic, and the story of Rome is defiantly synchronised into an aetiology of Homeric Greece.

2 (Im)perfect timing: Epigonality and empire

The idea of merging different forms of time has a long and varied history across ancient epic. In Homeric poetry itself, whereas the *Iliad* is seen as strong, teleological, and closed — marking its end by the *topos* of the burial of Hector and the formal device of ring composition of a father coming to hostile territory to reclaim his child[15] — the *Odyssey* delights first in "aimless" episodes of wandering and digression before allowing itself to be organised by a quest that, however much it may be deferred by adventure, will finally achieve its goal.[16] These different courses are directly manifest in the subsequent development of the epic genre, as hexameter texts charted their own responses to this double pull of Homeric time. Apollonius, to take what is now the most extensively discussed

---

[15] See especially de Jong 2014, 90 and Lowe 2000.
[16] On this way of conceptualising the *Odyssey*'s temporality see Quint 1993, 9 (from whence comes "aimless") and Lowe 2000, 151.

example, shapes his entire voyaging epic around a twofold approach to the Homeric past. On the one hand, the *Argonautica* is focused on constructing distinct layers of embedded, distant time. The proem announces its epigonal subject matter — the topic of "earlier singers" (*Arg.* 18–19), and a story already old for Homer (cf. *Od.* 12.69–70), an "always already distanced model of excellence."[17] But at the same time, through the towering presence of the quasi-eternal god Apollo, from whom the narrator "begins" (*Arg.* 1.1), the proem — and, as it continues, the poem — also points to the essential *continuity* of the past, which is not hermetically sealed from the present.[18] So too in the Latin epic tradition, where poets found numerous ways to reveal how earlier models were both essentially and eternally 'old' and also part of their on-going present. Thus to take just two major examples, Ennius' Pythagorean treatment of Homer, moves away from a literary dependence on an earlier ancestor to create a Homer *redivivus*, which enacts the direct cultural transmission from Greek to Latin through the physical act of rebirth into another's body.[19] And Ovid's kaleidoscopic treatment of Vergil in his own epic-rewriting of the *Aeneid* in *Metamorphoses* 13–14 produces a situation where, in Hinds' words, "rather than constructing himself as an epigonal reader of the *Aeneid*, Ovid makes Vergil a hesitant precursor of the *Metamorphoses*."[20]

These various techniques of epigonality acquired a special valence in the wider literary culture of Quintus' era, and became strongly associated with the writings and performances of the Second Sophistic: an epoch which, as many scholars have finely shown, was intent on forging a close connection with the mythological and classical past. A number of studies have revealed the emphasis placed on role-playing and play-acting in Second Sophistic declamations: the re-enactment of scenes from history and the close immediate representation of figures from the mythological and historical past.[21] Surviving works also bear witness to "close encounters"[22] with resurrected figures from myth and history. Homer or Socrates was available to be consulted in speeches; famous figures would appear in dreams, and even in the less fleeting, waking world via epiphany. Many traditions also found ways to refract later intellectual and cultural production into an earlier origin and source, most often by citing Homer as the

---

[17] Goldhill 1991, 284.
[18] See, e.g., Klooster 2007, 64 f.
[19] See Zeitlin 2001, 236 f. and Hardie 1993, 103.
[20] Hinds 1998, 106.
[21] See Anderson 1993; Zeitlin 2001; Schmitz 1997 and 1999, 71–92; Konstan/Saïd 2006.
[22] A term used productively in late antique contexts by Lane Fox 1986.

container of all subsequent knowledge and truth. Thus Pseudo-Plutarch's *Essay on the Life and Poetry of Homer* presents the poet as ἡ ἀρχή of all things, from politics to medicine, drama, and literature.[23] The later exponents of Neoplatonist *allegoresis* sought to reconcile the views of their two heroes, Homer and Plato, by conceiving of Homer as a divine sage privy to the most fundamental forms of philosophical truth.[24] And a number of imperial writers also drew associations between specific Homeric characters and later intellectual movements; such as the popular notion that Homer's "much enduring" Odysseus was a proto-Stoic, with authors such as Seneca, Epictetus, Musonius, and Dio Chrysostom all transmitting a Stoicising version of the hero.[25]

All of these writers, thinkers, and works, then, practised a particularly bold form of temporal mixology: they explored different ways of colliding the distant past and the contemporary present, with seams, the methodology, and the justifications often unapologetically on show. These ideas of course have a political as well as literary significance. In the epic sphere, this political dimension has been explored most influentially by David Quint in *Epic and Empire*.[26] In his account of how the epics of the western tradition responded to the two different narrative modes offered by the *Iliad* and *Odyssey*, Quint splits the history of the epic genre into two political strands — two different forms of response to imperialism: the Vergilian epics of teleology, conquest, and empire that take the victors' side[27] and the countervailing, loose, wandering epics of the defeated and of republican liberty:[28]

> The victors experience history as a coherent, end-directed story told by their own power; the losers experience a contingency that they are powerless to shape their own ends.[29]

The 'antiquarianism' of the Greek Second Sophistic has an equally imperial inflection. As David Konstan and Susan Saïd have emphasised, not all epochs are engaged in such a reflexive relationship with the past. Moments of 'crisis'

---

23 See Keaney/Lamberton 1986; Pontani 2005.
24 Lamberton 1986.
25 This concept of a proto-Stoic Odysseus did not begin in the imperial era (see, e.g., Buffière 1956, 316–317) but it certainly increased in popularity and inventiveness. See Montiglio 2011, 66–94. For the relevance of this vision of Odysseus to Quintus' epic see Maciver 2012a and Bär's chapter in this volume.
26 Quint 1993.
27 Quint 1993 focuses on the *Aeneid* itself, Camoes' *Lusíadas*, Tasso's *Gerusalemme liberata*.
28 Lucan's *Pharsalia*, Ercilla's *Araucana*, and d'Aubigné's *Les tragiques*. On politicised time in Lucan see also Masters 1992.
29 Quint 1993, 9.

tend in particular to elicit a tendency to imitate one's forebears so directly.[30] After the *Pax Romana*, the Greek east was involved in a complex version of such a crisis, of cultural as well as political identity.[31] As a result, this was an age intensely self-conscious about its relation to 'the before'; which manifested itself in an ironic but intense reverence for antique models.[32] As they memorably put it, "continuities were perceived and invented, differences were grafted onto the past to create new figures, in the way that grids on two superimposed transparencies produce elaborate and unexpected moiré patterns."[33]

Quintus reveals himself to be fully immersed in these twin traditions of temporality (epic and Second Sophistic).[34] However, he moves with them in a different way. This difference is rooted in the most central aspect of the *Posthomerica*, an aspect which makes it unique among surviving imperial Greek epic: its implicit claim to Homeric authorship, and to being the missing middle part of Homer's epic canon — Iliadic sequel, Odyssean prequel.[35] The direct continuity with the *Iliad* is announced by the unexpected absence of a Muse invocation at the beginning of book 1, while the connection to the *Odyssey* is secured by an increase in Odyssean allusions in the final books of the poem, and a direct intertextual gloss of its opening (*PH* 14.665–668; *Od.* 1.11–12). Quintus also repeats defining Homeric set pieces, most strikingly the Shield of Achilles, stressed as being the very same artefact as that in *Iliad* 19. This self-positioning as 'still Homer' — not a transmission from one language and culture to another, *qua* Ennius, but a direct continuation of the Homeric voice; a Greek Homer 'in his own words' — must affect our interpretation of Quintus' whole intertextual programme, the tone in which we take his engagement, or non-engagement with any later literary works. This poet, in other words, cannot 'signal' his use of the *Aeneid*, he cannot flaunt his Vergilian influence in the way that Roman writers do with their Greek models, because according to the conceit of his poem, to do so would be to veer outside of the rules of time. In this poem of the Homeric

---

[30] Konstan/Saïd 2006, x.
[31] This crisis has been well delineated by a number of studies: particularly Alcock 1993 and 1997; Hekster 2008 and Ando 2012.
[32] Konstan/Saïd 2006.
[33] Konstan/Saïd 2006, x.
[34] For the potential relationship between the *Posthomerica* and the Second Sophistic, Baumbach/Bär/Dümmler 2007 and Bär 2010 remain the seminal works, with critiques and challenges in Maciver 2012b and Greensmith 2020.
[35] This is by now the standard reading of Quintus' poetics, stretching at least as far back as Köchly 1850. See especially the recent treatments in Maciver 2012a and Greensmith 2020.

interval, Aeneas' story has not happened yet, and Vergil is long yet to be born. This is a story that Homer's characters cannot know; that Homer cannot tell.

We shall now see how Quintus uses this self-constructed position to his unique advantage — to retroject his Roman context, and (a key part of this context) his Latin literary inheritance, into a *Homeric* framework and form. This process is most clearly perceived in the two episodes of the *Posthomerica* usually considered by scholars to be the most explicit moments of 'imperialness' and 'anachrony': where the poem breaks through its Homeric veneer and alludes to events which are incompatible with it.[36] These are also among two of the passages of Quintus most strongly (but problematically) connected with Vergil's *Aeneid*: parts of the story of the sack of Troy where this Latin hypotext 'should' be there, but where its presence is notoriously hard to pin down. By reframing these passages as Odyssean emblems — making the connection not (just) to the Roman 'future present' but to the next part of Homer's own story which, after the final lines of this poem, is just about to unfold — Quintus profoundly changes the terms of engagement. Allusivity and anachrony become issues of fast-forward into Homeric, not Vergilian territory, and the Greek *aetion* of Roman imperial ideas (literary, military, and cultural) is inventively re-emphasised. Given the political significations of epic time, then, the effects of this process offer a powerful illustration of how the *Posthomerica* represents a different, more positive response to the challenges of this particular period of identity-negotiation. If, for Quint, closed epic belongs to the victors, and open-ended narratives to the conquered, then considered as a product of Greek culture under Rome, the *Posthomerica*'s unified view of Roman and Homeric time unsettles both sides of this equation, to reclaim an open *and* closed narrative for so-called *Graecia capta*.

3 A Family affair: Aeneas escapes Troy

In book 13 of the *Posthomerica*, amidst the fiery carnage of Troy's downfall, Aeneas makes his way to safety out of the burning city (*PH* 13.300–332). This episode has unsurprisingly become a major crux in the Vergil debate surrounding the *Posthomerica*, as scholars working from a traditional perspective have

---

[36] I analyse these two passages alongside their so-called "imperial" signals in Greensmith 2020, 328–335. This volume has provided the welcome opportunity for me to expand the arguments first made there, specifically in light of the question of Vergilian textual inheritance.

struggled to agree over specific references or allusions to Aeneas' own account of his dramatic escape (*Aen.* 2.250–804). Particularly vexing are the possible links between Aeneas' tale and Quintus' image of Aeneas carrying his aged father on his shoulders, with the young Ascanius holding his hand, barely able to keep up; and, in the lines immediately following, the description of the flames and the enemies' weapons making way for Aeneas, as he is led (in Quintus) by Venus:

>...ὡς πάις ἐσθλὸς ἐύφρονος Ἀγχίσαο   315
> ἄστυ λιπὼν δηΐοισι καταιθόμενον πυρὶ πολλῷ
> υἱέα καὶ πατέρα σφὸν ἀναρπάξας φορέεσκε,
> τὸν μὲν ἐπὶ πλατὺν ὦμον ἐφεσσάμενος κρατερῇσι
> χερσὶ πολυτλήτῳ ὑπὸ γήραϊ μοχθίζοντα·
> τὸν δ' ἀπαλῆς μάλα χειρὸς ἐπιψαύοντα πόδεσσι   320
> γαίης, οὐλομένου δὲ φοβεύμενον ἔργα μόθοιο
> ἐξῆγεν πολέμοιο δυσηχέος...
>
>   *PH* 13.315–322

So the noble son of wise Anchises abandoned his blazing city to the foe, seized his father and his son, and set off carrying them, lifting the old man, enfeebled by grievous age, on his broad shoulders with his mighty arms, and leading his son by his tender hand, barely touching the ground with his feet and terrified of those acts of deadly war, out of the furore and the fighting.

> *Haec fatus latos umeros subiectaque colla*
> *veste super fulvique insternor pelle leonis,*
> *succedoque oneri; dextrae se parvus Iulus*
> *implicuit sequiturque patrem non passibus aequis.*
>
>   *Aen.* 2.271–274

So I spoke, and over my broad shoulders and bowed neck I spread the cover of a tawny lion's pelt and stoop to the burden. Little Iulus clasps his hand in mine, and follows his father with steps that match not his.

>...Κύπρις δ' ὁδὸν ἡγεμόνευεν
> υἱωνὸν καὶ παῖδα καὶ ἀνέρα πήματος αἰνοῦ
> πρόφρων ῥυομένη· τοῦ δ' ἐσσυμένου ὑπὸ ποσσὶ
> πάντη πῦρ ὑπόεικε, περισχίζοντο δ' αὐτμαὶ
> Ἡφαίστου μαλεροῖο, καὶ ἔγχεα καὶ βέλε' ἀνδρῶν   330
> πῖπτον ἐτώσια πάντα κατὰ χθονὸς ὁππόσ' Ἀχαιοὶ
> κείνῳ ἐπέρριψαν πολέμῳ ἐνὶ δακρυόεντι.
>
>   *PH* 13.326–332

Cypris led the way, eager to protect her grandson, her son and her husband from that dreadful disaster: as he rushed along, the fire everywhere gave way beneath his feet, Hephaestus' raging flames were parted, and all the Achaean warriors' spears and missiles thrown at him in that grievous battle missed their target and fell to the ground.

Descendo, ac ducente deo flammam inter et hostis
expedior; dant tela locum, flammaeque recedunt.
Aen. 2.632–633

I descend and, guided by a god, make my way amid fire and foes. Weapons give me passage and the flames retire.

Now, it is easy to see why Vergilian correspondence-hunting has proven an unsatisfying exercise for this scene: the lack of even bilingual 'quotation' and the number of divergent details (especially in the second example, where in Vergil's account Aeneas parts the enemy fire as he is returning home alone) mean that, as Alan James remarks, "this [set of passages] could hardly suffice to prove Vergil's direct influence if it were not established independently."[37] It is therefore crucial to approach the scene with a more capacious, Greek-and-Latin form of 'intertextuality.' The fact is that to any post-Augustan reader, it is impossible *not* to see a Vergilian footprint on this scene; but this footprint does not need to take the form of an echo — it can be a gesture, a trope, a refusal, or a *substitution*, as Aeneas' tale is turned into something else. It is equally crucial to re-read the scene through the lens of Quintus' still-Homer position. The confined parameters of the *Posthomerica*'s inter-Homeric story in which Aeneas has not yet set sail from Troy, not yet been shipwrecked, is nowhere near ready to take his seat in Carthage and beguile Dido and her banqueters with the *bella exhausta [quae] canebat* (*Aen.* 4.14). Quintus knowingly marks this temporality in the lines immediately following this crux passage. The Greeks attempt to stop Aeneas from escaping — to overhaul the trajectory of the story after Troy's fall, and of Roman imperial glory, by cutting short Aeneas' aftermath which for Quintus and his readers, *has to happen*.

Cypris prevents this revolution. And Calchas then explains why. He stops the Greeks in their pursuit of the family by foretelling the glorious aftermath, and predicting Aeneas' Roman destiny:

καὶ τότε δὴ Κάλχας μεγάλ' ἴαχε λαὸν ἐέργων·
'ἴσχεσθ' Αἰνείαο κατ' ἰφθίμοιο καρήνου
βάλλοντες στονόεντα βέλη καὶ λοίγια δοῦρα.   335
τὸν γὰρ θέσφατόν ἐστι θεῶν ἐρικυδέι βουλῇ
Θύμβριν ἐπ' εὐρυρέεθρον ἀπὸ Ξάνθοιο μολόντα

---

[37] James 2007, 150.

> τευξέμεν ἱερὸν ἄστυ καὶ ἐσσομένοισιν ἀγητὸν
> ἀνθρώποις, αὐτὸν δὲ πολυσπερέεσσι βροτοῖσι
> κοιρανέειν· ἐκ τοῦ δὲ γένος μετόπισθεν ἀνάξειν   340
> ἄχρις ἐπ' ἀντολίην τε καὶ ἀκάματον δύσιν ἐλθεῖν·
> καὶ γάρ οἱ θέμις ἐστὶ μετέμμεναι ἀθανάτοισιν,
> οὕνεκα δὴ πάις ἐστὶν ἐυπολοκάμου Ἀφροδίτης.'
>
> PH 13.333–343

> Then Calchas gave a loud shout restraining the army: "Stop hurling your deadly missiles and murderous spears at mighty Aeneas' head! By the glorious will of the gods he is destined to leave Xanthus and go to Tiber's broad streams, there to found a holy city that will be a marvel even to future men; he himself shall be ruler of a people far and wide, and his descendants shall be lords of an empire extending from the tireless sun's eastern rising to where it sets in the west. And it is right that he should have a place among the immortals, since he is the son of Aphrodite of the beautiful tresses.

This is one of the three most 'direct' references to the Roman empire in Quintus' epic. Together with the arena simile (*PH* 6.532–537), which describes the use of wild beasts in amphitheatre executions, and the *testudo* episode in 11.358–399 (more of which later), this passage, so the usual interpretation goes, breaks with the mythic fiction of the Trojan War and places the *Posthomerica* more firmly in the context of the imperial era.[38] Through the self-distancing vehicle of a prophecy, Quintus comes closest to positioning himself in the context of Roman rule: the prediction describes the lived present of the poet and his readers, and offers a near-direct expression of Roman hegemony in a political sense, by not only pointing, in general terms, to the myth of Rome's origins, but also to the mythologised genealogy of the Julian imperial family, and its complex legacies in Quintus' own time. Scholars have also highlighted two possible (or probable, or doubtful...) intertexts with the *Aeneid* here, both centred on the prophecy of Creusa (*Aen.* 2.776–789), which occurs in the same narrative context as Calchas' premonition. Creusa's speech also contains a proleptic reference to the Tiber (*Aen.* 2.781–782) and a number of phrases which may (or may not) be recognised in Quintus' terms of description (e.g., *leni* [...] *agmine* at *Aen.* 2.782 possibly alludes to the adjective εὐρυρέεθρον, "with broad streams", of *PH* 13.337; and the beginning of Creusa's speech at *Aen.* 2.777 contains a similar proclamation to *PH* 13.336: θέσφατόν ἐστι θεῶν ἐρικυδέι βουλῇ, "by the glorious will of the gods").[39]

---

38 See, e.g., Baumbach/Bär 2007, 3, James 2004, xviii–xix, and especially Tomasso 2010.
39 See Gärtner 2005, 245. There are further possible parallels between Calchas' prediction here and Jupiter's famous prophecy in the first book of the *Aeneid*: for instance, the resounding

More important, however, than any tentative allusions, is how this scene *creates* the myth to which it refers: it allows Aeneas' story, as it is, by Quintus' time, enshrined in Vergil's imperial foundational text, to come into being and take hold. The Calchas of the *Posthomerica*, with his unique insight into the future as a seer, and his consequent ability to break the usual bounds of temporality, intervenes to stop the Greeks' attempt to forestall this myth — he ensures that the momentary glimpse at what a revolutionised imperial epic world would look like if Aeneas had not been allowed to escape remains unfulfilled. So the narrative stays on its ordained course, and the progression from Trojans to Romans (from the Xanthus to the Tiber, the start and end point of Aeneas' journey, [*PH* 13.337: ἀπὸ Ξάνθοιο... Θύμβριν ἐπ' εὐρυρέεθρον, "from Xanthus'... to Tiber's broad streams"]) continues as it must.

There are many potential tensions between Greek and Roman latent in this scene.[40] Is this Hellenic poet making way for the Roman reality which the prophecy inscribes? Does he rail against his lived subjugation — an "indication of resistance to full cultural integration"[41] — or rather describe it with a pointed resignation displaying an all-engulfing hegemony which he, like everyone else, is powerless to stop? In fact, Quintus activates all such tensions, but he reshapes them to articulate a very different message. For once again, and here more than anywhere, we can see how the obsessive search for contemporary signs and Latin intertexts in the *Posthomerica* downplays the significance of two types of *Homeric* texturing at work. The first is the close alignment with the *Iliad*'s own prophecy regarding Aeneas, in which Poseidon prevents Achilles from killing him because of his future role as the salvation of Priam's race:

ἀλλ' ἄγεθ' ἡμεῖς πέρ μιν ὑπὲκ θανάτου ἀγάγωμεν,	300
μή πως καὶ Κρονίδης κεχολώσεται, αἴ κεν Ἀχιλλεὺς	
τόνδε κατακτείνῃ· μόριμον δέ οἵ ἐστ' ἀλέασθαι,	
ὄφρα μὴ ἄσπερμος γενεὴ καὶ ἄφαντος ὄληται	
Δαρδάνου, ὃν Κρονίδης περὶ πάντων φίλατο παίδων	
οἳ ἕθεν ἐξεγένοντο γυναικῶν τε θνητάων.	305
ἤδη γὰρ Πριάμου γενεὴν ἔχθηρε Κρονίων·	
νῦν δὲ δὴ Αἰνείαο βίη Τρώεσσιν ἀνάξει	
καὶ παίδων παῖδες, τοί κεν μετόπισθε γένωνται.	
Il. 20.300–308	

---

imperium sine fine (*Aen.* 1.279) with (especially) *PH* 13.338–339; and *populum late regem* (*Aen.* 1.21) with *PH* 13.339–340.
40 For a differently-focused account of the ambivalences of this scene see Ozbek 2018, 150–154.
41 Hadjittofi 2007, 365.

Come, let us lead him away from death, lest the son of Cronos grow angry in any way, if Achilles slays him; for it is fated for him to escape, so that the race of Dardanus will not perish without seed and be seen no more — of Dardanus whom the son of Cronos loved above all the children born to him from mortal women. For at length the son of Cronos has come to hate the race of Priam; and now truly shall the mighty Aeneas be king among the Trojans, and his sons' sons that shall be born in days to come.

This prophecy — brief, vague, and of course, 'un-Roman' — may seem an unlikely primary model for the *Posthomerica*'s account.⁴² And yet the ancient reception of this passage already paves the way for a more imperial reading of its politics. Part of the manuscript tradition records the variant 'πάντεσσιν ἀνάξει' for line 307; a reading which is also reported by Strabo (13.1.53), and which finds its most emphatic echo in yet another Vergilian prophecy — as the prophetic voice when Delos welcomes the Trojan refugees with yet more premonitions about their as-yet-uncertain future:

'Dardanidae duri, quae vos a stirpe parentum
prima tulit tellus, eadem vos ubere laeto
accipiet reduces. Antiquam exquirite matrem:
hic domus Aeneae cunctis dominabitur oris,
et nati natorum, et qui nascentur ab illis.'
                                    Aen. 3.94–98

Long-suffering sons of Dardanus, the land which bore you first from your parent stock shall welcome you back to her fruitful bosom. Seek out your ancient mother. There the house of Aeneas shall lord it over all lands, even his children's children and their race that shall be born of them.

As Charles McNelis demonstrates, this Vergilian prophecy pointedly starts by addressing Aeneas' men as *Dardanidae*, evidently a nod to the emphasis in the Homeric prophecy that the line of Dardanus must not perish. However, in the following generalising phrase *cunctis orbis*, Vergil reflects the more expansive view of the Trojan line enshrined in the variant reading with πάντεσσιν.⁴³ It therefore seems likely that such a variant may have been preferred in Roman times precisely in light of Aeneas' post-Trojan career, as is celebrated in the *Aeneid*. Quintus reflects this less specific vision of Aeneas' future empire as

---

42 Or at least, a model which Quintus updates entirely. Other versions which may, in my view, less programmatically, lie behind the prophecy include the prophecies in *Homeric Hymn to Aphrodite* and Lycophron's *Alexandra*. See James 2004, 337.
43 McNelis 2018, especially 12–13. See also Hadjittofi 2007, 359.

moving beyond 'just' Troy,[44] but refracts it *back* into a distinctly Homeric-style scene, still within the timeframe of the Trojan War itself. Indeed, Quintus connects his version of this prophecy structurally, thematically, and lexically to the original Iliadic moment of prolepsis; far more tightly than to the Vergilian Creusa scene. His emphasis on γένος suggests Poseidon's repeated γενεή, γενεήν; and θέσφατόν ἐστι reworks the god's fatalistic warning μόριμον δέ οἵ ἐστ'. The mention of the Xanthus (*PH* 13.337) with its strong Homeric associations not just with Troy in a general sense, but also with Achilles' *aristeia* at and with the river[45] also evokes by transferral Achilles' own role in Poseidon's prophecy; where it is from his rage specifically that Aeneas is saved.

This Iliadic connection paves the way for an even more pivotal Homeric allusion, as Calchas adds a second reason why Aeneas must be allowed to escape:

καὶ δ' ἄλλως τοῦδ' ἀνδρὸς ἐὰς ἀπεχώμεθα χεῖρας,
οὕνεκά οἱ χρυσοῖο καὶ ἄλλοις ἐν κτεάτεσσιν   345
....[46]
ἄνδρα σαοῖ φεύγοντα καὶ ἀλλοδαπὴν ἐπὶ γαῖαν,
τῶν πάντων προβέβουλεν ἑὸν πατέρ' ἠδὲ καὶ υἷα·
νὺξ δὲ μί' ἧμιν ἔφηνε καὶ υἱέα πατρὶ γέροντι
ἤπιον ἐκπάγλως καὶ ἀμεμφέα παιδὶ τοκῆα.
PH 13.344–349

For another reason, too, we should offer this man no violence: instead of all his gold and other possessions <. . . . .> which might keep an exile safe even in a foreign land, he preferred his father and his son: this one night has shown us the extraordinary piety of a son toward his father and the blameless love of a parent toward his son.

On the one hand, this praise of Aeneas' paternal and filial piety seems perfectly in-keeping with the 'Roman context' of the scene: it affiliates Quintus' Aeneas with the idealised family figure of Augustan politics and rhetoric, which was so often centred on the promotion of generational continuity and the importance of producing and maintaining a *familia*, all embodied in the *Aeneid*'s metonymic *pater Aeneas*. But on the other hand, the family-centredness as specifically expressed in these lines is reminiscent not just of Augustan Rome, but also of

---

[44] For a more negative reading of Quintus' Calchas' precise terms of praising the empire, and a focus on what is left out and *not* praised (e.g., the eternity of the empire to match its vast spatial scope), see Hadjittofi 2007, 364–365; though she wisely veers away from terming such omissions a fully-fledged anti-Roman agenda.
[45] A connection also made much of by Nonnus during Aeacus' fight with the river (*Dionysiaca* 22, particularly 384–389).
[46] On the probable lacuna here see Vian 1969, 142.

the Homeric Greek world.[47] The image of a hero who is simultaneously a father and a son finds earlier parallel in the figure of Odysseus, whose story starts with a son's anguished search for his father and ends with an anguished father's reunion with his son. This filial triad is instantiated in the final book of the *Odyssey*, which provides the first and only scene where the three generations act together (*Od.* 24.359–364).

Calchas' speech in fact points strikingly to this Odyssean paradigm. The theme of fleeing and entering a foreign land is, we are here reminded linguistically, an original *topos* of Odysseus' wandering. Ἀλλοδαπός (*PH* 13.346) is found most frequently in the *Odyssey* in the context of the central hero's wayward travelling.[48] The reference to gold can also evoke Odysseus' interaction with Laertes, where he discusses the prospect of gifts whilst cruelly testing him (*Od.* 24.274: χρυσοῦ μέν οἱ δῶκ' εὐεργέος ἑπτὰ τάλαντα, "and I gave to him seven talents of finely-wrought gold"). And in the mention of Ascanius as a παῖς (*PH* 13.349) we may hear Odysseus' recollection of himself as a child during this same conversation with his father (*Od.* 24.338: παιδνὸς ἐών, "when I was a child") – a moment which allows us a rare glimpse at his own Telemachean anxieties: now a fully grown hero, Odysseus too was once a naïve and emergent son. More provocatively still, Calchas describes Aeneas as a υἱέα ἤπιον (*PH* 13.348–349). Now, ἤπιος as a Homeric epithet for a person is used most frequently in a specific formula about the family: πατὴρ ὣς ἤπιος αἰεί (and similar variants) is found once in the *Iliad* (24.770, as Helen, addressing Hector in lament, describes Priam's kindness to her) and twice in the *Odyssey*, where it is on both occasions about Odysseus. In the Ithacan assembly, Telemachus remembers his father's kindness:[49]

...τὸ μὲν πατέρ' ἐσθλὸν ἀπώλεσα, ὅς ποτ' ἐν ὑμῖν
τοίσδεσσιν βασίλευε, πατὴρ δ' ὣς ἤπιος ἦεν·
Od. 2.46–47

First, I have lost my noble father who was once king among you here, and was gentle as a father.

---

[47] On the reformulation of the myth of Troy in Greece and Rome more broadly see Erskine 2001.
[48] Odysseus uses the adjective in direct speech (to describe himself or others he has met) at *Od.* 8.211, 9.36, and 14.231; and it is used about him at *Od.* 9.255 and 17.485. The only other occurrences are at *Od.* 3.74, 20.220, and 23.219.
[49] Telemachus here arguably performs his own act of selective memory: reaching, perhaps, beyond the bounds of what he could feasibly remember from his early-year interactions with his father before he left for Troy.

In the same meeting, Mentor agrees:

μή τις ἔτι πρόφρων ἀγανὸς καὶ ἤπιος ἔστω
σκηπτοῦχος βασιλεύς, μηδὲ φρεσὶν αἴσιμα εἰδώς,
ἀλλ' αἰεὶ χαλεπός τ' εἴη καὶ αἴσυλα ῥέζοι·
ὡς οὔ τις μέμνηται Ὀδυσσῆος θείοιο
λαῶν οἷσιν ἄνασσε, πατὴρ δ' ὣς ἤπιος ἦεν.
                                    Od. 2.230–234

> Never henceforth let sceptered king of his own good will be kind and gentle, nor let him heed due measure in his heart, but let him always be harsh and do injustice, seeing that no one remembers divine Odysseus of the people whose lord he was; yet gentle was he as a father.

Vergil's Aeneas never receives a similar description: he is not termed a gentle or kind son to his father *or* father to his son.[50] The quality of paternal or filial kindness is, no doubt, dubiously accurate for either hero, but it is telling that it is only Odysseus who is internally recalled in this way — in the words of his son and his loyal supporters. *Pater Aeneas* receives no such transmitted praise. He has in fact no real personal relationship with his son at all: the only Vergilian scene which describes father and son alone together is when Aeneas is leaving for battle (*Aen.* 12.432–441), based on the famously touching moment in *Iliad* 6, where Hector removes his helmet to embrace Astyanax. But in a cold (mis)reading of his cousin's poignant paternity, Aeneas embraces his son only through his helmet![51] In this seemingly innocuous phrase, Quintus thus exploits all of the thematic, linguistic, and narratological differences between Vergil's account of the sack and his own — including the fact that Aeneas' Vergilian story is in the first person, so he could not easily describe himself in similar terms without seeming (even by his standards) excessively narcissistic — to make the *Odyssey* the dominant sequel at play. This dominance, and the comparative taciturnity about the *Aeneid*, ultimately reverses the assumed implications of the prototyping in this scene. In reframing the Trojan panorama from his still-Homeric *and* deeply imperial perspective, Quintus does not make the

---

50 The closest equivalents are descriptions of Aeneas' *patrius amor* (e.g., at *Aen.* 1.643–644) and *cura parentis* (e.g. 1.646). However, these are both connected to external substantive nouns, and do not have the same force as a direct adjectival epithet. Thanks to Talitha Kearey for an interesting conversation about this point.
51 See especially Lyne 1987, 145–206.

obvious move of establishing Aeneas as a proto-Odyssean figure,[52] but rather shows how this relationship can work both ways, giving it a renewed Greek, as well as a 'new' Roman, subjective effect. Aeneas' famously Augustan father-son duties here find literary precedent, but mythic *fulfilment*, in the workings of the *Odyssey*.

4 Learning to be Roman (a Greek Class): The *Testudo*

The scene discussed above must now be read with a further instance of combination between Odysseus and Aeneas, which takes place during the deadlock battle of book 11. During the fighting, Odysseus devises a trick which tries — and ultimately fails — to break the stalemate. His plan involves the soldiers arranging their shields in a 'familiar' type of formation:

> καὶ τότ' ἄρ' ἀμφ' Ὀδυσῆα δαΐφρονα κύδιμοι ἄνδρες
> κείνου τεχνήεντι νόῳ ποτὶ μῶλον Ἄρηος
> ἀσπίδας ἐντύναντο, βάλον δ' ἐφύπερθε καρήνων   360
> θέντες ἐπ' ἀλλήλησι· μιῇ δ' ἅπαν ἥρμοσεν ὁρμῇ·
> φαίης κεν μεγάροιο κατηρεφὲς ἔμμεναι ἕρκος
> πυκνόν, ὃ οὔτ' ἀνέμοιο διέρχεται ὑγρὸν ἀέντος
> ῥιπὴ ἀπειρεσίη οὔτ' ἐκ Διὸς ἄσπετος ὄμβρος·
> τοῖαι ἄρ' Ἀργείων πεπυκασμέναι ἀμφὶ βοείαις   365
> καρτύναντο φάλαγγες…
>
> *PH* 11.358–366

> It was then that the renowned warriors around warlike Odysseus made their shields ready for Ares' combat at his ingenious suggestion: they set them together above their heads and arranged the whole structure. You would have thought it was the tightly made, protective roof of a hall, impervious to the violent blasts of moist storm winds and to Zeus' most torrential downpours: so strong a defence did those Argive phalanxes have with their ox-hide shields.

This description has multiple models and allusive strands. It echoes, for instance, Apollonius' account of how the Argonauts used shields and helmets to protect themselves from the birds on the Island of Ares (*Arg.* 2.1047–1089); an

---

[52] Cf., e.g., Squire 2011 who read the Iliac Tablet's depiction of this same scene as "repackaged as the prequel to a distinctly Roman cultural, social and literary history" (thus Squire 2011, 148). Relevant discussion too in Petrain 2014.

association strengthened by the uncommon meaning of the noun ἕρκος in the roof simile (*PH* 11.362), which may be read as a nod to ἑρκίον at *Arg.* 2.1073.[53] However, the exact formation as described here is also quintessentially Roman: Quintus is depicting the *testudo*, the device whereby a body of soldiers covered themselves with shields interlocked above their heads. Many Latin poets and historians make reference to this technique.[54] However there is something distinctively Vergilian about this particular case. Not only does Quintus' passage appear closely analogous with the two mentions of this tactic in the *Aeneid* — in book 2 (438–444) where the Greeks attack Priam's palace in such a configuration, and in book 9 (505–518) where the Trojan defenders first fail and then succeed against a Volscian *testudo* —[55] but it also, and more profoundly, seems to take up the device's poetological function as it was established in Vergil's poem. For as many critics have noted, from the time of the *Aeneid* onwards, the *testudo* became a typical anachronism of Latin epic: it was a traditional, even old-fashioned military technique by the third century, inseparably associated with Roman martial power and the representation of empire, and as a symbol of this imperial power, it could readily be transplanted into the incongruous setting of the deep mythological past.[56] In his own use of the formation in this Homerising, Trojan timescape, Quintus is thus gesturing to the passages where the *Aeneid* was engaged in the same sort of paradoxical temporal manoeuvres as the *Posthomerica*: pointing to Vergil, as Hinds would put it of Ovid, where he was at his most Quintan.[57]

For a brief moment, then, Quintus appears to break his silence: in this out of place detail and "inherited anachronism,"[58] he inserts a reminder of the later

---

53 See Keydell 1954, 294–295 and James 2004, 32–36.
54 List of passages in Gärtner 2005, 115.
55 See Gärtner 2005, 243–251 and Tomasso 2010, 142–146 for further discussion of the 'closeness' between the passages.
56 Cf. Vian 1969, 44–45 and Gärtner 2005, 116. The *Ilias Latina* (c. 1st cent. CE) provides ancient testimony to the significance of this anachronism in the *Aeneid*: composed as a summary of the *Iliad*, the work also references aspects of Latin literature, including anachronisms. Among these anachronisms is a *testudo* (*Ilias Latina* 766–768) that verbally alludes to several passages of the *Aeneid*, and especially to *Aen.* 2.441 and 9.505. See Reitz 2007, 350 and Scaffai 1982, 66–73, with cogent discussion in relation to the *Posthomerica* in Bärtschi 2016, 15–16.
57 Cf. Hinds 1998, 106–109 on Ovid's synthesis and correction of the *Aeneid*'s own latent metamorphic moments (e.g., the Caieta story) in *Met.* 13–14: "what Ovid's mock-pedantic correction is really designed to do, I think, is to show his enjoyment of a very (dare I say it?) Ovidian moment in his predecessor." (109).
58 Phrase used by Bärtschi 2016, 15.

Vergilian inheritance underlying his overwhelmingly Homeric tenor. Then, however, he steers the scene a different way:

ὥρμηναν δὲ πύλῃσι θεηγενέος Πριάμοιο
ἀθρόοι ἐγχριμφθέντες ὑπ' ἀμφιτόμοις πελέκεσσι
ῥῆξαι τείχεα μακρά, πύλας δ' εἰς οὖδας ἐρεῖσαι   390
θαιρῶν ἐξερύσαντες. εἶχεν δ' ἄρα μῆτις ἀγαυὴ
ἐλπωρήν· ἀλλ' οὔ σφιν ἐπήρκεσαν οὔτε βόειαι
οὔτε θοοὶ βουπλῆγες, ἐπεὶ μένος Αἰνείαο
ὄβριμον ἀμφοτέρῃσιν ἀρηρότα χείρεσι λᾶαν
ἐμμεμαὼς ἐφέηκε, δάμασσε δὲ τλήμονι πότμῳ,   395
ἀνέρας οὓς κατέμαρψεν ὑπ' ἀσπίσιν....
                             PH 11.388–396

> They meant to approach all together the gates of Priam, descendant of the gods, to smash the great walls with their double-edged axes, and to demolish the gates by tearing them from their hinges. This admirable plan held hopes of success; but neither their ox-hide shields nor their fast-moving axes availed them when the mighty Aeneas picked up a great rock in both hands and furiously flung it at them, and a wretched death befell the men whom he caught unawares beneath their shields.

The *testudo* is now given vocabulary of an Odyssean flavour. With μῆτις (391) Quintus uses the paradigmatic noun associated with Homer's cunning hero. The epithet ἀγαυός is most often found in the *Odyssey* to describe the suitors, who are destroyed by Odysseus' wiles.[59] The device is also linked via foreshadowing to Odysseus' later, successful weapon-trick at Troy: the Wooden Horse, the subject of the very next book of the *Posthomerica*. This link is forged firstly through the symmetry of the image which the two devices produce — the individual heroes are joined in the *testudo* into one animalistic formation (cf. 13.391) just like, Quintus will soon tell us in his delayed proem and catalogue, they will be in the Horse (*PH* 12.307: ὅσοι κατέβησαν ἔσω πολυχανδέος ἵππου, "those who went inside the cavernous horse"; *PH* 12.327–328: ἄλλοι δ' αὖ κατέβαινον ὅσοι ἔσαν ἔξοχ' ἄριστοι / ὅσσους χάνδανεν ἵππος ἐΰξοος ἐντὸς ἐέργειν, "and went inside all those who were the best, so many as that beautifully crafted horse could hold"); and secondly by that loaded word μῆτις. After its use in this passage, the noun next occurs in the poem to describe Odysseus' new plan that results in the construction of the Horse: *PH* 12.19–20: τῷ νῦν μήτι βίῃ πειρώμεθα Τρώιον ἄστυ / πέρσεμεν, ἀλλ' εἴ πού τι δόλος καὶ μῆτις ἀνύσσῃ ("therefore let us not smite Troy by force, but let cunning stratagem avail").

---

59 *Od.* 2.209, 247; 4.681; 14.180; 17.325; 18.99; 19.488, 496; 21.58, 174, 213, 232; 22.171; 23.63.

This deep association between Roman stratagem, Homeric Odysseus, and cyclic *dolos* makes all the more dramatic the fact that Quintus attributes the ultimate *failure* of the Greeks' use of this device to none other than Aeneas. Agamemnon and Menelaus had been initially optimistic about the tactic (386–387), and the bellicose description of 391–393 contains further counterfactual hints at the success that it might have been. The fact that Aeneas puts a stop to it — bypasses the possibility of Troy falling before its mythically-allotted time, and has all too often been taken as another sign of Quintus' 'defeatist' pandering to Roman imperial victory: just like the Greeks and the Volsci in the *Aeneid* examples, the Greeks ultimately cannot, and do not, win this fight.[60] However, such a reading pays insufficient attention to Odysseus' central role in this scene, as inventor, primary practitioner and main intertextual reference point. The founder of Rome and the hero of the *Aeneid* thus discovers this trick, and learns how to counter it, only by watching Odysseus create it. A definitive Roman military invention is thus retrojected into an instance of Odysseus' heroic craftiness, and the Odyssey's poetic craft; and it is through this context that it enters into Aeneas' proto-Roman ideology. The success of the *testudo*, and thus of Roman prowess, is placed into a chain of heroic learning which makes the Trojans, Greeks, Volscians, and Romans *all* inextricably connected, in spite of their various — and bilingual — professions of difference. The forces of foreshadowing and retrospection are here most defiantly collapsed into one another, as in Quintus' new epigonal vision, Aeneas *learns how to be Roman* through copying Homer's Greek hero at Troy.

5 Coda: Questioning the Latin Question...

The interplay between Odysseus and Aeneas provides the strongest indication of Quintus' engagement with teleology in an ideological form. If, to evoke for a final time Quint's enduring typology, myth could be co-opted to serve either an '*Aeneid*-based' or an '*Odyssey*-derived' framework of imperial response, then by co-opting these epics' two representative heroes, the *Posthomerica* juxtaposes these two different forms of inevitability, and ultimately reconciles them. By emphasising the Aeneas story as the thread connecting Greek and Roman cul-

---

60 See, e.g., Bärtschi 2016, 19–20 ("In the case of the Rutuli [*Aen.* 2.516–520], who are progenitors of the future Romans just like the Trojans, this failure is particularly ironic as their descendants will know how to use a *testudo* properly") and Tomasso 2010, 145–146.

tural aetiologies, Quintus recognises and recalibrates the political implications of an open versus closed, Greek-conquered versus Roman-conqueror conception of epic time. The way in which these scenes collide the Roman-Vergilian and the Homeric-Odyssean dimensions — through characters, inventions, cultural symbols, and plots — becomes in fact not the poem's most overt 'contemporary' nod, nor its strongest indication of Latin indebtedness; but rather (or perhaps, a better understanding of 'contemporary' and 'Latin indebtedness' for Quintus) its strongest expression of the possibilities for incorporation between the imperial Greek obsession with the 'past' and the literary and political realities of the Roman present.

I shall end by returning to the more 'contemporary' exegetical politics with which I began: of *Quellenforschung*, Latin literature, and intertextuality in imperial Greek epic studies. For Quintus, as for all imperial Greek poetry, 'The Latin Question' is always in fact a series of questions: self-conscious, self-generating, at times still frustratingly elliptical, but always worth confronting, posing differently, and asking again. The answers have the potential to yield so much more than disciplinary cross-fertilisation (important as this process doubtless is). These are issues which test and pressurise the motifs surrounding cultural stand-off, assimilation, and appropriation, and which suggest the continued need to find alternative narratives to resistance in order to characterise Greek identity politics under Rome — all crucial steps in the endeavour of re-writing the story of imperial Greek history in poetry as well as prose. Silence in the *Posthomerica* is a language, but so too is substitution, as the voices of Homer and Vergil find different ways to communicate across the divides of space and time: non-violent, but no less forceful, pressing, and alive.[61]

Bibliography

Adams, J. (2003), *Bilingualism and the Latin Language*, Cambridge.
Adams, J./Janse, M./Swain, S. (eds.) (2002), *Bilingualism in Ancient Society: Language Contact and the Written Text*, Oxford.
Alcock, S.E. (1993), *Graecia Capta: The Landscapes of Roman Greece*, Cambridge.
Alcock, S.E. (ed.) (1997), *The Early Roman Empire in the East*, Oxford.
Anderson, G. (1993), *The Second Sophistic: A Cultural Phenomenon in the Roman Empire*, London/New York.

---

[61] I am grateful to Arnold Bärtschi and Simon Goldhill for sharing draft versions of forthcoming work with me and to Silvio Bär for his helpful comments on an earlier draft of this piece.

Ando, C. (2012), *Imperial Rome AD 193 to 284: The Critical Century*, Edinburgh.
Bärtschi, A. (2016), "Fighting Anachronisms: Interaction with the Roman Empire in the *Posthomerica* of Quintus Smyrnaeus". Quintus Workshop, University of Cambridge. [Unpublished paper].
Bär, S. (2010), "Quintus of Smyrna and the Second Sophistic", in: *Harvard Studies in Classical Philology* 105, 287–316.
Bär, S./Greensmith, E./Ozbek, L. (eds.) (2022), *Writing Homer Under Rome: Quintus of Smyrna in and Beyond the Second Sophistic*, Edinburgh.
Baumbach, M./Bär, S. (eds. in collaboration with Dümmler, N.) (2007), *Quintus Smyrnaeus. Transforming Homer in Second Sophistic Epic*, Berlin/New York.
Baumbach, M./Bär, S. (2007), "An Introduction to Quintus Smyrnaeus' *Posthomerica*", in: Baumbach/Bär/Dümmler (2007), 1–26.
Bowie, E. (1989), "Poetry and Poets in Asia and Achaia", in: Av. Cameron/S. Walker (eds.), *The Greek Renaissance in the Roman Empire*, London, 198–205.
Buffière, F. (1956), *Les myths d'Homère et la pensée grecque*, Paris.
Carvounis, K. (2019), *A Commentary on Quintus of Smyrna, Posthomerica 14*, Oxford.
Cuypers, M. (2005), Review of James/Lee (2000), in: *Mnemosyne* 58, 605–614.
de Jong, I. (2014), *Narratology and Classics: A Practical Guide*, Oxford.
Erskine, A. (2001), *Troy Between Greece and Rome: Local Tradition and Imperial Power*, Oxford.
Fairclough, H.R/Goold, G.P. (1999), *Virgil. Eclogues, Georgics, Aeneid 1-6 (vol. 1), Aeneid 7-12 (vol. 2); ed. and trans. by H.R. Fairclough; rev. by G.P. Goold*, Cambridge, MA/London.
Fisher, E.A. (1982), "Greek Translations of Latin Literature in the Fourth Century A.D.", in: *Yale Classical Studies* 27, 173–215.
Gärtner, U. (2005), *Quintus Smyrnaeus und die Aeneis. Zur Nachwirkung Vergils in der griechischen Literatur der Kaiserzeit*, Munich.
Goldhill, S. (1991), *The Poet's Voice: Essays on Poetics and Greek Literature*, Cambridge.
Goldhill, S. (forthcoming), "Latin and Greek: Language and the Mirror of the Other", in: R. Gibson/C. Whitton (eds.), *Cambridge Critical Guide to Latin Literature*, Cambridge.
Greensmith, E. (2020), *The Resurrection of Homer in Imperial Greek Epic: Quintus Smyrnaeus' Posthomerica and the Poetics of Impersonation*, Cambridge.
Habicht, C. (1985), *Pausanias' Guide to Ancient Greece*, Berkeley/Los Angeles/London.
Hadjittofi, F. (2007), *"Res Romanae*: Cultural Politics in Quintus and Nonnus", in: Baumbach/Bär/Dümmler (2007), 357–378.
Hardie, P. (1993), *The Epic Successors of Virgil: A Study in the Dynamics of a Tradition*, Cambridge.
Heinze, R. (1915), *Vergils epische Technik*. Third Edition, Leipzig.
Hekster, O. (2008), *Rome and Its Empire, AD 193-284*, Edinburgh.
Hinds, S. (1998), *Allusion and Intertext: Dynamics of Appropriation in Roman Poetry*, Cambridge.
Hopkinson, N. (2018), *Quintus Smyrnaeus: Posthomerica*, Cambridge, MA/London.
James, A.W. (2004), *Quintus of Smyrna, The Trojan Epic*, Baltimore/London.
James, A.W. (2006), Review of Gärtner (2005), in: *Classical Review* 56, 328–329.
James, A.W. (2007), "Quintus of Smyrna and Virgil: a Matter of Prejudice", in: Baumbach/Bär/Dümmler (2007), 285–306.
Keaney, J./Lamberton, R. (1996), *Essay on the Life and Poetry of Homer (Plutarch)*, Atlanta.
Keydell, R. (1931), "Die griechische Poesie der Kaiserzeit (bis 1929)", in: *Jahresbericht über die Fortschritte der klassischen Altertumswissenschaft* 231, 41–161.
Keydell, R. (1954), "Quintus von Smyrna und Vergil", in: *Hermes* 82, 254–256.

Keydell, R. (1961), Review of Vian (1959a), in: *Gnomon* 33, 278–284.
Keydell, R. (1963), "Quintus von Smyrna", in: *Real Enzyclopaedie* XXIV.1, 1271–1296.
Klooster, J. (2007), "Apollonius of Rhodes", in: I. de Jong/R. Nünlist (eds.), *Time in Ancient Greek Literature: Studies in Ancient Greek Narrative* (Vol. 2), Leiden, 63–80.
Köchly, H. (1850), Κοΐντου τὰ μέθ' Ὅμηρον. *Quinti Smyrnaei Posthomericorum libri XIV. Relegit Armenius Koechly. Accedit index nominum a Francisco Spitznero confectus*, Leipzig.
Konstan, D./Saïd, S. (eds.) (2006), *Greeks on Greekness: Viewing the Greek Past under the Roman Empire*, Cambridge.
Lamberton, R. (1986), *Homer the Theologian: Neoplatonist Allegorical Reading and the Growth of the Epic Tradition*, Berkeley.
Lane Fox, R. (1986), *Pagans and Christians*, Harmondsworth.
Lowe, N.J. (2000), *The Classical Plot and the Invention of Western Narrative*, Cambridge.
Lyne, R.O.A.M. (1987), *Further Voices in Virgil's Aeneid*, Oxford/New York.
Maciver, C.A. (2011), "Reading Helen's Excuses in Quintus Smyrnaeus' 'Posthomerica'", in: *Classical Quarterly* 61.2, 690–703.
Maciver, C.A. (2012a), *Quintus Smyrnaeus' "Posthomerica": Engaging Homer in Late Antiquity*, Leiden.
Maciver, C.A. (2012b), "The Flyte of Odysseus: Allusion and the *Hoplōn Krisis* in Quintus Smyrnaeus, *Posthomerica* 5", in: *American Journal of Philology* 133.4, 601–628.
Masters, J. (1992), *Poetry and Civil War in Lucan's Bellum Civile*, Cambridge.
McNelis, C. (2018), "Mythical and Literary Genealogies: Aeneas and the Trojan Line in Homer, Ennius and Virgil", in: P. Knox/P. Hayden/A. Sens (eds.), *They Keep it All Hid: Augustan Poetry, its Antecedents and Reception*, Berlin.
Montiglio, S. (2011), *From Villain to Hero: Odysseus in Ancient Thought*, Ann Arbor.
Most, G. (2016), "The Rise and Fall of Quellenforschung", in: A. Blair/A. Goeing (eds.), *For the Sake of Learning: Essays in Honor of Anthony Grafton*, Leiden, 933–954.
Mullen, A./Elder, O. (eds.) (2019), *The Language of Roman Letters: Bilingual Roman Epistolography from Cicero to Fronto*, Cambridge.
Murray, A.T./Dimock, G. (1998), *Homer Odyssey 1–12 (vol. 1) and 13–24 (vol. 2); ed. and trans. by A.T. Murray; rev. by G. Dimock*, Cambridge, MA/London.
Murray, A.T./Wyatt, W.F. (1999), *Homer Iliad 1–12 (vol. 1) and 13–24 (vol. 2); ed. and trans. by A.T. Murray; rev. by W.F. Wyatt*, Cambridge, MA/London.
Ozbek, L. (2018), "(Almost) like a God: Depicting Aeneas in Quintus Smyrnaeus' *Posthomerica*", in: *Studi Italiani di Filologia Classica* 16.2, 133–156.
Petrain, D. (2014), *Homer in Stone: The 'Tabulae Iliacae' in their Roman Context. Greek Culture in the Roman World*, Cambridge.
Pontani, F. (2005), *Eraclito. Questioni omeriche sulle allegorie di Omero in merito agli dei*, Pisa.
Quint, D. (1993), *Epic and Empire*, Princeton.
Reitz, C. (2007), "Verkürzen und Erweitern — literarische Techniken für eilige Leser? Die "Ilias Latina" als poetische Epitome", in: *Hermes* 135.3, 334–351.
Scaffai, M. (1982), *Baebii Italici Ilias Latina. Introduzione, edizione critica, traduzione italiana e commento*, Bologna.
Scheijnen, T. (2018), *Quintus of Smyrna's Posthomerica: A Study of Heroic Characterization and Heroism (Vol. 421)*, Leiden.
Schmitz, T. (1997), *Bildung und Macht. Zur sozialen und politischen Funktion der zweiten Sophistik in der griechischen Welt der Kaiserzeit*, Munich.

Schmitz, T. (1999), "Performing history in the Second Sophistic", in: M. Zimmermann (ed.), *Geschichtsschreibung und politischer Wandel im 3. Jh. N. Chr.*, Stuttgart, 71–92.

Squire, M. (2011), *The Iliad in a Nutshell: Visualizing Epic on the Tabulae Iliacae*, Oxford.

Tomasso, V. (2010), *"Cast in Later Grecian Mould", Quintus of Smyrna's Reception of Homer in the Posthomerica*. PhD Dissertation, Stanford University.

Tychsen, T. (1807), *Quinti Smyrnaei Posthomericorum libri XIV*, Strasbourg.

Vian, F. (1959), *Recherches sur les "Posthomerica" de Quintus de Smyrne*, Paris.

Vian, F. (1963–9), *Quintus de Smyrne. La suite d'Homère*. Texte établi et traduit par F. Vian. Tome I. Livres I–IV, 1963; Tome II. Livres V–IX, 1966; Tome III. Livres X-XIV, 1969, Paris.

Wilamowitz-Moellendorf, U. (1905), *Die griechische Literatur des Altertums*, Berlin.

Zeitlin, F. (2001), "Visions and Revisions of Homer", in: S. Goldhill (ed.), *Being Greek Under Rome*, Cambridge, 195–268.

Giampiero Scafoglio
Triphiodorus and the *Aeneid*: From Poetics to Ideology

Abstract: In Triphiodorus' *Sack of Troy*, it is possible to find traces of a "dialectical" confrontation with the *Aeneid*: a kind of silent dialogue with a text that is not a model in the usual meaning of the word, but rather an unavoidable interlocutor. I try to detect some of these traces, starting from an issue of poetics, then focusing on two episodes as case studies, notably Triphiodorus' treatment of Sinon and Cassandra. Finally, I deal with an ideological point, that is, the curtailment of Aeneas' heroism in the *Sack of Troy*. I will therefore show that Triphiodorus establishes a polyvalent relationship with *Aeneid* 2 that goes from a partial convergence about poetics up to a marked difference, almost bordering on open opposition, on the ideological ground.

Keywords: Triphiodorus' *Sack of Troy*; Vergil's *Aeneid* 2; poetics; ideology; Sinon; Cassandra; Laocoon; Aeneas.

1 Introduction: A Judgement of Triphiodorus' intentions

Triphiodorus' small-scale epic poem, the *Sack of Troy* (Ἰλίου ἅλωσις),[1] narrates the conquest of the city (as announced by its title), beginning with the construction of the Wooden Horse (57–107), after a summary of the hard situation of both Greeks and Trojans, exhausted by their tiredness of many years of fighting (6–39). The story includes the episode of Sinon, who convinces Priam and the Trojans to accept the Horse into their city to find favour with Athena (258–303), in spite of Cassandra, who tries in vain to warn her fellow citizens (358–443). The poem culminates in the night battle and the massacre of the Trojans by the Greeks (506–663) who, the next day, set fire to Troy, sacrifice Polyxena on Achilles' grave, distribute the booty among themselves, and leave to return home (668–691).

---

[1] Cf. the excellent commentary by Miguélez-Cavero 2013.

Triphiodorus' literary activity can be dated between the mid-3rd and the mid-4th century CE (after Quintus Smyrnaeus and before Nonnus of Panopolis).[2] The subject of his poem coincides with the lost Ἰλίου πέρσις dating from the 7th century BCE and belonging to the Epic Cycle: it is unknown whether Triphiodorus read this text or not, but he undoubtedly knew its content from later summaries; one might even think that he wanted to write an epic in the same fashion.[3] Anyway, Homer seems to be the *auctor princeps* for Triphiodorus, who has probably taken Demodocus' song (*Od.* 8.499–520) as his starting point, and has imitated several passages and motifs from the *Iliad* and the *Odyssey* throughout his poem.[4] The author of the *Sack of Troy* shows in fact not only a deep understanding of the Homeric epics, but also a solid knowledge of their interpretation in the grammatical tradition.[5] Furthermore, Triphiodorus establishes a complex relationship with Quintus Smyrnaeus: I would call it an antagonistic or oppositional imitation (*oppositio in imitando*), all the more since his *Sack of Troy* overlaps with book 12 of the *Posthomerica*, telling the same events with substantial differences.[6]

However, the most controversial point concerning Triphiodorus' sources and models is about the *Aeneid*. The *Sack of Troy* indeed deals with the same subject as Aeneas' tale to Dido in book 2 of Vergil's poem, but there is no clear evidence of a direct relationship of imitation, given that the major events are reported differently in the two texts, while their common ground can be traced back to the literary tradition and/or to a specific model (or more than one) that they both followed. For this reason, several leading scholars from the beginning of the last century until today (as Richard Heinze, W.F. Jackson Knight, Francis Vian, Malcolm Campbell, Wendell Clausen)[7] have denied Vergil's influence on

---

[2] Cf. Cameron 1970, 478–482; Gerlaud 1982, 6–9; Miguélez-Cavero 2013, 4–6. The major evidence comes from *P.Oxy.* 41.2946, containing lines 301–402 of the *Sack of Troy* and related to the 3rd/4th century. Most scholars agree on Quintus' chronological priority to Triphiodorus, yet it is not rigorously proven: Gärtner 2005, 25, speaks of "kaum stichhaltige Argumente." Carvounis 2019, xxii–xxiii, makes an effective point on Quintus' priority.
[3] Actually, scholars (as Gerlaud 1982, 37–39) are more inclined to put Triphiodorus in relation with the Ἰλιὰς μικρά than with the Ἰλίου πέρσις. Cf. the balanced assessment by Baumbach/Bär 2015, 614–618.
[4] Cf. Ypsilanti 2007; Tomasso 2012.
[5] Cf. Miguélez-Cavero 2013, 38–51.
[6] A direct link between the two poems is taken into account by Vian 1959, 61–64, 70–71, and Maciver 2012, 3, 29; while Campbell 1981, 46–47, 176–177, is sceptical.
[7] Cf. Heinze 1915, 78–81; Jackson Knight 1932; Vian 1959, 98–101 (mainly on Quintus Smyrnaeus, and only marginally on Triphiodorus); Gerlaud 1982, 46–47; Campbell 1984; Dubielzig 1996, 26; Clausen 2002, 60.

Triphiodorus. Other scholars (including Alan Cameron)[8] have chosen the opposite direction, but without bringing compelling proofs, since the search for *loci similes* (structural and verbal intertexts) has not given reliable results, thus leaving open the problem and further fuelling scepticism.

A reconsideration of the issue cannot but start from an assessment about the diffusion of the Latin language and culture in 3rd-century Egypt. The papyri bear direct and concrete witness to the Latin learning process, preserving the texts and the tools used by students to acquire the language of the Roman Empire: Egypt has provided in fact a huge quantity of educational material that allows us to gather information on the everyday practice of teaching and learning Latin.[9] There is little doubt that Egyptian citizens were exposed to the language of Rome, which was used by the army and the public administration;[10] but their grade of familiarity with Latin literature varied from one person to another. Yet we have reason to think that an exponent of the intellectual class, a learned poet like Triphiodorus, had a good level of acquaintance with the Roman culture and could not but know Vergil, its major representative. Several copies of the *Aeneid* (especially the early books, as the second) survive on papyri in bilingual format: this means that they were exploited for didactic purposes, and even by beginners.[11] The audience of cultural products as the *Sack of Troy* must have known Latin language and, at least to some extent, the *Aeneid* too: Triphiodorus could not compose his poem, and (some of) his readers might not enjoy it, without recalling some corresponding episodes in Vergil's story.[12]

Anyway, Triphiodorus does not imitate the *Aeneid* in an open and evident way; we may even say that he does not imitate it at all, if we understand imitation as a process resulting in structural and verbal analogies helping and even encouraging the reader to recognise the model, to which the poet pays tribute and with which he eventually competes (*aemulatio*).[13] Triphiodorus carries out this kind of imitation on Homer and maybe occasionally on Quintus Smyrnaeus, the tribute prevailing with the former, the competition (mainly through *variationes*) with the latter.[14] His approach with Vergil reflects the general attitude of

---

8 Cf. Cameron 1970, 478–482; but also D'Ippolito 1976 and 1990.
9 Cf. Rochette 1997, 177–206; Cribiore 2003/4 and 2007, 57–62.
10 Cf. Rochette 1997, 105–126, 147–150; Adams 2003, 527–641; Fournet 2009, 421–430; Evans 2012.
11 Cf. Rochette 1990 and 1994; Kramer 1996; Dickey 2015, 43–48.
12 On allusions and reminiscences of Vergil in other Greek authors of Late Antiquity: Rochette 1997, 272–279, 320–323.
13 On Triphiodorus' models and sources cf. Gerlaud 1982, 10–47.
14 Cf. Gerlaud 1982, 40–41; Miguélez-Cavero 2013, 72–74.

the Greek poets of the imperial period (Quintus Smyrnaeus not the least)[15] towards Latin literature, which they ignore, or better pretend to ignore, with a keen sense of independence and even of superiority, turning instead to the Hellenic cultural tradition that they feel they belong to. Such an attitude fits in the context of the contemporary Greek mindset towards Rome: the upper class and the intellectuals accepted Roman domination and even cooperated with the rulers, while resisting cultural integration and keeping a disdainful distance from Latin culture.[16]

Nevertheless, considering that Triphiodorus shared with his audience a certain knowledge of the *Aeneid* and notably of book 2, it is highly unlikely that he wrote about the same subject, and that his readers read his writing, without bearing in mind Vergil's tale (with its content innovations compared to the traditional legend, its effective narrative structure, and its strong ideological meaning) along with other texts of authors from different periods (from Homer to Quintus Smyrnaeus). In the *Sack of Troy*, then, it is possible to find traces of a confrontation with the *Aeneid* activated by cultural memory: a kind of silent dialogue with a text that is not a model in the usual meaning of the word, but rather an unavoidable interlocutor. This is why it is so hard to provide evidence to such an intertextual relationship that assumes an atypical and elusive form, due not only to the overlapping of several models and the language difference between hypotext and hypertext, but also, and especially, to Triphiodorus' choice to follow the *Aeneid* as little as possible (still paying attention not to highlight his debt to Vergil) and, in general, to keep distance from Latin literature and its main poem.

I will try to detect some of these traces, starting from an issue of poetics, then focusing on two episodes as cases studies, and finally dealing with an ideological point.

---

15 On Quintus Smyrnaeus' approach to Latin poetry, and to Vergil in particular, cf. Holloway 2004; Hadjittofi 2007, 358–370; James 2007; as well as the contributions by Bär, Greensmith, and Papaioannou in this volume.
16 Cf. Brunt 1990, 267–281, 515–517; Woolf 1994; Swain 1996, 1–100.

2 Between Homer and the Alexandrians

Triphiodorus introduces his *Sack of Troy* with a short proem that blends the invocation to the Muse with a synthetic overview of the subject:

> Τέρμα πολυκμήτοιο μεταχρόνιον πολέμοιο
> καὶ λόχον, Ἀργείης ἱππήλατον ἔργον Ἀθήνης,
> αὐτίκα μοι σπεύδοντι πολὺν διὰ μῦθον ἀνεῖσα
> ἔννεπε, Καλλιόπεια, καὶ ἀρχαίην ἔριν ἀνδρῶν
> κεκριμένου πολέμοιο ταχείῃ λῦσον ἀοιδῇ.
>
> *Sack* 1–5

> Tell me quickly, O Calliope, avoiding a long speech, as I am in a hurry, the long delayed end of the painful war and the ambush, the equestrian work of Argive Athena, and resolve with a rapid song the ancient quarrel of men, when the war decided the outcome.[17]

Triphiodorus announces his subject through three keywords: τέρμα, the turning point of the war (quite different from the war as a whole); λόχον, the stratagem of the Wooden Horse that represents precisely this turning point and occupies most of the poem (57–541, from its construction to its crucial work); ἔριν, the final battle (542–691) that constitutes the culmination of the events triggered by the Horse and leads the war to its end. The reference to Homer as the *auctor princeps* is clear and strong, beginning with the phrasing and the lexical choice.[18] If the last keyword would be appropriate (in its narrower meaning of "quarrel") to designate the topic of the *Iliad*, the term λόχος refers to the Wooden Horse in three passages of the *Odyssey*, including Demodocus' song (*Od.* 8.515) which is a sort of miniature reproduction of the same tale developed much more widely in Triphiodorus' poem.[19] More importantly, Triphiodorus programmatically announces a selective and targeted approach to the mythical matter, as he will focus on the final phase of the war and not on the war as a whole; just like Homer, who extrapolated from the entire war a specific episode (sc. Achilles' wrath and his quarrel with Agamemnon) with all its consequences, taking place within less than two months. Aristotle praises Homer for this very reason, while criticising the authors of the Epic Cycle who cover an all-

---

[17] The Greek text is quoted according to Gerlaud 1982; the translation of the *Sack* throughout is mine. On Triphiodorus' poetics and in particular on the programmatic meaning of the proem cf. Maciver 2020, who highlights the claim for "speed and brevity," as well as the Callimachean intertexts that articulate "the dual nature" of the poem, "both conservative and innovative."
[18] Cf. Miguélez-Cavero 2013, 130–134.
[19] Cf. Miguélez-Cavero 2013, 120–126.

encompassing account of the myth, "formed by many distinct parts" (πολυμερῆ), lacking unity and coherence (*Poet.* 1459a30–b2).[20] Triphiodorus thus follows Homer and Aristotle at the same time, since he takes from the former the compositional and architectural criterion appreciated by the latter; he chooses a subject exploited in the Epic Cycle, but develops it in the Homeric fashion.

The invocation to the Muse is an (almost)[21] unavoidable conventional feature of the epic genre from Homer onwards:[22] this is why it can be traced back to Homer in a broad sense, but not precisely. However, Triphiodorus' invocation closely looks like the structure of the proem of the *Odyssey*, with which it also shares the verb ἐννέπω in the specific meaning "to tell of/to tell the tale of,"[23] referring to the rhapsodic practice: the phrase τέρμα κτλ. ἔννεπε, Καλλιόπεια, recalls *Od.* 1.1, ἄνδρα μοι ἔννεπε, Μοῦσα. On the other hand, the reference to the song (ἀοιδῇ) connects to the cognate verb ἄειδε, from *Iliad* 1.1. Nevertheless, there is a difference that cannot go unnoticed, and which in fact stands out even more evidently through the structural and lexical analogy: Homer invokes the Muse (the only one, or just any of the Muses),[24] while Triphiodorus addresses Calliope as the patron of epic poetry. As a γραμματικός, Triphiodorus knows only too well the distinction between the Muses and their identity, which appears in Hesiod's *Theogony* (notably at 75–80); besides, he follows a widespread poetic trend since the Hellenistic era, consisting in invoking a single, specific Muse (or goddess) as the authority governing the subject of the work just about to begin.[25] In this outlook, Triphiodorus' invocation to Calliope points out the literary genre, as well as the topic and the ethos of the poem, that fully adheres to the epic statute.

In addition, however, I recognise in that invocation an allusive reference to Quintus Smyrnaeus, who makes Calliope a character in the *Posthomerica*: if the Muses mourn all together Achilles' death (as already happened in the lost Ἰλίου

---

20 Cf. Scafoglio 2007a.
21 Quintus Smyrnaeus' *Posthomerica* lack the initial invocation of the Muse, but introduce the story *in medias res* in order to highlight the continuity with the *Iliad*: cf. Bouvier 2005.
22 Cf. Schindler 2019.
23 Cf. Cunliffe 1924, s.v. ἐννέπω; Dettori 1994.
24 Cf. Scafoglio 2017, 57–60.
25 E.g., Apollonius Rhodius in the proem of his third book (3.1–5) invokes Erato, referring to the erotic matter of that part of the poem; [Oppian], in the proem of his *Cynegetica*, jointly appeals to Calliope and Artemis, because of the hunting as didactic subject (1.16–40).

πέρσις, belonging to the Epic Cycle), it is Calliope 'in person'[26] who addresses a *consolatio* to Thetis (*PH* 3.631–654), affirming the transience and the fragility of human life, but also the power of poetry that immortalises the glory of the heroes. The metaliterary meaning of this scene, confirming the role of Calliope as the patron of epic poetry and the guarantor of its immortalising power,[27] has not escaped Triphiodorus: this is one more reason to invoke her by name, specifying her identity. But this is also an occasion of confrontation with Quintus Smyrnaeus: Triphiodorus' *Sack of Troy* shares the literary genre and partly the subject as well as several stylistic features with the *Posthomerica*, while being at the extreme opposite as for length and overall structure. Both poems are conceived in the wake of Homer, but each in a different way, the *Sack of Troy* complying with Aristotle's praise of Homer and criticism of the Epic Cycle, the *Posthomerica* rather conforming to the cyclic fashion, with their all-encompassing architecture.[28]

What about Vergil? His discreet and almost hidden presence can be detected in the proem of the *Sack of Troy*, not without consequences on its programmatic meaning. Triphiodorus asks Calliope to speak "quickly" (αὐτίκα), "putting away a long speech" (πολὺν διὰ μῦθον ἀνεῖσα), since he is "in a hurry" (μοι σπεύδοντι), and still to bring up the topic "with a rapid song" (ταχείῃ... ἀοιδῇ). All this is already found, albeit in a more synthetic form, in the words pronounced by Aeneas at the beginning of his tale of the fall of Troy, that is the proem to book 2 of the *Aeneid* (3–13), notably in the last part:

> *sed si tantus amor casus cognoscere nostros*
> *et breviter Troiae supremum audire laborem,*
> *quamquam animus meminisse horret luctuque refugit,*
> *incipiam.*
>
> Aen. 2.10–13

> However, if you feel such a strong desire to know our downfall and to hear in few words the extreme suffering of Troy, even though my heart shudders at the memory and turns away from tears, I will start.

The adverb *breviter* is a keyword with metaliterary implications, as it refers to the aesthetic principle of *brevitas*, which goes back to Callimachus and the Al-

---

26 Cf. *PH* 3.631–632: [...] ἣ δέ οἱ αὐτὴ / Καλλιόπη φάτο μῦθον ἀρηραμένη φρεσὶ θυμόν, "Calliope herself spoke to her [sc. Thetis], with firm wisdom set in her heart."
27 Cf. Zanusso 2013, xxv, and 2014, 6.
28 Cf. Scafoglio 2022.

exandrians, and partly corresponds to the precept of λεπτότης.[29] Aeneas tells Dido that he cannot go on for too long remembering such painful events, while Vergil takes a poetological position in the wake of the Alexandrians through his words.[30] In my view, Triphiodorus develops the same point in a more extensive and articulated form, still in a proem, that is the right place for a poetological statement. If the conceptual coincidence between the Latin adverb and the Greek phrases does not seem to be enough to identify an intertextual relationship, we can pay attention to other similarities and resonances that bring together the two texts, confirming their proximity on the metaliterary side. Triphiodorus' τέρμα πολυκμήτοιο μεταχρόνιον πολέμοιο, "the long-delayed end of the painful war," corresponds to Vergil's *supremum... laborem*. The impatience of the Greek poet, who is eager to hear the tale from the Muse (μοι σπεύδοντι), is a feeling similar in many respects to Dido's strong desire to know Aeneas' story (*tantus amor*). A conceptual and syntactical analogy is to be found in the immediately following lines, which describe the exhausting duration of the war as a premise to the construction of the Wooden Horse: Triphiodorus' genitive absolute ἤδη μὲν δεκάτοιο κυλινδομένου λυκάβαντος, "the tenth year already rolling away" (6), matches Vergil's ablative absolute *tot iam labentibus annis* (*Aen*. 2.14); but one may also think of the adjective μεταχρόνιον, agreeing with τέρμα, at the very beginning of the *Sack of Troy*.

Within this framework of consonances, the correspondence between Vergil's adverb *breviter* and Quintus' phrases cannot be considered accidental. There are some differences of course, and not only in the conceptual formulation. Indeed, Aeneas expresses a reason for his haste within the narrative fiction (it is late night and "the setting stars induce to sleep"):[31] the metaliterary meaning takes over as an added significance, a second reading level; while Triphiodorus claims the need to hurry as a poetic choice, stated by the authorial voice in a true proem that takes place before the beginning of the tale. Triphiodorus shows a deep understanding of Vergil's proemial scene: hence he draws the aesthetic principle of *brevitas*/λεπτότης, but he puts it in a form that is at the same time easier (clear and open, without a double reading level) and more articulated and elaborate in lexicon and phrasing. Through Vergil, anyway, Triphiodorus goes back to Alexandrian poetics, to which he conforms his poem

---

29 I say "partly," because Greek λεπτότης is a polysemous term that also implies "lightness" and "finesse."
30 Cf. Deremetz 2000, 86–87; Horsfall 2008, 54.
31 Cf. *Aen*. 2.8–9: [...] *et iam nox umida caelo / praecipitat suadentque cadentia sidera somnos*, "and the dewy night is already spreading from the sky, while the setting stars urge sleep."

as a small-scale epic: one may say that he follows the steps of Homer in an Aristotelian and Alexandrian fashion (in opposition to Quintus Smyrnaeus, who adheres to the same main model, but in the archaic manner, drawing close to the Epic Cycle). All the more since Vergil, with the pregnant adverb *breviter*, marks the difference with the Homeric conception of epics, in a situation that is modelled on a famous Homeric scene, performing the same function of introducing a retrospective tale: the dialogue between Odysseus and queen Arete at the court of the Phaeacians (in *Odyssey* 7).[32] Here Odysseus qualifies the tale that the queen wants to listen to with the adverb διηνεκέως (241), which expresses the continuity, the full duration of the flashback, "from the beginning to the end": it can be viewed, therefore, almost as an antonym of Vergil's *breviter*, whose metaliterary meaning is confirmed by the comparison with the Homeric scene that is put into effect through the intertextual reference.[33]

As a γραμματικός, Triphiodorus read Homer with the mediation of Alexandrian poetics. Then, in his compositional work, he resorted to Alexandrian poetics to "adjust" the imitation process, so to say, to "correct" Homer. Actually, he found such an operation already realised, *mutatis mutandis*, in a small-scale epic poem that he silently (almost secretly) used as one of his models: book 2 of the *Aeneid*.[34]

3 Sinon's transformations

Sinon is unknown to Homer, but he was present in the legend of the capture of Troy since the Epic Cycle, from which he passed into Attic tragedy and hence landed to Roman drama.[35] He plays a major role in book 2 of the *Aeneid*, where he pretends to be a deserter and persuades the Trojans, with an astonishingly effective and deceptive eloquence, to take the Wooden Horse in the city walls.[36]

---

32 Cf. in particular the first words of Odysseus' answer to Arete: ἀργαλέον, βασίλεια, διηνεκέως ἀγορεῦσαι / κήδε', ἐπεί μοι πολλὰ δόσαν θεοὶ Οὐρανίωνες, "my queen, it is painful to tell my troubles from beginning to end, as the heavenly gods gave me so many" (*Od.* 7.241–242).
33 That comparison was carried out already by ancient scholars: cf. Macrobius, *Sat.* 5.5.2. On the programmatic character of the two passages see D'Ippolito 1976, 26–28.
34 We know that some books of the *Aeneid* circulated individually at least since the 2nd century CE, as we learn by Gellius, *Noct. Att.* 2.3, concerning exactly book 2. Cf. Mac Góráin 2018, 428, adducing other evidence.
35 Cf. Scafoglio 2008; synthesis and bibliography in Horsfall 2008, 92–94.
36 Cf. Dangel 2007; Scafoglio 2007b; Horsfall 2008, 95–183.

Vergil makes him a prominent example of disloyalty, unfaithfulness, and perjury that are typical of the Greek people,[37] while he depicts the Trojans (ancestors of the Romans) like reckless and thoughtless, but basically loyal and generous.[38] Quintus Smyrnaeus reverses the matter, making Sinon a brave and valiant warrior, who courageously endures tortures and mutilations that the Trojans inflict on him.[39] The Greek poet evidently pursues an aim that is symmetrically opposite to that of Vergil: the aim of rehabilitating and almost celebrating the ancestors of his people, while showing the savage cruelty of their enemies; maybe he pursues this objective in open opposition to the ideologically oriented tale by Vergil's Aeneas[40] (but Quintus' relationship with the *Aeneid* remains *sub iudice*).

Triphiodorus takes a middle way between Vergil and Quintus: maybe he keeps closer to the latter in making a hero of Sinon, but without demonising the Trojans. As soon as he enters the scene, Sinon is called ἀπατήλιος ἥρως, "deceptive hero" (220): an appellative that sounds like an oxymoron in Vergil's standpoint, but that fits Triphiodorus' ambivalent portrait of the character, who is a liar and a deceiver, but also a hero. The poet, who in general outlines a balanced picture of the two fighting peoples, shows that he knows about the tortures inflicted to Sinon by Quintus' Trojans, but he rejects such a version: he keeps in fact the wounds and mutilations from the account of the *Posthomerica*, but in the *Sack of Troy* it is Sinon who hurts himself, putting this on the Greeks' account, so as to increase his credibility in the eyes of the Trojans.[41] Scholars admit however that, "in the episode of Sinon, Triphiodorus and Vergil are particularly close in a number of areas," starting from the profile of the false deserter as an "accomplished speaker who plays upon the curiosity and childishness of his Trojan listeners."[42] It is true that Sinon's speech is shorter and bipartite in Triphiodorus' poem; it is instead longer and divided into three parts in *Aeneid* 2. In both works, however, he opens a part of his speech with a claim to sincerity, imbued with sneaky irony, stating that he does not wish to deny his identity and his belonging to the Greek people (which is already evident in it-

---

[37] Cf. *Aen.* 2.65–66: *accipe nunc Danaum insidias et crimine ab uno / disce omnis*, "now learn the trickery of the Danaans and, from one crime, get to know all of them."
[38] Cf. *Aen.* 2.145: *his lacrimis vitam damus et miserescimus ultro*, "for those tears, we grant him his life and we even take pity of him."
[39] Cf. *PH* 12.360–373, with Campbell 1981, 117–126.
[40] Cf. Hadjittofi 2007, 365–370. See also the contributions by Bär and Greensmith in this volume; the two critics further explore Quintus' relationship with the *Aeneid*.
[41] Cf. lines 227–229, 258–261, 275–277.
[42] Cf. Miguélez-Cavero 2013, 68–69.

self!): *Sack* 292–293: ἐξερέω καὶ ταῦτα· σὺ γάρ μ' ἐθέλοντα κελεύεις. / Ἄργός μοι πόλις ἐστί, Σίνων δέ μοι οὔνομα κεῖται ("I will also speak out these things: in fact, I willingly obey your order to speak out. Argos is my city, my name is Sinon"), can be compared to *Aen.* 2.77–78: *cuncta equidem tibi, rex, fuerit quodcumque fatebor / vera — inquit — neque me Argolica de gente negabo* ("I shall confess to you the whole truth, o king, come what may — he said — and I shall not deny that I am of Argive birth").

Vergil's Sinon explains his break with the Greeks by making up a dramatic and compelling story, filled with elements coming from Greek and Roman tragedy (including human sacrifice).[43] In doing so, he takes the cue from Ulysses' underhanded vengeance against Palamedes (*Aen.* 2.81 ff.). In Triphiodorus' poem, Sinon recalls the evil deeds committed by the Greeks against their own fellow soldiers: the judgment of Achilles' arms that led to Ajax' suicide, the abandoning of the wounded Philoctetes on the island of Lemnos, and the killing of Palamedes "out of envy" (*Sack* 270–272).[44] The latter reference could come from the tale by Vergil's Sinon, that may even have given Triphiodorus the general idea of the Greeks' hostility to their fellows used as an argument by the false deserter. Actually, all three evil deeds can be traced back to Odysseus: this seems a little suprising, considering that he is exalted as a great hero by Triphiodorus.[45] The strangeness of this passage compared to the context of the poem might plead in favour of its derivation from a model of different orientation — a model like the *Aeneid*. But it is also possible to think of a common (Greek) source that recorded all three evil deeds of Odysseus and therefore was hostile to him, from which Triphiodorus has drawn the whole list of wickedness, while Vergil has just taken a cue from it, developing widely only the story of Palamedes and building on it the deception contrived by Sinon.[46]

---

43 Cf. Scafoglio 2007b, notably 88–95.
44 Here is the text: ὣς μὲν Ἀχιλλῆος γέρας ἥρπασαν Αἰακίδαο, / ὣς δὲ Φιλοκτήτην ἔλιπον πεπεδημένον ὕδρῳ, / ἔκτειναν δὲ καὶ αὐτὸν ἀγασσάμενοι Παλαμήδην. I understand the first phrase (with Vian and Gerlaud) as "thus they snatched from the Aeacid (Ajax) the reward (sc. the weapons) of Achilles" (given that the patronymic "Aeacid," which referred only to Achilles in the Homeric epics, perfectly fits Ajax too); while Mair 1928 translates "even so they snatched away his reward from Achilles, son of Peleus," referring to the quarrel with Agamemnon, the γέρας being Briseis. Miguélez-Cavero 2013, 208, does not take a firm position, but inclines towards the latter interpretation.
45 On Odysseus' positive portrait and role of undisputed leader of the Greeks in the *Sack of Troy* cf. Tomasso 2012, 393–394, who calls into question the influence of the *Odyssey*.
46 The shared source has been said to be a tragedy or a poem on the ὅπλων κρίσις: cf. Vian 1959, 64; Gerlaud 1982, 131.

In both poems, Sinon says that the Greeks will be happy if the Trojans kill him (as an argument to persuade them not to do it): Triphiodorus' lines 279–280, χάρμα γὰρ Ἀργείοισι γενήσομαι, εἴ κεν ἐάσῃς / χερσὶν ὕπο Τρώων ἱκέτην καὶ ξεῖνον ὀλέσθαι ("I shall be a joy to the Argives, in fact, if you let a suppliant and a stranger die at the hands of the Trojans"), correspond (despite the different wording) to *Aen.* 2.103–104, *iamdudum sumite poenas: / hoc Ithacus velit et magno mercentur Atridae* ("but now take your vengeance: this is what the Ithacan wants and what the sons of Atreus would pay dearly for"). The kind answer of Priam, αἰεὶ δ' ἡμέτερος φίλος ἔσσεαι, οὐδέ σε πάτρης / οὐδὲ πολυκτεάνων θαλάμων γλυκὺς ἵμερος αἱρεῖ, "from now on, you will be our friend, nor will sweet desire for your homeland and for your large and rich halls seize you" (*Sack* 286–287), recalls both the answer of the king in Vergil's tale, *quisquis es, amissos hinc iam obliviscere Graios: / noster eris*, "from now on, whoever you are, forget the Greeks, lost to you: you will be one of us" (*Aen.* 2.148–149), and the words of Sinon himself, evoking his lost homeland and family to move his interlocutors to compassion, *nec mihi iam patriam antiquam spes ulla videndi / nec dulcis natos exoptatumque parentem*, "by now I have lost any hope to ever seeing my ancient homeland, my sweet children and my father, whom I missed so much" (*Aen.* 2.137–138). So far, one can still think of a shared model. Nevertheless, an allusive intention implying a direct relationship is probably to be detected in what I would call an "inverted correspondence" between Sinon's wistful complaint about his home in *Aeneid* 2 (*nec mihi iam patriam antiquam spes ulla videndi* etc.) and the reassurance that Triphiodorus' Priam addresses to him, when claiming that he will not suffer from nostalgia (*Sack* 286–287: οὐδέ σε πάτρης / οὐδὲ πολυκτεάνων θαλάμων γλυκὺς ἵμερος αἱρεῖ, "nor shall sweet desire for your fatherland and for your large and rich halls seize you"). It is almost like Triphiodorus' Priam is talking directly to Vergil's Sinon, in order to comfort and reassure him. There seems to be a dialogue between the characters of two different texts, which is in reality a dialogue between the texts themselves.

Yet, the most interesting point is the correspondence between the Latin phrase *noster eris* and the Greek ἡμέτερος φίλος ἔσσεαι: scholars have not failed to acknowledge the analogy, but have not drawn some important implications and have rather turned to other parallels from the *Odyssey*.[47] Here is Servius' commentary on the phrase *noster eris* (*ad Aen.* 2.148): *et sunt, ut habemus in Livio, imperatoris verba transfugam recipientis in fidem*, "as we find in Livy, they are the words of the military leader receiving a deserter in his trust." Vergil at-

---

47 Cf. Miguélez-Cavero 2013, 68 and 273–274.

tributes to Priam a formulaic sentence belonging to military and juridical language, notably the words usually pronounced by the generals of the Roman army to welcome deserters into their troops: Servius recalls Livy, who quoted this phrase in a lost book of his historical work (fragment 61 Weissenborn–Müller).[48] Vergil inserts an anachronism that foreshadows the relationship of descent and kinship between Trojans and Romans.[49] In view of the distinctly Roman character of this sentence, it is not probable that Triphiodorus drew it from a lost Greek text, a common model for both him and Vergil: it is instead more likely that he found it (not necessarily understanding its meaning) in book 2 of the *Aeneid*.

There is another common point between Triphiodorus and Vergil that scholars have noticed in broad terms, without further exploring the comparison and consequently without giving it much credit. Both in the *Sack of Troy* and in book 2 of the *Aeneid*, Sinon presents the Horse "as ambivalent for the Trojans, depending on what they decide to do with it": if they do not accept it, the Greeks will come back and capture Troy; conversely, if the Trojans consecrate it to Athena, bringing it into the city walls, they should be the winners.[50] This is what Triphiodorus' Sinon explains to Priam:

εἰ μὲν γάρ μιν ἐᾶτε μένειν αὐτοῦ ἐνὶ χώρῃ,
Τροίην θέσφατόν ἐστιν ἑλεῖν πόλιν ἔγχος Ἀχαιῶν·
εἰ δέ μιν ἁγνὸν ἄγαλμα λάβῃ νηοῖσιν Ἀθήνη,
φεύξονται προφυγόντες ἀνηνύστοις ἐπ' ἀέθλοις.
                                                    Sack 296–299

Now, if you allow it to stay here in its place, it is decreed that the spear of the Achaeans will capture the city of Troy; if, on the contrary, Athena gets it as a holy offering in her shrine, they will flee away, leaving their deed unaccomplished.

The dynamics are not clear: the Greeks already went away (or better, pretended to go away, hiding in the island of Tenedos), leaving Sinon alone (220–221); but he says that they "will flee away," if the Trojans welcome the Horse as a votive offering to Athena. If the Greeks have already left (as the Trojans believe), Sinon's words must mean that they will come back, in the event that the Trojans do not accept the Horse, while they will not, on condition that the Trojans would accept it. The lack of clarity is an argument in itself in favour of the provenance of this passage from a model that Triphiodorus did not fully understand.

---

48 Cf. Delvigo 2016, 362, who confirms Servius' reliability.
49 On the anachronisms in the *Aeneid* cf. Horsfall 1984 and 1991.
50 Cf. Miguélez-Cavero 2013, 68 (hence the quotation) and 261–262.

The dynamics are much clearer in Vergil's account: there, Sinon claims that Calchas advised the Greeks to return home in order to seek favourable omens because they had offended Athena by stealing the Palladium from Troy; and he says that, after appeasing the gods, they will come back unexpected to resume the war (*Aen.* 2.176–182).[51] The construction of the Wooden Horse also fits in this story, which does not lack likelihood and internal consistency: Sinon explains that the Greeks built it in atonement for the theft of the Palladium (*Aen.* 2.183–194); hence the ambivalence of the votive gift, which would allow the Greeks to win the war, unless the Trojans welcome it into their city, turning its power in their favour. In this context, the outward and return journey to and from Greece finds a clear and convincing explanation; while Triphiodorus' Sinon does not give a reason for the weird behaviour of the Greeks going away and possibly coming back; indeed, he even speaks as if they had not yet left, while slightly before, the poet said that they had pretended to return home (actually hiding in Tenedos). These inconsistencies can be easily explained as awkward imitation of a superficially approached and not well understood model, which might be recognised in Vergil's episode of Sinon.

Nevertheless, one may still argue that both poets followed a lost Greek text as a shared source, which Vergil imitated more closely, and that Triphiodorus did so summarily. Anyone can judge how far-fetched a servile imitation on Vergil's part is; moreover, such misunderstanding and clumsy reshuffling of a Greek model seems too demeaning even for a poet like Triphiodorus, who has been commonly regarded as dull and undistinguished. If this is yet not enough to neutralise the objection (as classical scholars are often more tenacious than lawyers), a closer look on the story made up by Vergil's Sinon will provide further evidence. In the tale of the false deserter, Calchas prophesies that the Greeks cannot conquer Troy *omina ni repetant Argis*, "if they do not (come back home to) seek omens at Argos" (*Aen.* 2.178). The account of the prophecy ends with this concise sentence: *ita digerit omina Calchas*, "so Calchas interprets the omens" (*Aen.* 2.182). Vergil uses the term *omen* (twice in 5 lines) and the verb *digero* in the specific meaning of "explaining/interpreting (an omen or a portent),"[52] both belonging to the technical language of Roman religion. Servius

---

51 Cf. in particular *Aen.* 2.180–182: *et nunc quod patrias vento petiere Mycenas, / arma deosque parant comites pelagoque remenso / improvisi aderunt*, "and now they have headed for their native Mycenae with the sails to the wind, and they are preparing weapons and getting the friendship of the gods, and re-crossing the sea they will suddenly come back."
52 The verb is paraphrased by Servius, *ad Aen.* 2.182: *interpretatur numinis commotionem*. Cf. Ovid, *Met.* 12.21: *novem volucres in belli digerit annos*, "he (sc. Calchas) interpreted the nine birds as the years of the war." Gudeman, *TLL* 5.1.1118, misses the mark.

again provides valuable help with his comment *ad Aen.* 2.178: *et respexit Romanum morem: nam si egressi male pugnassent, revertebantur ad captanda rursus auguria,* "this reflects the Roman customs: indeed, if once landed they fought out of luck, they came back home to take again the auspices." This identifies another anachronism, namely the Roman custom of the *repetitio auspiciorum*, which is also attested by historical sources, such as Livy: during a war, when the Roman army was in serious troubles or in a deadlock, the general had to come back to Rome to renew military auspices (*auspicia militaria*).[53] Vergil has inserted this Roman custom in Sinon's false story to make it look familiar to his audience and to provide a valid reason for the Greeks' journey back and forth (valid, I mean, in the eyes of Roman readers).[54] Vergil did not take such a Roman mark from, and Triphiodorus could not have found it in, a lost Greek text. It is much more likely that Triphiodorus imitated Vergil, without necessarily understanding the dynamics connected to the religious and military traditions of Rome: precisely for this reason, Triphiodorus outlines an oversimplified, rough, and not entirely consistent account of the same story made up by Vergil's Sinon. Anyway, it is worth remembering that book 2 of the *Aeneid* is only one of the sources exploited by Triphiodorus in the episode of the false deserter,[55] and that in other cases he proves to be able to rework the matter coming from the literary tradition in an original and effective way.[56]

4 Cassandra versus Laocoon

One of the main differences highlighted by scholars between the *Sack of Troy* and *Aeneid* 2 in order to deny an intertextual relationship is the character who warns the Trojans on the danger from the Wooden Horse: Laocoon in the *Aeneid*, Cassandra in the *Sack of Troy*. First of all, it must be said (in fact, it would not even be necessary to say) that such difference proves exclusively that Triphiodorus did not imitate Vergil's narrative in that particular point; but he could have imitated this model (as he actually did) in many other parts of the story. Moreover, the difference between both texts, which nevertheless have some

---

[53] On this Roman custom cf. Livy 8.30.2, 10.3.6, 21.63.11 and *passim*, with Oakley 1998, 708 and 2005, 583–584; cf. Phillips 1997, 46–49.
[54] Cf. Horsfall 2008, 171; Casali 2017, 161–162.
[55] Cf. Campbell 1981, 121–122 (tragic influence); Ypsilanti 2007, 94–99 (Homeric background).
[56] Triphiodorus "is still a poet with his own ideas about the Trojan War, not a simple versifier who pulls together strings from other poems," as rightly claimed by Miguélez-Cavero 2013, vii.

shared points, can say a lot about their relationship. All the more that, as I shall try to show, the overall difference between these two episodes hides some subtle connections that work as allusive hints, aiming at stimulating the comparison, underlining the diversity of the whole design, and ultimately confirming Triphiodorus' intertextual approach with book 2 of the *Aeneid*, although in the distinctive form that can be defined as *oppositio in imitando*.

The episode of Laocoon killed with his sons by the sea snakes as punishment for warning the Trojans of the danger posed by the Wooden Horse seems to be an invention by Vergil, who reworked *suo Marte* the mythical matter.[57] He gave Laocoon the role carried out by Cassandra in the literary tradition, though he did not completely remove the warning prophecy of Priam's daughter, but relegated it, instead, to the margins of the tale (*Aen.* 2.246–247), so as to recall the "orthodox" version of the legend and thus to throw light on his innovation. Triphiodorus in turn follows the common route, relying on Cassandra and totally ignoring Laocoon. This is not surprising: the Laocoon episode in *Aeneid* 2 is so markedly Vergilian, and so markedly Roman,[58] that Triphiodorus could never imitate it without assuming a large (and evident) debt to the Latin poet; and this is exactly what he wanted to avoid, as we have seen. Still, Triphiodorus could develop the Laocoon episode in the traditional way (from the Epic Cycle onwards), setting it within the city walls, after bringing the Horse into Athena's temple;[59] but he prefers to follow the example of Homer, who does not mention that horrible killing in Demodocus' song at the Phaeacian court.[60] So, he stays close to Homer, while turning away from non-Homeric tradition(s), and especially from Vergil.

A closer look reveals nevertheless unexpected similarities. Triphiodorus' Cassandra enters the scene in a similar way to Vergil's Laocoon: she is out of her mind (*Sack* 359 ff.) and runs (ἔδραμεν, 360); Laocoon likewise *ardens... decurrit* (*Aen.* 2.41). The speeches of both characters open with (three-line) questions full of surprise and indignation that they address to their fellow citizens (*Aen.* 2.42–44; *Sack* 376–378). At the beginning of her intervention, the maiden calls them "miserable" (376: ὦ μέλεοι) and accuses them of behaving as if "in the grip of madness" (377: δαιμόνιοι μαίνεσθε); Laocoon speaks to the Trojans in similar terms: *o miseri, quae tanta insania, cives?* "wretched citizens, what madness is

---

[57] Cf. Zintzen 1979, 15–66; Scafoglio 2006.
[58] Cf. the old but still useful Kleinknecht 1944, who considers the killing of Laocoon and his sons in Vergil's account as a *prodigium* in the typical Roman fashion.
[59] Cf. Severyns 1963, 91 (on the Ἰλίου πέρσις); Zintzen 1979, 18–21 and 68–70.
[60] The episode of Laocoon is omitted from Demodocus' song in the *Odyssey* because of the relative realism, self-restraint, balance, and dignity that distinguish Homeric poetry from the Epic Cycle, which more faithfully reproduced the oral tradition: cf. Griffin 1977.

this?" (*Aen.* 2.42). Cassandra's exhortation to destroy the Horse with axes or to set it on fire (*Sack* 412–413: ῥηγνύσθω πελέκεσσι δέμας πολυχανδέος ἵππου / ἢ πυρὶ καιέσθω, "let the body of the big horse be torn apart with axe blows or burnt with fire") recalls not Laocoon's speech, but the debate of the Trojans just before the arrival of Laocoon, notably the advice of Capys and other fellow citizens, who wanted "to fire (the horse) with flames heaped beneath, or to pierce and to probe its secret inner cavities," *subiectisque urere flammis, / aut terebrare cavas uteri et temptare latebras* (*Aen.* 2.37–38).

At the end of the prophecy, Triphiodorus recalls the extraordinary status of Cassandra, whom the Trojans never believe, "since Apollo made her a prophet as truthful as unbelieved" (*Sack* 417–418: τῇ δ' οὔτις ἐπείθετο· τὴν γὰρ Ἀπόλλων / ἀμφότερον μάντιν τ' ἀγαθὴν καὶ ἄπιστον ἔθηκεν). This has nothing to do with Laocoon, of course; but Vergil says the same about Cassandra, *dei iussu non umquam credita Teucris*, "who was never believed by the Trojans, by decree of the god" (*Aen.* 2.247). One may object that the two poets only describe the main feature of the maiden, her ambivalent prerogative, which is well known to everyone: did Triphiodorus need to imitate Vergil in this regard? Definitely no; all the more so because there is no precise analogy in vocabulary nor in syntax. But the following description of the Trojans adorning the temples to celebrate the alleged end of the war: *nos delubra deum miseri, quibus ultimus esset / ille dies, festa velamus fronde per urbem*, "we unfortunate ones, for whom that day was our last, adorned the temples of the gods with festive branches, throughout the city" (*Aen.* 2.248–249), leaves a recognisable sign in the first words told by Cassandra in the *Sack of Troy*: ὦ μέλεοι [...] ὑστατίην ἐπὶ νύκτα / σπεύδετε, "O wretched men [...] you hasten to your last night" (*Sack* 376–378). This makes it probable that Triphiodorus bore in mind the whole passage, including the immediately preceding account of Cassandra's useless prophetic faculty. This also applies to the metaphor of the pregnant Horse giving birth to warriors that is a topos of Greek tragedy,[61] taken up by Triphiodorus in Cassandra's prophecy (*Sack* 379–390); but here too the mediation of Vergil, who uses the same metaphor (*Aen.* 2.237–238),[62] cannot be excluded.

The episode of Laocoon and its surroundings in *Aeneid* 2 seem therefore to be the object of Triphiodorus' subtle and intermittent imitation, which serves to highlight the difference from, rather than the likeness with, Vergil's narrative, as a claim of literary dignity and flaunted independence from the Roman cultural influence.

---

61 Cf. Aeschylus, *Ag.* 824–826; Euripides, *Tr.* 11, 519–521 and 534; Rodari 1985.
62 Cf. also *Aen.* 6.515–516; Scafoglio 2001, 79–81.

5 What about Aeneas? A Conclusion on intertextuality and ideology

Triphiodorus devotes only 5 lines to Aeneas' flight from Troy and to the bright future of his descendants:

> Αἰνείαν δ' ἔκλεψε καὶ Ἀγχίσην Ἀφροδίτη
> οἰκτείρουσα γέροντα καὶ υἱέα, τῆλε δὲ πάτρης
> Αὐσονίην ἀπένασσε· θεῶν δ' ἐτελείετο βουλὴ
> Ζηνὸς ἐπαινήσαντος, ἵνα κράτος ἄφθιτον εἴη
> παισὶ καὶ υἱωνοῖσιν ἀρηιφίλης Ἀφροδίτης.
> *Sack* 651–655

> Aphrodite pulled out Aeneas and Anchises, feeling pity for the old man and the son, and took them away to Ausonia, far from their homeland. The will of the gods was thus realised, under the approval of Zeus, so that the children and grandchildren of Aphrodite dear to Ares would get an endless power.

Aeneas and his father (Aeneas' son is not mentioned at all) are 'pulled out' by Aphrodite from the city that was occupied and ravaged by the Greeks. It is all too clear that Triphiodorus has no interest in celebrating the ancestor of the Romans, even if he announces their greatness in a sort of prophecy, spoken by the authorial voice, that sounds as a (short and debatable) eulogy. At first glance, this version of Aeneas' story is quite different from Vergil's ideologically oriented account in *Aeneid* 2, where the hero fights desperately in a last attempt to defend the city or to die gloriously in battle (in spite of the warnings that Hector had just given him in a dream).[63] Even Venus' intervention, which is apparently a common ground, actually works in different ways, as the goddess just saves her son in the *Sack of Troy*, while she must first persuade him to leave Troy, giving up the fight and a glorious death, in the *Aeneid*.[64] Vergil portrays Aeneas as a valiant warrior, combining the Homeric conception of heroism with the civic and military virtue belonging to Roman tradition.[65] Triphiodorus makes him a dull and bland character, completely managed by his mother: this can only be an ideological choice, aimed at belittling Aeneas' heroism: even the

---

[63] Cf. Casali 2017, 19–25.
[64] Cf. Casali 2017, 27–35.
[65] Cf. La Penna 2005, 294–301.

praise to his descendants is just made to downsize their glory, as far as their "endless power" is the result of the divine will and not of their own merits.[66]

The impression that Triphiodorus is responding to Vergil's version of the legend with a veiled dissent against the celebration of Rome that is at the centre of the *Aeneid* is unquestionable: this would be a (complex and refined) form of intertextuality, still based on the *oppositio in imitando*, not without delicate ideological overtones. But are we really sure that Triphiodorus' polemical attitude is directed against Vergil's poem and not just against Roman political propaganda that finds expression in many (not only literary) forms? In the latter case, Triphiodorus' refusal and rework of the Roman (or better, Romanised) legend of Aeneas would not be a dialogue with Vergil, but a merely ideological stance, as well as a response to a broader cultural phenomenon.

Actually, if Triphiodorus only wanted to deny Aeneas' heroism, completely ignoring the *Aeneid*, all he had to do was to follow the most ancient version of the legend, which was told in the Epic Cycle and, for this reason, was also the closest to the Homeric epics: he just had to tell that Aeneas left the city before and not during the last night, remembering and following the warnings that Aphrodite had given Anchises long before (at the time of their love).[67] Furthermore, if he wanted to defame Aeneas, he could opt for the slanderous version proposed by a historian of the 4th century BCE, Menecrates of Xanthus, who made the hero a traitor, responsible for the fall of his city:[68] a version that came back in vogue in the imperial period (within the movement of the Second Sophistic) and especially in the Late Antiquity.[69] But likely such a defamation went far beyond Triphiodorus' intentions, as polemical as they were. Anyway, he made Aeneas flee from the city in the last night of Troy, without fighting and without any act of heroism: not even his escape is his own work (at least with the paltry merit to have faced some enemies on the way), since he is passively taken away by his mother. Triphiodorus, then, does not deal with the literary tradition, but with a precise version of the legend, which is exactly that of book 2 of the *Aeneid*: as far as we know, no other Greek text shares this version; and if ever it was in some Latin poem or historic work before Vergil (the leading candidate being Ennius' *Annales*, but without any certainty),[70] it is quite obvious

---

66 Cf. Miguélez-Cavero 2013, 69–70 and 455–456.
67 Cf. the summary of the Ἰλίου πέρσις in Proclus' *Chrestomathy*, namely 250–251 Severyns; Hyginus, *Fab*. 135; Servius, *ad Aen*. 2.201; but especially Dionysius of Halicarnassus, *Ant. Rom*. 1.48.2.
68 Cf. Scafoglio 2013; Bettini/Lentano 2013, 190–221 and 278–289.
69 Cf. Chiappinelli 2007, 27–41; Lentano 2020.
70 Cf. Skutsch 1985, 71–72, 142, and 171–183.

that only the *Aeneid* could be the "controversial idol" of Triphiodorus, the target of the (intertextual) confrontation that he carries on reworking the legend.

In short, Triphiodorus establishes a polyvalent relationship with *Aeneid* 2, that goes from a partial convergence about poetics (with the corresponding metaliterary hints) up to a marked difference, almost bordering on open opposition, on the ideological ground. All this, without carrying on an avowed allusive and/or emulative imitation, in the traditional and conventional sense. Scholars' discomfort resulting in a sceptical reaction, faced with such a complex and elusive issue, is perfectly understandable; but it is not the right answer. Rather, it must be acknowledged that Triphiodorus embraces different approaches with different models (this falling within his relative creativity, which must not be overestimated), and that he reserves a subtle and nuanced one for Vergil, who turns out to be the less loved and the most controversial of his *auctores*.

Bibliography

Adams, J.N. (2003), *Bilingualism and the Latin Language*, Cambridge.
Baumbach, M./Bär, S. (eds. in collaboration with N. Dümmler) (2007), *Quintus Smyrnaeus. Transforming Homer in Second Sophistic Epic*, Berlin/New York.
Bettini, M./Lentano, M. (2013), *Il mito di Enea: Immagini e racconti dalla Grecia a oggi*, Turin.
Bouvier, D. (2005), "Penthésilée ou l'absence de la Muse au début des *Posthomériques* de Quintus de Smyrne", in: A. Kolde/A. Lukinovich/A.L. Rey (eds.), Κορυφαίῳ ἀνδρί. Mélanges offerts à André Hurst, Geneva, 41–52.
Brunt, P.A. (1990), *Roman Imperial Themes*, Oxford.
Cameron, A. (1970), *Claudian. Poetry and Propaganda at the Court of Honorius*, Oxford.
Campbell, M. (1981), *A Commentary on Quintus Smyrnaeus, Posthomerica XII*, Leiden.
Campbell, M. (1984), Review of Gerlaud (1982), in: *Journal of Hellenic Studies* 104, 220.
Carvounis, K. (2019), *A Commentary on Quintus of Smyrna, Posthomerica 14*, Oxford.
Casali, S. (2017), *Virgilio, Eneide 2*, Pisa.
Chiappinelli, F. (2007), *Impius Aeneas*, Acireale/Rome.
Clausen, W. (2002), *Virgil's Aeneid. Decorum, Allusion, and Ideology*, Munich/Leipzig.
Cribiore, R. (2003/4), "Latin Literacy in Egypt", in: *KODAI Journal of Ancient History* 13/14, 111–118.
Cribiore, R. (2007), "Higher Education in Early Byzantine Egypt: Rhetoric, Latin, and the Law", in: R.S. Bagnall (ed.), *Egypt in the Byzantine World, 300–700*, Cambridge, 47–66.
Cunliffe, R.J. (1924), *A Lexicon of the Homeric Dialect*, London.
Dangel, J. (2007), "L'énigme du savoir et du pouvoir médiatiques: le mensonge de Sinon virgilien (*Én.* II)", in: M. Ledentu (ed.), *Parole, 'media,' pouvoir dans l'Occident romain. Hommages offerts au professeur Guy Achard*, Lyon, 105–124.
Delvigo, M.L. (2016), "Virgilio e Servio alla ricerca del *mos Romanus*", in: A. Garcea/M.-K. Lhommé/D. Vallat (eds.), *Servius et le savoir antique*, Hildesheim/New York, 353–367.

Deremetz, A. (2000), "Le livre II de l'*Énéide* et la conception virgilienne de l'épopée. Épopée et tragédie dans l'*Énéide*", in: *Revue des Études Latines* 78, 76–92.
Dettori, E. (1994), "Un'ipotesi su ἐννέπω (storia di una radice)", in: *AION(ling)* 16, 117–169.
Dickey, E. (2015), "Teaching Latin to Greek Speakers in Antiquity", in: E.P. Archibald/W. Brockliss/J. Gnoza (eds.), *Learning Latin and Greek from Antiquity to the Present*, Cambridge, 30–51.
D'Ippolito, G. (1976), *Trifiodoro e Virgilio: il proemio della Presa di Ilio e l'esordio del libro secondo dell'Eneide*, Palermo.
D'Ippolito, G. (1990), "Trifiodoro", in: *Enciclopedia Virgiliana* V, Rome, 268–271.
Dubielzig, U. (1996), Τριφιοδώρου Ἰλίου ἅλωσις / Triphiodor, *Die Einnahme Ilions*, Tübingen.
Evans, T. (2012), "Latin in Egypt", in: C. Riggs (ed.), *The Oxford Handbook of Roman Egypt*, Oxford, 516–525.
Fournet, J.-L. (2009), *The Multilingual Environment of Late Antique Egypt: Greek, Latin, Coptic, and Persian Documentation*, in: R.S. Bagnall (ed.), *Oxford Handbook of Papyrology*, Oxford, 418–451.
Gerlaud, B. (1982), *Tryphiodore, La prise d'Ilion*, Paris.
Griffin, J. (1977), "The Epic Cycle and the Uniqueness of Homer", in: *Journal of Hellenic Studies* 97, 39–53.
Hadjittofi, F. (2007), "*Res Romanae*: Cultural Politics in Quintus Smyrnaeus' *Posthomerica* and Nonnus' *Dionysiaca*", in: Baumbach/Bär/Dümmler (2007), 357–378.
Heinze, R. (1915), *Vergils epische Technik*. Third Edition, Leipzig/Berlin.
Holloway, R.R. (2004), "Arctinus, Virgil, and Quintus Smyrnaeus", in: P.-A. Deproost/A. Meurant (eds.), *Images d'origines – Origines d'une image. Hommages à Jacques Poucet*, Louvain-la-Neuve, 73–80.
Horsfall, N. (1984), "Anacronismi", in: *Enciclopedia Virgiliana* I, Rome, 151–154.
Horsfall, N. (1991), "Virgil and the Poetry of Explanations", in: *Greece and Rome* 38, 203–211.
Horsfall, N. (2008), *Virgil, Aeneid 2. A Commentary*, Leiden/Boston.
Jackson Knight, W.F. (1932), "Iliupersides", in: *Classical Quarterly* 26, 178–189.
James, A.W. (2007), "Quintus of Smyrna and Virgil. A Matter of Prejudice", in: Baumbach/Bär/Dümmler (2007), 145–158.
Kleinknecht, H. (1944), "Laokoon", in: *Hermes* 79, 66–111.
Kramer, J. (1996), "Der lateinisch-griechische Vergilpalimpsest aus Mailand", in: *Zeitschrift für Papyrologie und Epigraphik* 111, 1–20.
La Penna, A. (2005), *L'impossibile giustificazione della storia. Un'interpretazione di Virgilio*, Rome/Bari.
Lentano, M. (2020), *Enea: L'ultimo dei Troiani, il primo dei Romani*, Salerno.
Mac Góráin, F. (2018), "Untitled / *Arma virumque*", in: *Classical Philology* 113, 423–448.
Maciver, C.A. (2012), *Quintus Smyrnaeus' Posthomerica. Engaging Homer in Late Antiquity*, Leiden/Boston.
Maciver, C.A. (2020), "Triphiodorus and the Poetics of Imperial Greek Epic", in: *Classical Philology* 115, 164–185.
Mair, A.W. (1928), *Oppian, Colluthus, and Tryphiodorus*, London/Cambridge, MA.
Miguélez-Cavero, L. (2013), *The Sack of Troy. A General Study and a Commentary*, Berlin/Boston.
Oakley, S.P. (1998), *A Commentary on Livy, Books VI–X*, vol. II, *Books VII–VIII*, Oxford.
Oakley, S.P. (2005), *A Commentary on Livy, Books VI–X*, vol. IV, *Book X*, Oxford.
Phillips, D. (1997), "Seeking New Auspices: Interpreting Warfare and Religion in Virgil's *Aeneid*", in: *Vergilius* 43, 45–55.

Rochette, B. (1990), "Les traductions grecques de l'*Énéide* sur papyrus", in: *Les Études Classiques* 58, 333–346.
Rochette, B. (1994), "Traducteurs et traductions dans l'Egypte gréco-romaine", in: *Chronique d'Egypte* 69, 313–322.
Rochette, B. (1997), *Le latin dans le monde grec. Recherches sur la diffusion de la langue et des lettres latines dans les provinces hellénophones de l'Empire romain*, Brussels.
Rodari, O. (1985), "La métaphore de l'accouchement du cheval de Troie dans la littérature grecque", in: *La Parola del Passato* 40, 81–102.
Scafoglio, G. (2001), "La tragedia di Eschilo nel libro II dell'*Eneide*", in: *L'Antiquité Classique* 70, 69–86.
Scafoglio, G. (2006), "Le *Laocoon* de Sophocle", in: *Revue des Études Greques* 119, 406–420.
Scafoglio, G. (2007a), "Aristotele e il ciclo epico. Una nota a *Poet*. 1459a 37", in: *Revue d'Histoire des Textes* 2, 287–298.
Scafoglio, G. (2007b), "Elementi tragici nell'episodio virgiliano di Sinone", in: *Antike und Abendland* 53, 76–99.
Scafoglio, G. (2008), "Sinon in Roman Drama", in: *Classical Journal* 104, 11–18.
Scafoglio, G. (2013), "The Betrayal of Aeneas", in: *Greek, Roman and Byzantine Studies* 53, 1–14.
Scafoglio, G. (2017), *Ajax. Un héros qui vient de loin*, Amsterdam.
Scafoglio, G. (2022), "Quintus and the Epic Cycle", in: S. Bär/E. Greensmith/L. Ozbek (eds.), *Quintus of Smyrna's Posthomerica: Writing Homer Under Rome*, Edinburgh, 298–318.
Schindler, C. (2019), "The Invocation of the Muses and the Plea for Inspiration", in: C. Reitz/S. Finkmann (eds.), *Structures of Epic Poetry*, vol. I, *Foundations*, Berlin/Boston, 489–530.
Severyns, A. (1963), *Recherches sur la Chrestomathie de Proclos*, vol. IV, *La Vita Homeri et les sommaires du Cycle*, Paris.
Skutsch, O. (1985), *The Annals of Quintus Ennius. Edited with an Introduction and Commentary*, Oxford.
Swain, S. (1996), *Hellenism and Empire. Language, Classicism, and Power in the Greek World, AD 50–250*, Oxford.
Tomasso, V. (2012), "The Fast and the Furious: Triphiodorus' Reception of Homer", in: Baumbach/Bär/Dümmler (2007), 369–409.
Vian, F. (1959), *Recherches sur les Posthomerica de Quintus de Smyrne*, Paris.
Woolf, G. (1994), "Becoming Roman, Staying Greek: Culture, Identity and the Civilizing Process in The Roman East", in: *Proceedings of the Cambridge Philological Society* 40, 116–143.
Ypsilanti, M. (2007), "Triphiodorus Homericus. People in the Ἰλίου Ἅλωσις and their Forebears in the *Iliad* and *Odyssey*", in: *Wiener Studien* 120, 93–114.
Zanusso, V. (2013), "Quinto e la tradizione letteraria: fonti e modelli", in: E. Lelli (ed.), *Quinto di Smirne, Il seguito dell'Iliade*, Milan, XXII–LVI.
Zanusso, V. (2014), "Quinto di Smirne e la tradizione mitica di argomento troiano : *imitatio, variatio*, allusività", in: E. Amato/É. Gaucher-Rémond/G. Scafoglio (eds.), *La légende de Troie de l'Antiquité Tardive au Moyen Âge. Variations, innovations, modifications et réécritures = Atlantide. Cahiers de l'EA 4276, L'Antique, le Moderne* 2, 1–17 (http://atlantide.univ-nantes.fr/IMG/pdf/atlantide-2-zanusso.pdf).
Zintzen, C. (1979), *Die Laokoonepisode bei Vergil*, Wiesbaden.

Markus Kersten
ἄντρα περικλυτά: Revisiting Mythical Places in the Orphic *Argonautica*

Abstract: This chapter deals with intertextuality in the *Orphic Argonautica* by analysing the mythical places mentioned in the poem (the cliffs of the Sirens, the caves of Orpheus and Chiron, the wood of the nymphs, the realm of the Cimmerians, and the sphere of Sleep). It is argued that reading the poem against the Latin epic tradition, without necessarily speculating about its immediate sources or its philosophical intricacies, will at least help us map the (literary) journey that the text records and thus describe the possible significance of metapoetics for a poem that defies categorisation.

Keywords: Argonauts; Bauform; Chiron; Cimmerians; Flavian Poetry; intertextuality; mytho-chronology; *Quellenforschung*; Ps-Orpheus; Sirens; Vergil.

et quae loca viderat ante, / cuncta recognoscit

(Ov. *Met.* 11.61–62)

The anonymous late antique poem that retells, in some 1,400 Greek hexameters, the quest for the Golden Fleece as a first-person narrative spoken by Orpheus, raises at least three profound difficulties in interpretation. In terms of genre, it is unclear what the text actually is (a hymn, an epyllion, or rather a kind of elaborate epitome?) and what it aims at.[1] In terms of content, it can be argued (and doubted) that it has an allegorical Neoplatonic meaning.[2] In terms of literary criticism, one has to ask about the poet's technique and the poem's relation to the literary tradition. This third issue may appear less important by comparison, and yet it could present the angle from which the poem is most accessible.

I am most grateful to the editors for the invitation to contribute to the present volume and for their comments on this paper. Moreover, I wish to thank my colleagues in Basel for their help and Henry Tang (Cambridge) for his very valuable proofreading.

---

[1] Cf. Hunter 2005, Schelske 2011, 11–28; Zuenelli 2019, 28: "a literary experiment."
[2] Cf. Schelske 2011. Cecchetti 2013, Burges Watson 2015, and Hopkinson 2015 appreciate Schelske's interpretive attempt, but express some general doubt.

Like the two other problems, that of intertextuality hinges on our extremely limited knowledge of and, hence, our various prejudices about the author ('Ps-Orpheus,' as I shall say in contrast to his autodiegetic narrator) and the original audience of the poem. Unlike 'purpose' and 'meaning,' however, the intertextual network at the interface of the *Orphic Argonautica* (*OA*) can be traced with (relative) certainty.[3] Already at the outset, Orpheus mentions his former songs: θυμὸς ἐποτρύνει λέξαι τά περ οὔ ποτε πρόσθεν / ἔφρασ', ὅταν... φρικώδεα κῆλ' ἐπίφασκον, "my spirit rouses me to tell of things of which I have never before spoken, when... I uttered words that were like terrible shafts" (*OA* 8–10).[4] On the one hand, the author thus inscribes his work into an 'Orphic' tradition,[5] thereby implicitly claiming to be the oldest poet.[6] On the other hand, through Homeric and Apollonian material, he positions himself in the epic tradition, and thus points to his literary dependence.[7] The latter implication is the stronger one. The tale of Jason and his comrades is one of the most popular myths in antiquity;[8] readers may feel immediately compelled to compare any new version of this myth with a previous one. The lists of testimonia offered by Venzke and Vian leave no doubt that such a comparison could be fruitful for reading the *OA*. Indeed, I think that these lists can even be extended.

Needless to say, a parallel in phrasing or motif does not automatically imply interpretive significance: it does not have to appear as anything other than accidental. But since there are many parallels to Latin literature, in particular to Valerius Flaccus,[9] and since, as said, the poem is so decidedly repetitive in reporting yet another voyage of the Argo we must ask what we are to make of them.

In a study of the poem's major intertextual features, including some interesting details of Orpheus' κατάβασις, Damien Nelis has been duly hesitant to

---

[3] But see the remarks made by Gärtner in this volume (pp. 12–23).
[4] I have cited the Greek text from Vian 1987a. Translations of the *OA* are from Colavito 2011 (with occasional adaptations). For all other texts, I either refer to the translations of the Loeb Classical Library or produce my own.
[5] See West 1983, 37–38; Luiselli 1993. Consequently, the issue of the author's Orphism has become a focal point of academic interest; see Schelske 2011, 4–9.
[6] On the issues of time see Schelske 2011, 12–20; Madeła 2020.
[7] Cf. Venzke 1941, 111–112; Vian 1987a, 22–28; Karanika 2017.
[8] In fact, it is an important narratological precondition of the subject matter that any *Argonautica* can only be a repetition to some extent; cf. Hom. *Od.* 12.70; A.R. 1.18. Epitomising remarks are found at *OA* 476 and 1191.
[9] See Rovira Soler 1978 and Schelske 2011, 30, who argue that Valerius was known to Ps-Orpheus; however, see Vian's scepticism (1987a, 27 n. 3).

infer "direct imitation" of Latin poetry, arguing instead for a common pre-Apollonian source now lost.[10] In fact, this evaluation is correct in terms of *Quellenforschung*. There are no marked allusions to Latin authors and, given the difference of language, we cannot easily speak of paraphrases, let alone prove them — although this is, of course, what we often do with Greek models of Latin literature. Nonetheless, the lack of immediate echoes cannot preclude the possibility that Roman readers or Greek readers with some knowledge of Latin literature could have noticed and even interpreted the very parallels we see.[11] It is, in any philological case, not only reasonable, but also necessary to reckon with lost sources. Yet whenever there are multiple different parallels within a certain corpus, questions will implicitly arise about the nature of these sources (whether they are poems, prose, translations, discourses etc.) and their number. In some cases, this can ultimately provoke assumptions that are likely to be as speculative as those regarding direct imitation.

Another methodological concern would be the parallels to features that were particularly popular in Rome (or even specific to Rome) as well as to features that do not seem to be of certain relevance to Orphism. Accordingly, in a recent article on the authorial voice of the *OA*, Andromache Karanika was fairly confident that "throughout the Orphic *Argonautica* we see affinities with the Latin epic tradition."[12] But what these affinities are, needs, I think, to be described in more detail.

In this chapter, I do not strive to show that Ps-Orpheus necessarily emulated certain passages of Latin epic poetry. Rather, I intend to demonstrate that, regardless of what the author knew, a reading with an eye on the Latin epic tradition will lead to some more differentiated description of the text and make it appear more interesting in terms of metapoetics.[13] This, in fact, may imply that Ps-Orpheus had some contact with this tradition. However, what is at issue then is intertextuality in a broader sense: if we consider that our author was somehow aware of Roman literature, this does not necessarily require an explanatory model on how this awareness was achieved. Nelis is right in claiming "the burden of proof should lie with those who would agree for direct imitation." But what about indirect imitation? As an intermediate step, it seems sensible not to

---

10 Nelis 2005.
11 On this matter as well as on the knowledge of Latin in the East see, e.g., the discussion and bibliography in Gärtner 2005, 13–22.
12 Karanika 2017, 127.
13 On cross-cultural metapoetics in Late Greek poetry, see the contributions by Bär, Carvounis, and Papaioannou in this volume.

exclude the possibility that Ps-Orpheus was influenced by Roman literature. On this basis, we might get closer to assessing the challenging text of the *OA*, without, however, opening the discussion on its philosophical intricacies.

One of the poem's most conspicuous intertextual features is the descriptions of mythical places. Both in relation to the length of the poem and the demands of myth, mythical places are quite frequent in the *Orphic Argonautica*.[14] I shall confine myself to only a number of them here (the cliffs of the Sirens, the caves of Orpheus and Chiron, the wood of the nymphs, the realm of the Cimmerians, and 'Sleep').

As a *Bauform* of epic poetry,[15] a description of a mythical place like a cave, a location in the woods, an island (etc.) often serves to convey a certain atmosphere to an episode, which in turn can provide a spatial portrait of the inhabitants or foreshadow the events to come. Think of the garden of Alcinous or of the island of Polyphemus. Like these Odyssean archetypes, mythical places, as I understand the feature, regularly appear as a sort of detached otherworld even within the fictional universe of the narrative. Moreover, they tend to be 'diegetic' places; that means they often serve as the setting of a certain episode. Accordingly, as structural elements, mythical places are often configured by deictic formulas (e.g., ἔστι δέ τις νῆσος; *est locus* ...). Narratologically speaking, the main impact of such descriptions, which are by no means an exclusively epic phenomenon, lies in their contribution to the texture — literally their mapping — of the narrative.[16]

Mythical places have a special significance in Latin epic. Whereas it is of rather little importance that Apollonius' Argonauts, like Odysseus, but mythochronologically before him, visit the island of Circe, and whereas Apollonius' Phaeacians do not dwell at Scheria, but at Drepane,[17] revisitation of places is quite frequent in Latin epic, and it is often meaningful. Aeneas, to name just one well-known example, experiences Polyphemus through the speech of the Greek Achaemenides, who was left behind by Odysseus. In Rome, mythical places function as literary crossroads, as poetic *lieux de mémoire*, and, quite literally, as *loci* of imitation. Quintus and Nonnus seem to avoid extensive repetition of mythical places, though they exploit singular topoi of spatial descrip-

---

14 On Ps-Orpheus' mythico-geographical interests see Vian 1988. A literary structure deserving similar interest is the proem, cf. Luiselli 1993; especially its *recusatio*, cf. Hunter 2005.
15 On the term see Reitz/Finkmann 2019, I, 1–9.
16 Cf. Kersten 2019. In terms of definition, there is some overlap with geographical ecphrasis and set pieces like *loca amoena*.
17 Cf. A.R. 4.922–929; on the difference see Hunter 2015 *ad loc*.

tion at different instances.[18] Ps-Orpheus, however, makes ample use of intertextual (p)revisitation.

1 The Cliff of the Sirens

The most obvious and most provoking example for Ps-Orpheus' engagement with mythical places and their inhabitants is the defeat of the Sirens (*OA* 1264–1290). On the one hand, this episode clearly functions as a repetition of the Homeric and Apollonian mythical place. Ps-Orpheus offers no detailed description, but refers only to the rock, σκόπελον (*OA* 1265–1267), on which the Sirens sit. Since the place is well known from literary sources,[19] it is up to the audience to imagine the actual setting from their memories.[20] On the other hand, though, in terms of mytho-chronology, the episode is something like an unrealistic analepsis to the *Odyssey*, since the voyage of the Argo took place before Odysseus' return from Troy.

Our poet follows Apollonius inasmuch as he describes (albeit differently) the creatures, whose appearance would remain notoriously unclear in the *Odyssey*,[21] and inasmuch as he has Orpheus defeat them by a more elaborate means than the Homeric wax — namely by poetic quality. In Ps-Orpheus' version, however, not only are the Sirens vanquished, but also their place undergoes a spectacular and definite change. Overwhelmed by the song of the bard, they throw away their instruments and turn into stones — leaving no adventure for Odys-

---

18 Cf. Kersten 2019, 401–402. Traditional mythical places like the bedchamber of Anchises (Hom. *Il.* 2.819–821; Quint. *PH* 8.97–98), Niobe's rock (Hom. *Il.* 24.602–617; Ov. *Met.* 6.310–312; Quint. *PH* 1.294–306), or the serpent's grove near Thebes (Ov. *Met.* 3.28–49; Nonn. *Dion.* 4.356–359) rather appear as encyclopaedic references that do not serve a certain diegetic purpose, and they often lack description. What is frequent in these poems, though, is allusive description of newly invented places; Emathion's home (Nonn. *Dion.* 3.134–179), for example, is compared to the palace and the garden of Homer's Alcinous.
19 Either a beautiful λειμών, covered with the corpses of men, cf. Hom. *Od.* 12.45–46, or an εὔορμος περιωπή, cf. A.R. 4.900.
20 In terms of scenery, Ps-Orpheus makes use of elements from several different Homeric places; see Schelske 2011 *ad loc.* (also Danek 1998, 253), but this does not effect the narrative function of the episode.
21 Cf. A.R. 4.898–899: τότε δ' ἄλλο μὲν οἰωνοῖσιν, / ἄλλο δὲ παρθενικῆς ἐναλίγκιαι ἔσκον ἰδέσθαι; *OA* 1269: κοῦραι. The visual artistic tradition is inconsistent as well; winged Sirens are found in the 7th century BCE, but there are also other iconographic strands; see, e.g., Hofstetter 1997, Nünlist/Bäbler 2001.

seus to be experienced. This, in contrast to Apollonius' version, makes this analepsis appear 'unrealistic.'

The legend of the Sirens' death is of course no invention by Ps-Orpheus,[22] but what matters is its appearance in a hexametrical poem where it is incommensurable with Homer's account. There is a metapoetic dimension in contradicting the authoritative predecessor,[23] and it seems to be an interesting footnote that this mythological aberration agrees with Roman epic, where the Sirens tend to be remarkably silent. In Vergil, Aeneas only passes the rocks, *scopuli* (!), on which the monsters once sat:[24]

> *iamque adeo scopulos Sirenum advecta subibat,*
> *difficilis quondam multorumque ossibus albos*
> *(tum rauca adsiduo longe sale saxa sonabant)*
>
> Aen. 5.864–866

> And now, onward borne, the fleet was nearing the cliffs of the Sirens, once perilous and white with the bones of many men (at this time with the ceaseless surf the rocks afar were sounding hoarsely) …

The Sirens are apparently gone; at least, they are silent: only the rocks seem still to sing. The absence causes no (narrato)logical problems in the *Aeneid* — Aeneas is indeed a late visitor, so commentators can easily assume that the κοῦραι have died after Odysseus escaped them.[25] However, the Sirens' obvious silence also draws attention to an issue of authenticity. These creatures are not only mysterious; they and their story are logically indescribable, so to speak, when no one can return from their island to tell the truth. This is, at least, what their literary history suggests. Since there exist many different versions of their genealogy and their fate,[26] their story and their appearance must always remain as vague as the particular content of the sweet song they promise Odysseus. Apol-

---

22 See Vian's (1987a) note on the episode and Madeła 2020, 7–8. On Homer's Sirens in reference to other variants of the myth see Danek 1998, 252–255.
23 See Schelske 2011, 40–42. The interpretation by Madeła (2020, 8) is one way to deal with metapoetics here: "Following that literary fiction [i.e. the seniority], it is conceivable that Homer, when composing the *Odyssey*, looked for inspiration in the epic of 'Orpheus,' since it predated his birth. Homer, then, would have read the passage about the Sirens in the Orphic Argonautica." See, however, Hunter's (2005, 165–166) remarks on Orpheus' problematic reliability as narrator and the metapoetic implications of this.
24 Translation by Fairclough/Goold 1999, slightly adapted.
25 Cf. Serv. *Aen.* 5.864: *Vlixes contemnendo deduxit ad mortem* (cf., e.g., Hyg. *fab.* 141). Ov. *Met.* 14.87–88 and Sil. 12.33–36 require a similar explanation. See, also, n. 22 above.
26 See, e.g., the overview in Nünlist/Bäbler 2001.

lonius alludes to the fact that the different legends transmitted about them imply a certain chronology: τότε δ' ἄλλο μὲν οἰωνοῖσιν, / ἄλλο δὲ παρθενικῆς ἐναλίγκιαι ἔσκον ἰδέσθαι, "by this time, though, they looked partly like birds and partly like maidens" (A.R. 4.898–899).[27] The presumed reason for their transformation is hidden, as it were, behind this factual τότε. Vergil apparently reacts to this kind of implicit reference, as he equally cuts short what must or could have happened after Odysseus' escape by the parenthetical *tum* (*Aen.* 5.866).[28] There is a similar structure in Ps-Orpheus: Δὴ τότε δὴ Μινύαισιν ἐφήνδανε πύστις ἀοιδῆς / Σειρήνων, "Then it happened that the Minyans wanted to experience the song" (*OA* 1270–1271).[29] Here, however, the temporal continuum concerns the Argonauts rather than the perilous maidens, for there is no further evidence of any kind of mythological history in that passage.[30] These Sirens seem to have no past. But maybe they have a future: the poet explicitly mentions the surges beneath their rock which would remain the only remembrance of the Sirens in Vergil: χαροπὸν δ' ἄρ' ὑποβρέμει ἔνδοθι κῦμα, "within which the dark waves resounded terribly" (*OA* 1267).

In fact, Ps-Orpheus' localisation of the rock near Scylla and Charybdis is much more in line with the tradition followed by Vergil than with that of Apollonius' (Campanian?) island Anthemoessa.[31] And perhaps there is even more: for some readers, Ps-Orpheus' surprising myth, according to which the Sirens finally turn to stones (*OA* 1287–1290),[32] will probably function as an explanatory note to Vergil's *saxa sonantia*.

Be that as it may. The Sirens obviously draw attention to the difficulties of mythical chronology and the relationship between certain myths. Ps-Orpheus seems particularly interested in these things. There is, above all, the question whether Orpheus accompanied the Argonauts before or after the death of Eurydice. Ps-Apollodorus, for example, mentions both myths independently of one

---

27 Translation by Race 2009.
28 Note also the correlatives ποτε (A.R. 4.896) and *quondam* (Verg. *Aen.* 5.865).
29 My translation.
30 The Sirens are introduced with a conventional formula, as if the narrator thinks that they are unknown to the audience: Ἔνθα δ' ἐφεζόμεναι λιγυρὴν ὄπα γηρύουσι (*OA* 1268).
31 It is hardly possible to pinpoint the Sirens from Homer's account. On these issues see Hunter 2015 *ad* A.R. 4.891–892.
32 It is difficult to determine whether Ps-Orpheus invented this metamorphosis or not. Regarding the rocks, Vian (1987a, 194) refers to Stephanus of Byzantium, who could, however, be younger than our poet. On the possibly Roman implications of the Sirens' metamorphosis see Karanika 2017.

another and thus avoids an explanation.[33] Ps-Orpheus, by mentioning the singer's κατάβασις, deliberately arranges the stories (see section 2).[34] The former journey to Hades could even be relevant to the present passage, for the Sirens often function as a symbol of death.[35] When Orpheus successfully defeats 'death' here, the audience is, of course, reminded of his failure with Eurydice. However, as we will see, the significance of death and life in the *Orphic Argonautica* always remains an issue of interpretation.

2 The Cave of Orpheus

The beginning of the poem is set in a cave. Ps-Orpheus describes a location closely connected to song:

> καί μ' ἐκίχανε χέλυν πολυδαίδαλον ἐντύνοντα,
> ὄφρα κέ τοι μέλπων προχέω μελίγηρυν ἀοιδήν,
> κηλήσω δέ τε θῆρας ἰδ' ἑρπετὰ καὶ πετεηνά.
> Ἡνίκα δ' εἰς ἄντρον πολυήρατον εἰσεπέρησε ...
>
> *OA* 72–75

> [sc. Jason] found me occupied playing my cithara skilfully and singing sweet songs, beguiling wild animals and winged serpents. But when he had entered into my pleasant cave ...

The Thracian cave where Jason finds Orpheus when he comes to invite him to the adventure and to which Orpheus finally returns after the journey is described as πολυήρατον, "much loved" (*OA* 75) and, respectively, as περικλυτόν, "famous" (*OA* 1375).[36] Both adjectives classify the cave as an important place, but at no point in the narrative does Ps-Orpheus tell his audience what this place looks like – just as if it were known. To some extent, a detailed description seems indeed unnecessary; a cave is a *topos*, the archetype of a sacred, detached place.[37] In terms of religious symbolism, one might even feel tempted

---

[33] Cf. Apollod. *Bibl.* 1.14–15; 1.110–111.
[34] On Ps-Orpheus' encyclopaedic technique in general see Schelske 2011, 42–51, especially 48: "Das Bestreben, die verschiedenen Details, die mit dem Namen Orpheus verbunden sind, zu vereinen, ist deutlich."
[35] See, e.g., Nünlist/Bäbler 2001.
[36] See also *OA* 110: ἄντρον ἐπήρατον; and [Orph.] *Lith.* 18: ἐς πολυήρατον ἄντρον ἐσελθέμεν Ἑρμείαο.
[37] Cf. Schelske 2011, 112–113; van Opstall 2013.

to relate every literary cave to that of Circe or that of the Ithacan nymphs.³⁸ In fact, the latter place (and the profound allegoresis to which it has led) might be an important clue to the significance of our poem,³⁹ but Homer's ἄντρον νυμφῶν is a different locality and it has nothing directly in common with the abode of Orpheus.⁴⁰ If this specific cave can be assumed to be loved and known by many, it is not just because it is a typical cave.

The word πολυήρατον connects a certain place with a certain emotion, an individual *myth* so to speak. It can thus function as an 'Alexandrian footnote': if the narrator chooses not to explain why the cave is loved, readers may seek an intertextual explanation. The most natural one is, however, hardly meaningful. Though a cave is mentioned by Apollonius as Orpheus' birthplace,⁴¹ it neither plays a role in the *Argonautica*, nor does it receive any particular description. Instead, having mentioned it, Apollonius comes to the legend (A.R. 1.26: ἐνέπουσιν) according to which Orpheus has enchanted rocks and trees in the mountains.

Is there an established tradition of an *Orphean* cave? As stated above, the image of the singer who moves beasts, trees, and even stones is topical. That the singer is singing in a cave, however, is not; the motif (actually a combination of Apollonius' two remarks) is not common until Vergil uses it in his account of Orpheus' grief:⁴²

> *Septem illum totos perhibent ex ordine menses*
> *rupe sub aëria deserti ad Strymonis undam*
> *flesse sibi et gelidis haec evoluisse sub antris*
> *mulcentem tigres et agentem carmine quercus.*
>
> G. 4.507–510

Of him they tell that for seven whole months day after day beneath a lofty crag beside lonely Strymon's stream he wept, and in the shelter of cool caves unfolded this his tale, charming tigers and drawing oaks with his song.

---

38 Cf. Hom. *Od.* 5.59–74; 13.96–112.
39 Cf. Schelske 2011, 112–115, 217, 306–307.
40 Porphyry's interpretation of that cave has often been the subject of scholarly interest; see, for example, the recent works of Akçay 2019 and Dorandi *et al.* 2019.
41 A.R. 1.23–25: τόν ῥά ποτ' αὐτὴ / Καλλιόπη Θρήικι φατίζεται εὐνηθεῖσα / Οἰάγρῳ σκοπιῆς Πιμπληίδος ἄγχι τεκέσθαι ("whom once Calliope bare, it is said, wedded to Thracian Oeagrus, near the Pimpleian height").
42 Translation by Fairclough/Goold 1999, slightly adapted.

As it happens, this passage contains one of the few problems of textual criticism in Vergil: do we have to read *antris* (**M**) or *astris* (**R**)?[43] It seems that *antris* is to be preferred; yet even if we chose *astris*, this would hardly affect the image of the singer sitting beneath some sort of stony arch (*rupe sub aëria*).[44] Vergil refers to the scene as a matter of narration (*perhibent*), which reflects, as in Apollonius, the legendary status of Orpheus' song. As said, however, the cave (with Vergil's plural taken as poetic) is not canonical as far as I can see.[45] In the iconographic tradition, idyllic scenes are not uncommon and Orpheus often sits on a rock beneath a tree.[46]

Whereas woods traditionally feature as poetic environment,[47] caves often serve as oracular places. In the *Georgics*, Orpheus' cave may thus reflect the exceptional, larger-than-poetic status of his song; apart from this religious dimension, it probably serves — being cold and stony — as an apt backdrop for his grief and his eventual death.[48] It is precisely here that Orpheus spends his last days before being ripped apart by the Maenads.[49] For whatever reason Vergil invented that peculiar place,[50] the motif itself apparently has had some influence on later Latin poetry. The *antrum* becomes a place associated with (prophetic) poets.[51] In one of Claudian's panegyrical poems *ad Serenam*, Orpheus has a cave as well:[52]

---

[43] For *astris* see Thomas 1988 *ad loc*. For *antris* see the editions of Mynors 1969 and Conte in Ottaviano/Conte 2013, the latter referring to Ov. *Trist*. 5.1.61; Sil. 3.203. In Horace, the 'Orphean' Haemus has the epithet *gelidus* (*Carm*. 1.12.6).

[44] *Pace* Mynors 1990 *ad loc.*: "probably in the sense of 'valley'" with reference to Prop. 1.1.11.

[45] At least, the mountains of Thessaly are often in the backdrop of Orpheus' singing. Euripides refers to Orpheus singing ἐν ταῖς πολυδένδρεσσιν Ὀλύμπου θαλάμαις (*Bacch*. 561); Iamblichus says that Orpheus was instructed by his mother κατὰ τὸ Πάγγαιον ὄρος (*Vita Pyth*. 146.18). However, the fact that Apollonius mentions the cave and the song so closely one after another (A.R. 1.24–27) may suggest the idea that both motifs belong together.

[46] Cf. Jesnick 1997, 73–74; Viellefon 2003, 253–268.

[47] Ovid exploits this, when, in his account of the myth, he uses a conspicuously varied formula of introduction: *collis erat collemque super planissimi campi / area* ("there was a hill and beneath it an open field," *Met*. 10.86–87). No distinctive environment at all: here, it is just through the trees elicited by the divine song that a mythical shadowy grove comes into existence (90–147: *umbra loco venit...*).

[48] Cf. Richter 1957 *ad loc*.

[49] Cf. Verg. *G*. 4.516–527.

[50] For instance, the parallel with Proteus' cave (*G*. 4.429) may be noted. On Vergil's reception of the Orphic tradition see the standard commentary of Eduard Norden (1927).

[51] On the cave see Sidon. *Carm*. 23.180–181: *non possim merita sonare laude, / nec si me Odrysio canens in antro...* ("I could not praise him worthily, even if [sc. Orpheus] singing in Odrysian

> *certavere ferae picturataeque volucres*
> *dona suo vati quae potiora darent,*
> *quippe antri memores, cautes ubi saepe sonorae*
> *praebuerant dulci mira theatra lyrae.*
>
> *Carm. min.* 31.4–6

The beasts and gay-plumaged birds strove among themselves what best gifts they could bring their poet, mindful of the cave whose sounding rocks had offered a wondrous theatre for his tuneful lyre.

It is impossible not to take the phrase *antri memores* as referential and to feel reminded of the Augustan image of a *vates in antro*. However, whereas in the *Georgics* the sad appearance of the landscape is highlighted, Claudian — referring to the 'happy' tradition that regards Orpheus above all as a culture hero — depicts the place rather as a cultured *locus amoenus*. He stresses the beautiful sound that has been heard in the *antrum*, but he has no tragic reason for that. Ps-Orpheus' πολυήρατον ἄντρον seems to reflect an idyllic scenario of this kind.

Apparently, however, Orpheus has lost Eurydice for ever (a particularly Vergilian notion)[53] and intends to die in the cave before Jason takes him to Colchis (*OA* 41-42, 105). For him, the quest can thus only be an interruption. Orpheus will have to come back to the place where, according to the Vergilian tradition, he must bemoan Eurydice and die. This idea gets some support when we read how Orpheus, on his way back to the "renowned cave," passes Taenarus, the entrance to the Underworld (*OA* 1370). An atmosphere of death (or, in somewhat more Orphic terms: "rebirth") dominates the ending.[54] In fact, then, Ps-Orpheus' ἄντρον may be as cold and stony as Vergil's. Jason, an independent focaliser, nearly repeats Vergil's description of the Thracian landscape: Αἱμονίους ὀχεὰς πρώτιστον ἱκάνω / Στρυμονίους τε ῥοὰς Ῥοδόπης τ' αἰπεινὰ πρὸς ἄγκη, "For the first time I come to the Haemonean caves and to the waters of Strymon and the steep ravines of Rhodope" (*OA* 79–80, cf. Verg. *G.* 4.508: *rupe sub aëria deserti ad Strymonis undam*, "under a lofty crag, by the waters of deserted Strymon").[55] But to the 'Orphean' Orpheus the lonely place of his immi-

---

cave… [had taught] me…"). On the issue of (Augustan) poetic self-representation connected with the image of Vergil's Orpheus see Kayachev 2017, 76–77.
52 Translation by Platnauer 1922. On Claudian's engagement with Orphic literature see Bernert 1938.
53 See Lee 1996, 9–14.
54 Cf. Schelske 2011 *ad loc.*
55 Cf. *OA* 1373: ὁρμηθεὶς ἐσύθην χιονώδεα Θρήκην ("I hurried to snowy Thrace").

nent death appears as a lovely *locus amoenus* to which he returns as if coming home.

Whereas Claudian speaks of the singer's *antrum*, ignoring the tragedy to which it is connected in the *Georgics*, Ps-Orpheus blends together the happy and the sad traditions. When he labels the cave as περικλυτόν he seems to evoke — at least for Latinist readers — precisely the cold place invented by Vergil. However, when it appears as "much loved" or indeed "very lovely" it serves an idyllisation of death that is remarkably different from Vergil's account. In referring to it in roughly the same manner as Claudian did, namely by stressing its *literary* fame, Ps-Orpheus not only expresses dependence, but also his ability to read Vergil's Aristaeus-Orpheus-epyllion in a different way than with sad compassion for Vergil's (or Proteus'?) *miserabilis Orpheus*.

Whatever the case is, the epithet clearly has a metapoetic dimension, as it concerns the problem of literary closure. For readers remembering the conventional form of the myth, the label περικλυτόν would mark the cave as the well-known ending point of the story. Here, Ps-Orpheus' narrative arrangement enables an observation on the modes of pseudepigraphy. When, as is known from the Vergilian tradition, Orpheus sings in Thessaly before he is slain by the Maenads, and when, as Ps-Orpheus' first-person narrator says, he returns to his cave after the Argonautic adventure, the last poem which Orpheus sang before his cruel death must be exactly the very poem we read, the *Argonautica*. There is no consensus in the literary tradition as to what the content of Orpheus' last song was. In Vergil, he sings a *miserabile carmen*; in Ovid, it seems that he sings of beautiful boys and their tragic fate.[56] Ps-Orpheus, in contrast, speaks of a song that is glorious and sweet (*OA* 3–6, 73); there is no evidence of grief at all. The choice of the unconventional narrator even suggests that Orpheus might not suffer his conventional death, but die peacefully after completing his œuvre, as 'he' prays at the end of the *Hymns*.[57] That would be a similar intervention in the canonical myth as in the case of the Sirens.[58] But if the famous cave really echoes the poetic κλέος of Ps-Orpheus' predecessors, we have to consider these interventions as ludic indications of fictionality rather than as irreverential references.

---

[56] Cf. Verg. *G*. 4.514; Ov. *Met*. 11.1 (apparently referring to the content of book 10).

[57] Cf. [Orph.] *Hymn*. 87.11. Yet the narrator is, of course, not reliable; Schelske 2011 sees a foreshadowing of Orpheus' death at *OA* 667–679.

[58] It has, however, been noted, that the *OA* lack eroticism (see Schelske 2011, *ad* 643–648). So, we could perhaps say that tradition is indeed respected if the narrator of this poem does what Orpheus is said to have done after Eurydice's death: to spurn love.

3 The Cave of Chiron

Ps-Orpheus provides an extended description of the cave on Mt Pelion where Chiron lives and educates Achilles. This passage further stresses the issue of mythographic consistency:

> [...] ἐνθάδε Χείρων
> ναίει ἐνὶ σπήλυγγι, δικαιότατος Κενταύρων
> [...]
> Αὐτὰρ ἔπειτ' αὐλὴν εἰσήλθομεν ἠεροειδῆ·
> καί οἱ κεκλιμένος μὲν ἐπ' οὐδαίοιο χαμεύνης
> κεῖτο μέγας Κένταυρος, ἀπηρήρειστο δὲ πέτρῃ   395
> ἱππείαισιν ὁπλαῖσι τανυσσάμενος θοὰ κῶλα·
> ἀγχοῦ δ' ἱστάμενος Θέτιδος καὶ Πηλέος υἱὸς
> χερσὶ λύραν ἤρασσε, φρένας δ' ἐπετέρπετο Χείρων.
> Ἀλλ' ὅτε δή ῥ' ἄθρησεν ἀγακλειτοὺς βασιλῆας
> ἀσπασίως ἀνόρουσε, κύσεν δ' ἄρα φῶτα ἕκαστον·   400
> δαῖτά τ' ἐπόρσυνεν· μέθυ δ' ἀμφιφορεῦσι κομίσσας,
> ῥωγαλέαις ἔστρωσεν ὑπὸ στιβάδεσσι πέταλα·
> κλινθῆναι δ' ἐκέλευσεν· ἀδαιδάλτοις δ' ἐπὶ πλεκταῖς
> κρεῖα χύδην προύθηκε συῶν ἐλάφων τε ταχειῶν,
> αὐτὰρ ἔπειτ' ἐπένειμε ποτὸν μελιηδέος οἴνου.   405
>   *OA* 378–379; 393–405

> In that cave lives Chiron, the most just of the Centaurs [...]
> We followed him into a dark hall. There lay recumbent the great Centaur, resting against a rock, his hooves and swift horse feet extended. Standing near, the son of Peleus and Thetis played the lyre with his hands, and lifted the spirits of Chiron. When he first caught sight of the famous lords, he stood up to greet them and kissed each and every man. He made food available and furnished amphorae of wine. He spread out a covering of torn leaves and commanded his guests to take a place. He swiftly placed ample deer and boar meat on rough plates; afterward he distributed sweet wine to drink.

The place, unmentioned in extant Greek epic,[59] is a very common feature in Flavian poetry. Valerius, who follows Apollonius in narrating how Chiron comes down from his mountain to see the Argonauts,[60] briefly names the Centaur's dwelling.[61] Silius has the singer Teuthras tell of Achilles studying epic

---

[59] The cave is, however, well-known in other poetic genres; Pindar, for instance, refers to it (*P.* 9.30) as well as Antisthenes (fr. 24A Decleva Caizzi).
[60] Cf. Val. Fl. 1.255–263; A.R. 1.553–558. In Apollonius, Chiron has told Jason to add Orpheus to his crew: see A.R. 1.33.
[61] *Chironis antrum*, cf. Val. Fl. 1.407–409.

poetry in the mountain (Sil. 11.449).⁶² Statius provides a detailed portrait of the cave in his *Achilleid*, as he narrates how Thetis brings her son back from Chiron to hide him in Scyrus. It is to this passage that Ps-Orpheus' description seems to refer:⁶³

> [...] *domus ardua montem*
> *perforat et longo suspendit Pelion arcu;*
> *pars exhausta manu, partem sua ruperat aetas.*
> *signa tamen divumque tori et quem quisque sacrarit*
> *accubitu genioque locum monstrantur; at intra*   110
> *Centauri stabula alta patent, non aequa nefandis*
> *fratribus: hic hominum nullos experta cruores*
> *spicula nec truncae bellis genialibus orni*
> *aut consanguineos fracti crateres in hostes,*
> *sed pharetrae insontes et inania terga ferarum.*   115
> *haec quoque dum viridis; nam tunc labor unus inermi*
> *nosse salutiferas dubiis animantibus herbas,*
> *aut monstrare lyra veteres heroas alumno.*
>   Ach. 1.106–118

High up his lofty dwelling bores through the mountain, upholding Pelion with its lengthy vault. Part was excavated by hand, part its own age had ruptured. But tokens and couches of the gods are to be seen, showing which place each deity had hallowed with his reclining and his familiar spirit. Within spread the Centaur's lofty stalls, a contrast to his villainous brethren. Here are no darts that have tasted human blood, no ash trees fractured in festive combats, nor mixing bowls shattered upon kindred foes, but innocent quivers and empty hides of wild beasts – these too of his salad days. For at this time unarmed his only labour was to know herbs that bring health to living things in doubtful case or to limn with his lyre the heroes of old for his pupil.

It comes as no surprise that in both poems the scene takes place in a rustic setting;⁶⁴ the same applies to the food that the centaur prepares.⁶⁵ Remarkably, however, both caves serve as backdrop for mythological memory. Statius' narrator mentions the wedding of Peleus and Thetis that was celebrated there (*Ach.*

---

62 Moreover, cf. Ov. *Met.* 2.630; Stat. *Silv.* 1.4.98.
63 Translation by Shackleton Bailey 2004.
64 Caves and similar hideouts of poor people often serve as the setting of epic hospitality scenes; see Reitz 2020 on Ps-Theocr. 21.6–13; Call. *Hecale* fr. 26 Hollis; Call. *Aet.* fr. 54–59 Pfeiffer; Lucan 5.504–549; Verg. *Aen.* 8.366–368.
65 Cf. *Ach.* 1.125: *pauperibus tectis* ("humble residence") and *OA* 394: ἐπ' οὐδαίοιο χαμεύνης ("on a strawbed on the ground"). *Ach.* 120–121: *properatque dapes largoque serenat / igne domum* ("and he hastens the meal and brightens the residence with a generous fire") and *OA* 401: δαῖτά τ' ἐπόρσυνεν ("and he prepared a meal").

1.101–103, 110 f.), and, by stressing the differences between Chiron's place and other *connubialia antra*, he intertextually reminds his audience of the fight between Lapiths and Centaurs.⁶⁶ Ps-Orpheus evokes the same 'epic' narrative when he has Chiron sing of that very fight (*OA* 415–418), even though he skips a detailed spatial description.⁶⁷ Both caves are places of culture and study,⁶⁸ where Achilles seems to learn the κλέα ἀνδρῶν that he will sing of at Troy (Hom. *Il.* 9.189).⁶⁹ Moreover, both Statius and Ps-Orpheus make use of the ironic dissonance that this cultivated home is but a stable (*Ach.* 1.111: *Centauri stabula*; *OA* 438: βοαύλια Κενταύροιο).⁷⁰

The scenery in Statius and Ps-Orpheus is roughly the same. The scene, however, is not, for Ps-Orpheus tells of an earlier event. According to the mythochronology, Peleus' son should be relatively young at this point in the action.⁷¹ Apollonius and Valerius say that Chiron presents the boy to his father; we have to imagine the centaur holding up an infant.⁷² In Ps-Orpheus, however, Achilles plays the lyre just like his predecessor in the *Achilleid*, even though he does not sing a specific song like his Statian counterpart.⁷³

---

66 See Kersten 2019, 398: "In Chiron's cave, one can still see the places where the gods sat when they attended the wedding (Stat. *Ach.* 1.110: *monstrantur*) ... And yet, another remembrance of an epic wedding, that of Pirithous (1.113–114, equally celebrated in a cave; cf. Ov. *Met.* 12.211), is present at this place; albeit *ex negativo*: Chiron's cave has nothing to do with the ordinary dwellings of his fellow Centaurs who fought the Lapiths."
67 Chiron as singer is prominent in Flavian epic, cf. Val. Fl. 1.139: *pulsatque chelyn post pocula Chiron* ("and after their drinking Chiron is striking his lyre"); Sil. 11.451: *Centauro dilecta chelys* ("the lyre that Chiron loves"). This motif may, however, be much older, cf. Nelis 2005, 174–178.
68 See also Schelske 2011, 267 on the contrast between Chiron's and Polyphemus' caves.
69 On the intertextual implication of priority see Hinds 1998, 123–129. Both texts mention how the lyre is handed over from one to the other: Stat. *Ach.* 1.187–188: *fila movet leviterque expertas pollice chordas / dat puero* ("[Chiron] played the strings and having lightly tried out a few chords with his thumb, he gave it to the boy"); *OA* 413–414: Κένταυρος ἀείρατο πηκτίδα καλήν, / ἥν ῥα τότ' ἐν χείρεσσι φέρων ὤρεξεν Ἀχιλλεύς ("the Centaur lifted the beautiful lyre, which Achilles then brought and handed to him"). For further correspondences see Hunter 2005, 154.
70 Whereas *stabulum* is not confined to a certain species (and not even to animals), βοαύλιον is strange (unless it indicates the stable of Chiron's cattle, cf. Schelske 2011 *ad loc.*); is there a kind of wordplay with κεν-ταῦρος? On this (improbable) etymology see Serv. *G.* 3.115: *qui dicti sunt Centauri* ἀπὸ τοῦ κεντᾶν τοὺς ταύρους, "to goad the bulls." As for *stabula Centauri*, cf. Verg. *Aen.* 6.286; Stat. *Theb.* 1.457.
71 Cf. A.R. 1.558–560; Val. Fl. 1.257–270.
72 Scholars have noted the relation between Valerius' Achilles and Homer's Astyanax (*Il.* 6.399–471); see Spaltenstein 2002 *ad loc.*
73 Statius has Achilles sing a *Heracleid* (*Ach.* 1.188–194).

Once more, there might be a metapoetic implication here. When Orpheus responds to Chiron's challenge with his cosmogonic song, as is obligatory, animals and trees arrive there (*OA* 435–439).⁷⁴ This significantly changes the place where Achilles is studying until his mother brings him to Scyrus. It is not difficult to imagine trees and birds increasing the amenity of Chiron's cave. We might even suspect that this affects how, from that moment on, poetry will be received and performed there. At any rate, it is apparent that Chiron, although he lives in a cave and sings, cannot not be *the* archetypical singer. This notion is further underpinned by the centaur's non-sublime reaction at his defeat: Αὐτὰρ ὁρῶν Κένταυρος ἐθάμβεε χεῖρ' ἐπὶ καρπῷ / πυκνὸν ἐπισσείων, οὖδας δ' ἤρασσεν ὁπλῇσι, "Seeing this, the Centaur was astounded and repeatedly struck hand upon hand and his hooves upon the ground" (*OA* 440–441).⁷⁵

On the other hand, Ps-Orpheus indeed sticks to the Argonautic chronology. Although he applies a similar setting as Statius, he clearly follows the tradition according to which the centauromachia has taken place before Jason's voyage,⁷⁶ whereas in Statius⁷⁷ it remains unclear when it happened precisely.⁷⁸ To be sure, this cannot prove that Ps-Orpheus has read Statius; but it may be valuable to see that he uses ecphrastic material quite similar to that developed by a Latin poet in the first century.

4 The Wood of the Nymphs

While Ps-Orpheus has inserted places into his narrative that are somewhat alien to the myth of the Argonauts, he also appears to have excised places that belong to its core repertoire. Hylas does not drown in water but is taken into a cave (*OA* 645: σπέος), since the nymphs dwelling there want to bestow immortality on

---

74 Note that the motif of 'Orpheus singing in a cave' is repeated here; the interesting parallel between Sil. 11.467 and *OA* 438–439 may be an old Orphic motif, cf. Nelis 2005, 176.
75 A similar image is found at Sidon. *Carm*. 1.17–20. The cultural superiority of Orpheus is precisely the theme of Teuthras' *Castalium carmen* in Sil. 11.440–480.
76 Cf. A.R. 1.101–104 (implicitly); Val. Fl. 1.137–148.
77 As in Ovid, cf. *Met*. 12.210–535.
78 In fact, the cave could serve as a marker for chronology, cf. Apollod. *Bibl*. 2.85: Χείρων [...] ὃς ἐξελαθεὶς ὑπὸ Λαπιθῶν ὄρους Πηλίου παρὰ Μαλέαν κατῴκησε; however, this idea is not canonical.

him (*OA* 643–648). Ps-Orpheus only gently alludes to the nymphs' erotic desire that is inherent in the myth.[79]

The "woodman" gets lost in the wood, ὕλῃ ἐνιπλαγχθείς (*OA* 645),[80] but does not, one might add, get to the famous spring called Πηγαί, "Fountain," that some readers probably expect.[81] On the other hand, the nymphs who capture him are apparently connected to water (*OA* 646: Λιμνακίδες).[82] This kind of change could insinuate that the definite place is indeed irrelevant to the story. At any rate, if we imagine the σπέος to be like that of Calypso (as said, one of the archetypical caves),[83] water might not be far off.[84] To think of Calypso might indeed be adequate, since she too promises immortality, albeit one that appears like death to Odysseus.[85] Odysseus' own complex attitude towards the gift of immortal life far away from his loved ones makes us question the exact nature of Hylas' gifts. As in the case of Orpheus' cave, the readers are offered different perspectives on death, love, and afterlife.

As regards tradition, grottoes fit well into a Hylean setting. In Propertius, it is at least uncertain, whether the nymphs dwell in the water or in a humid cave: *hic erat Arganthi pege sub vertice montis / grata domus Nymphis umida Thyniasin*, "beneath Mt Arganthus, there was (a) πηγή, a humid home dear to Bithynian nymphs" (Prop. 1.20.33).[86] Dracontius applies a similar ambiguity: *expavit sic raptus Hylas pavidusque petebat / herbida quod vitreum tellus perfuderat antrum*, "terrified by this kind of rape, Hylas fearfully went into the watery grotto that the grassy soil had opened here" (*Rom.* 2.129–130). Apart from that, there is evidence of a Greek epigram from Egypt, that mentions Hylas in a σπέος.[87] This could well imply that the motif was known to Ps-Orpheus.

---

79 Cf. *OA* 647–648: ὄφρα σὺν αὐταῖς / ἀθάνατός τε πέλῃ ("and that he may become immortal with them").
80 On the poetic potential for playing with Hylas and ὕλη / *silva* see Petrain 2000.
81 Cf. A.R. 1.1221–1222: κρήνη, ... ἣν καλέουσιν Πηγάς. Prop. 1.20.33 has the name as well (the singular is preferable to Scaliger's plural Pegae; does it underline the Greek pun?). Schol. A.R. 1221–1222a comments that this is indeed the name: ὄνομα κρήνης Πηγαὶ οὕτω κυρίως.
82 In Valerius, the nymph Dryope ("Oak," Val. Fl. 3.529) who draws him into the spring might actually live in a tree.
83 On Homer's Calypso and her σπέος (*Od.* 5.57) see Schelske 2011 *ad loc.*
84 Cf. Hom. *Od.* 5.70–71: κρῆναι δ' ἑξείης πίσυρες ῥέον ὕδατι λευκῷ, / πλησίαι ἀλλήλων τετραμμέναι ἄλλυδις ἄλλη ("and four neighbouring springs, channelled this way and that, flowed with crystal water").
85 Cf. Hom. *Od.* 5.152, 208–209.
86 For *nympharum domus* as a cave see Verg. *Aen.* 1.166–668, a passage modelled on the famous cave of *Odyssey* 13; cf. Kersten 2019, 379.
87 Cf. Agosti 1994.

It is not easy to determine whether the poet simply thought of a watery cavern like that in Propertius' elegy, or whether he intended to vary the scene profoundly and give hermeneutic significance to it. If so, religion could perhaps offer an explanation.[88] While in the mythological tradition it is Hylas' task to disappear, Ps-Orpheus offers a perspective on Hylas' later existence by explicitly mentioning his eternal youth (ἀγήραος ἤματα πάντα, *OA* 648). This version is, however, not entirely new (in Valerius, the boy is turned into a water deity),[89] and the significance of the cave for Hylas' transition into another sphere is anything but explicit. In fact, there is some ambiguity in Ps-Orpheus' account, depending on how much we tend to see Calypso's cave as a symbol of death (and on what we think death means).[90]

5 The Sphere of Sleep

The passage in *OA* 1004–1012 does not describe a mythical place in the strictest sense; however, it contains the motif of Sleep's invocation. This motif, originating from Hom. *Il.* 14.224–291, has a relatively stereotypical form: Sleep is visited by a deity – Sleep learns about his task – Sleep acts.[91] In Latin epic, the visit-scene is sometimes extended to a description of the god's house,[92] which may be called 'allegorical' since the abode symbolises the power of the abstract force that is personified into a god.[93] Dreams and Silence dwell here; and around Sleep's home, there is no wind, no birds sing, no animals can be heard, no water is murmuring, etc.

---

88 See Agosti 1994 and Schelske 2011, 307: "Die Darlegung des Porphyrios wird offensichtlich evoziert."
89 Cf. Val. Fl. 1.218–220; 4.25–37.
90 See Elliger 1975, 131–132. There is similar irony in Theocr. 13.72, when Hylas (apparently immortalised by the nymphs, but shedding tears under the water) is numbered among the blessed ones, οὕτω μὲν κάλλιστος Ὕλας μακάρων ἀριθμεῖται; cf. Hunter 1999 *ad loc.*
91 This structure is basically the same in Nonn. *Dion.* 31.123–196; however, descriptions of Sleep and his sphere are lacking.
92 Cf. Ov. *Met.* 11.592–615; Stat. *Theb.* 10.84–136. See also Sil. 10.337–356. In Ovid, there is even a structural link between Sleep and Orpheus, since Morpheus has to tell Alcyone of the death of Ceyx (*Met.* 11.671–676). Orpheus and Alcyone share similar miseries in books 10 and 11 after seeing at last a vain shade of their beloved ones.
93 On this term see Reitz 2000; on allegory in Ovid and Statius see Feeney 1991, 241–249; 364–391.

Ps-Orpheus does not apply the full motif; a proper visit-scene is lacking (no wonder, since Orpheus is but a human), and the apostrophe of the god is cut short by indirect speech. However, even if the poet does not describe the house of Sleep, he still names all the elements that are constitutive for the description of the sphere Sleep regularly brings with him when accomplishing his task. Above all, the poet represents Sleep's impact on nature:

> Κλῆξα γὰρ Ὕπνον ἄνακτα θεῶν πάντων τ' ἀνθρώπων
> ὄφρα μολὼν θέλξειε μένος βριαροῖο δράκοντος.   1005
> Ῥίμφα δέ μοι ὑπάκουσε, Κυτηίδα δ' ἵκτ' ἐπὶ γαῖαν.
> Κοιμίσσας δ' ὅ γε φῦλα πανημερίων ἀνθρώπων,
> καὶ ζαμενεῖς ἀνέμων πνοιὰς καὶ κύματα πόντου,
> πηγάς τ' ἀενάων ὑδάτων, ποταμῶν τε ῥέεθρα,
> θῆράς τ' οἰωνούς τε, τά τε ζώει τε καὶ ἕρπει,   1010
> εὐνάζων, ἤμειψεν ὑπὸ χρυσέαις πτερύγεσσιν.
> Ἷξε δ' ὑπὸ στυφελῶν Κόλχων εὐανθέα χῶρον.
>   OA 1004–1012

I called upon Sleep, king of gods and all men, to come and beguile the might of the immense snake. Yielding to me at once, he came to the land of Cyta, on his way causing sleep among tribes of men weary from the day's work, powerful blasts of winds, waves of the sea, springs of ever-flowing water, gliding rivers, beasts, and birds, and everything living and moving he persuaded to sleep under his golden wings. Thus he came to the blooming land of the harsh Colchians.

Orpheus fulfils the task traditionally carried out by Medea:[94] He sings a prayer to Hypnus until the dragon falls asleep (OA 1004: κλῆξα γὰρ Ὕπνον...). This may indicate that it is actually the power of the song of Orpheus that overcomes the guardian of the Golden Fleece. Yet even if Hypnus basically symbolises the singer's power, our poet, unlike his Argonautic predecessors, describes the god as an epic character, and his appearance corresponds to his poetic representation in Latin epic. Both Ovid and Statius make use of the iconographic tradition

---

94 Cf. A.R. 4.145–147: κατ' ὄμματα νίσσετο κούρη, / ὕπνον ἀοσσητῆρα, θεῶν ὕπατον, καλέουσα / ἡδείῃ ἐνοπῇ, θέλξαι τέρας ("the maiden came before his eyes, with sweet voice calling to her aid Sleep, highest of gods, to charm the monster"); see also Val. Fl. 8.68–108.

according to which Sleep is winged.⁹⁵ Moreover, Hypnus' voyage is closely reminiscent of that of Somnus as described by Statius:⁹⁶

> *illius aura solo volucres pecudesque ferasque*
> *explicat, et penitus, quemcumque supervolat orbem,*
> *languida de scopulis sidunt freta, pigrius haerent*
> *nubila, demittunt extrema cacumina silvae,*
> *pluraque laxato ceciderunt sidera caelo.*
>
> Theb. 10.141–145

> His air strews birds and cattle and wild beasts upon the ground; whatever part of the world he flies over, the waters subside in deepest languor from the rocks, the mists cling more lazily, the woods droop their treetops, and more stars fall from the loosened sky.

In both instances, the manner in which the god acts is described as a flyover (*supervolare* / ὑπὸ χρυσέαις πτερύγεσσιν), and both authors make use of the same rhetoric: Sleep affects even inanimate nature. However, whereas in Statius, even stars tiredly fall from heaven, Ps-Orpheus seems more realistic. Since he first mentions the πανημέριοι ἄνθρωποι, his description appears as a semantic hypallage: rather than that rivers and trees have fallen asleep, one does not hear anything when sleeping.

Ps-Orpheus decribes the effect of the song as a faint: κῶμα δ' ἄφαρ κατέμαρψε πελωρίου ὄσσε δράκοντος, / ἰσοπαλὲς θανάτῳ, "a deep sleep suddenly settled on the monstrous serpent's eyes, the likeness of death" (*OA* 1013 f.). Valerius has a similar remark in Medea's prayer: *Somne... ades fratrique simillime Leto* (Val. Fl. 8.74). On the one hand, this reference to the kinship of Death and Sleep might be nothing else than just a topical apostrophe originating from very ancient mythology.⁹⁷ In the context of Jason's theft, though, the similarity, if mentioned so explicitly, might also suggest that the serpent could never wake up again. In Pindar's version, it must be remembered, Jason indeed kills him.⁹⁸ In the light of that parallel, Orpheus' song not only serves to characterise once more the singer's exceptional abilities. If Orpheus does essentially the same as

---

95 Cf. Ov. *Met.* 11.650 (here it is Morpheus, to be precise); Stat. *Theb.* 10.148; Sil. 10.344. The image probably corresponds to the Homeric simile in *Il.* 14.290: ὄρνιθι λιγυρῇ ἐναλίγκιος. On Sleep's similarity with Hermes (which might be observed in Ps-Orpheus as well, cf. *OA* 593), see Wöhrle 1995, 33–34. Golden wings are also not uncommon for Amor; cf., e.g., Aristoph. *Av.* 697 (note the Orphic expressions in that passage); Ov. *Rem.* 39; Mart. 8.50.13 (ecphrastic).
96 Translation by Shackleton Bailey 2004, slightly adapted.
97 Cf., e.g., Hom. *Il.* 14.231; Hes. *Theog.* 212 (see also [Orph.] *Hymn.* 85.8). Statius has the two live in the same house: Stat. *Theb.* 10.105–106.
98 Cf. Pind. *P.* 4.249.

Apollonius' and Valerius' Medea,⁹⁹ a poetic and ethical comparison is drawn up. While Orpheus has no affinity to deadly magic, the witch is a traditionally ambiguous character. Unlike Medea, Orpheus does not make use of violence to help the Argonauts. Accordingly, he sings quite silently: βαρυχέα φωνὴν / σιγαλέοις ἄφθεγκτον ἐμοῖς ὑπὸ χείλεσι πέμπον, "I sent from my silent lips a weak and inaudible sound" (*OA* 1002–1003).¹⁰⁰ In Valerius, Medea mobilises hellish forces to narcotise the dragon (Val. Fl. 8.83–87), but what she does is effective, and she trusts at least not to have killed her dragon (8.99). Ps-Orpheus alludes to the cruelty of the traditional arrangement by referring to the pain-bringing roots Medea has plucked as if to perform her deathly rites in the grove (*OA* 1000: λυγρῶν ἀποθρίσματα ῥιζῶν, "bits of poisonous roots"). When Orpheus forestalls her fulfilling the task that is crucial for the entire enterprise, Medea loses much of her ambiguous appearance; what is left to her is but the role of the "deadly maiden", παρθένος αἰνή (1027).

Finally, readers remembering the narrative contexts of the house of Sleep in Ovid and Statius will note that, in the *OA*, the god's task is quite undramatic. In the *Metamorphoses*, Morpheus tells Alcyone of Ceyx's death and subsequently drives her to suicide; in the *Thebaid*, Sleep helps to commit the massacre of the sleeping Thebans; in the *Orphic Argonautica*, he helps gain the Fleece. Again, there is less spectacle and less violence when Hypnus obeys the son of Calliope.

6 The Realm of the Cimmerians

Different from Apollonius, but close to Valerius Flaccus,¹⁰¹ our poet mentions the land of the Cimmerians. In terms of imitation, Ps-Orpheus' Argonauts clearly revisit the dark city; there is, however, no narrative reason for this. No κατάβασις takes place here, as in the *Odyssey*, nor does any expiation, as in Valerius.¹⁰² The visit is thus wholly episodic or ornamental:

---

99 The πανδαμάτωρ-motif is present in all three texts: A.R. 4.146; Val. Fl. 8.70; *OA* 1004.
100 I deviate from Colavito's (2011) translation. On the matter of sound as well as on the differences to Valerius' Medea see Schelske 2011, 347.
101 On Valerius see Spaltenstein 2004, 121: "On peut ainsi nommer des raisons vraisemblables pour expliquer que Val. fasse intervenir les Cimmerii dans ce contexte, mais on ne voit pas pourquoi il a choisi cette péripétie complexe. En effet, il y avait sans doute d'autres moyens."
102 In Valerius, Celaenus expiates the Argonauts of the murder of Cyzicus.

> [...] αἰγιαλὸν δὲ
> ποσσὶν ἐπιστείβοντες, ἔπειτα δὲ Κιμμερίοισι   1120
> νῆα θοὴν ἐπάγοντες ἱκάνομεν, οἵ ῥά τε μοῦνοι
> αἴγλης ἄμμοροί εἰσι πυριδρόμου Ἠελίοιο.
> Ἐν μὲν γὰρ Ῥίπαιον ὄρος καὶ Κάλπιος αὐχὴν
> ἀντολίας εἴργουσιν· ἐπικρέμαται δὲ πελώρη
> ἆσσον ἐπισκιάουσα μεσημβρινὸν ἠέρα Φλέγρη·   1125
> δείελον αὖ κρύπτουσι φάος ταναήκεες Ἄλπεις
> κείνοισιν μερόπεσσιν, ἀχλὺς δ' ἐπικέκλιται αἰεί.
> Ἔνθεν ἀφορμηθέντες ...
>
>   OA 1119–1128

At the shore, we went on foot and pulling the swift ship, we then came to the Cimmerians, who are without the splendid light of the sun. For the Rhipaean mountains and the Calpius block the rising sun and shut out brightness. Phlegra overshadows the noontime sun, and the sharp-peaked Alps block the evening light. So the Cimmerians are always in darkness. From there, we once again went forth ...

This land of eternal gloom is very well known. There is an extensive description in the *Odyssey* (11.14–19),[103] which Ps-Orpheus seems to epitomise with the short relative clause οἵ ῥά τε μοῦνοι ... (*OA* 1121). However, not only is the darkness classical, but so is the remoteness. Unlike, say, the Cyclopes, the Cimmerians are difficult to localise. It cannot be determined from the Homeric texts whether they live in the east or the west.[104] The vagueness of the spatial details makes this an often-used topos in Latin poetry,[105] where it serves as a mythological décor that is relatively independent from any rational attempts at pinpointing the Cimmerians at the Black Sea.[106]

In this mythologising manner, Valerius includes the land into the geography of his poem (Val. Fl. 3.397–401).[107] Following Homer in positioning it somewhere near the Underworld (but not necessarily in the north), he is equally

---

103 The issue of intertextuality is particularly difficult at *OA* 1122: αἴγλης ἄμμοροί εἰσι πυριδρόμου Ἠελίοιο ("they are deprived of the glare of the fireraging Sun"). In vocabulary, it is close to the Homeric phrase οὐδέ ποτ' αὐτοὺς / ἠέλιος φαέθων καταδέρκεται ἀκτίνεσσιν ("the bright sun never shines down on them with his rays," *Od.* 11.15–16), while in terms of personification it is similar to Val. Fl. 3.400–401: *quo flammea numquam Sol iuga... mittit* ("where the Sun never drives his flaming car"). The adjective πυρίδρομος appears to be a particularly Orphean word; see LSJ on this issue.
104 Cf. Nakassis 2004; Kersten 2019.
105 Cf. [Tib.] 3.5.24; 3.7.64 [= 4.1.64]; Ov. *Pont.* 4.10.1; [Verg.] *Culex* 232.
106 Cf., e.g., Hdt. 1.15; Strab. 1.1.10. On the historical Cimmerians see Sauter 2000.
107 On the relation of this passage to the somewhat more scientific remark at 6.61 see Spaltenstein 2004, 121.

imprecise about where it lies.[108] Silius, however, is more concrete; for him it is in Campania. When Hannibal visits Cumae, he learns about the myths connected to the land:[109]

> ille, olim populis dictum Styga, nomine verso
> stagna inter celebrem nunc mitia monstrat Avernum
> [...]
> at iuxta caligantis longumque per aevum   130
> infernis pressas nebulis pallente sub umbra
> Cimmerias iacuisse domos noctemque profundam
> Tartareae narrant urbis.
>
> Sil. 12.120–133

[sc. A third man] pointed out Lake Avernus, formerly called Styx by the people, but now, under a new name, famous among healing waters. ... Then his guides tell Hannibal that close at hand, wrapped in gloom and sunk for long ages in subterranean mists, the city of the Cimmerians lay deep in earth under a pall of shade; and they describe the unfathomed night of that Tartarean city.

This is in line with the idea that Circe's island (which, in Homer, is not far off from the Cimmerians) should be sought in the west.[110] Silius' account also corresponds to some remarks by Strabo and Pliny the Elder about Campania.[111] The latter deserves special attention, since he connects the dark city with the Phlegraean Fields, the volcanic area around Mt Vesuvius:[112]

> in ora [...] lacus Lucrinus et Avernus, iuxta quem Cimmerium oppidum quondam, dein Puteoli colonia Dicaearchea dicti, postque Phlegraei campi, Acherusia palus Cumis vicina.
>
> Plin. Nat. 3.61

---

108 Cf. Spaltenstein 2004, 121.
109 Translation by Duff 1934.
110 Cf. A.R. 4.660–661. On the localisation of Aiaia see Kersten 2019.
111 Strab. Geogr. 5.4.5 [C244]: προσεμύθευον δ' οἱ ἐπιχώριοι καὶ τοὺς ὄρνεις τοὺς ὑπερπετεῖς γινομένους καταπίπτειν εἰς τὸ ὕδωρ, φθειρομένους ὑπὸ τῶν ἀναφερομένων ἀέρων, καθάπερ ἐν τοῖς Πλουτωνίοις. καὶ τοῦτο χωρίον Πλουτώνιόν τι ὑπελάμβανον, καὶ τοὺς Κιμμερίους ἐνταῦθα γενέσθαι ("The inhabitants affirm that birds, flying over the lake, fall into the water, being stifled by the vapours rising from it, a phenomenon of all Plutonian localities. They believed, in fact, that this place was a Plutonium, around which the Kimmerians used to dwell"). Both Strabo and Pliny know, however, of the Black Sea Cimmerians as well. Note that Valerius makes use at least of the motif, when he speaks of an Averna silva (3.402–403).
112 Translation by Rackham 1942, slightly adapted.

> On the coast are... the Lucrine lake, Lake Avernus near which formerly stood the town of Cimmerium, then Pozzuoli, formerly called the Colony of Dicaearchus; after which come the plains of Salpatara and the Lago di Fusaro near Cumae.

The volcano itself is sometimes also referred to as *Phlegra* (i.e. the place where the giants were struck by Jupiter's thunderbolt),[113] which further strengthens the underworldly atmosphere of the place. As a conflation of Homeric and Italian myths, the Campanian Cimmerians are especially apt for a historical narrative; Silius can offer a description that is both geographically precise and poetically sublime.

Ps-Orpheus shows a similar interest in localising the Cimmerians without giving up their otherworldly appearance. Yet a consistent mapping of his itinerary is impossible and may perhaps never be achieved. What is crucial in his account is not topographical exactitude, but rather physical probability. Ps-Orpheus is eager to offer a rational explanation for the darkness. When he claims that the city always lies in the shadow of huge mountains, this is obviously hyperbolic, but not absurd.[114] The mountains could indeed be located in 'opposite' directions: Mt Rhipaeus (taken as the Carpathian Mountains) lies in the east;[115] the Alps lie in the west, and Phlegra (taken as Mt Vesuvius) lies in the south. Given that the Cimmerians are mentioned jointly with Phlegra both in Ps-Orpheus and in the Latin tradition, we might wonder if Ps-Orpheus imagined his Cimmerians close to Lake Avernus. The mention of the Ἀΐδαο πύλαι καὶ δῆμος Ὀνείρων (*OA* 1142) supports this impression since Vergil's *geminae Somni portae* are located somewhere near Cumae (*Aen.* 6.893). The city of Hermioneia, however, hardly fits a Campanian site,[116] the more so as Italy is mentioned explicitly in a different context in *OA* 1248–1249; and apart from that, there are some other inconsistencies.[117]

Another, maybe more convincing explanation is that the author, illustrating the Argonauts' return with Valerian details, re-Hellenises the 'Roman' Cimmerians and takes Φλέγρη as the Thessalian region of that name. We would then have to look for the Cimmerians somewhere in the north, maybe even in Jut-

---

113 Phlegra is usually located in the region of Chalcidice. On Phlegra for Vesuvius see Sil. 8.654; Claud. *Rapt.* 3.201. Lucan 7.145 probably refers to Pallene, but could be ambivalent.
114 See Schelske 2011 *ad loc.* on the rationalising impetus.
115 On the localisation see Schelske 2011 *ad loc.* On the difficulties concerning the identification of the Κάλπιος αὐχήν see Bacon 1931, 180–181.
116 Cf. Bacon 1931, 187; Vian 1987b, 257–258. Whereas Bacon locates Hermioneia in Greece, Vian rather thinks of Germany.
117 See Kalachanis *et al.* 2017.

land.¹¹⁸ But even in this case we might ask ourselves, whether we tend to take Ps-Orpheus' route as a sort of conflation of different geographical accounts or as a deliberate rework of Flavian narratives. Although it is not always clear exactly how, it is clear that Ps-Orpheus is weaving together lots of strands of poetic traditions.

7 Conclusion

I have argued that Ps-Orpheus makes use of poetic features prominent in descriptions of mythical places in Latin epic poetry. This concerns motifs (the cliff of the Sirens, the caves of Orpheus and Chiron), rhetorical structures (the effect of Sleep), and mythographical details (the Cimmerians). These passages contribute to the textures of Ps-Orpheus' mythical world. On a general level, they draw attention to the epic tradition and to the interrelations and contradictions within the fictional universe. On the level of detail, they offer room for sophistication.

The importance of these issues for the work as a whole — that is: the specific relationship between philology and philosophy and, hence, the impact of different 'parallels' — still needs scrutiny. Yet, it is important to note that the poem is full of learned details, which should prevent us from the temptation to explain them with 'probable' assumptions on the unknown author's (intellectual) biography or his religion. What Judith Bacon said about Ps-Orpheus ninety years ago is as true as it is self-evident:[119]

> He was, however, a very devout reader of poetry [...] Books, and not personal experience, were his guides. His mind was stored with the lines and phrases of other poets; he read his authors attentively, but he did not always understand them.

All books tend to be more learned than their writers, and references are at times wittier than the referees. Ps-Orpheus may not have read every passage I have discussed here, though I imagine that he had indeed some knowledge of Latin literature, even beyond Valerius' *Argonautica*. However, for the interpretation of the curious poem, which seems to praise the power of Orphic song and thought, it does not matter in the first place whether the author — an author *demi helléni-*

---

118 See Vian 1987b; Kalachanis *et al.* 2017; the latter, however, base their analyses on the improbable assumption that the poem was written in the 6th century BCE.
119 Cf. Bacon 1931, 172.

sé, according to Vian — knew Latin, or whether he knew people who knew Latin. It is for those of us who aim at an understanding of Greco-Roman culture as a whole that it matters to ask whether poetic motifs are widespread and whether mythical places can be revisited from both the West and the East.

Bibliography

Agosti, G. (1994), "Ila nella caverna (su Arg. Orph. 643–648)", in: *Materiali e Discussioni per l'Analisi dei Testi Classici* 32, 175–192.
Akçay, K.N. (2019), *Porphyry's 'On the Cave of the Nymphs' in its Intellectual Context*, Leiden.
Bacon, J.R. (1931), "The Geography of the *Orphic Argonautica*", in: *Classical Quarterly* 25, 172–183.
Bernert, E. (1938), "Die Quellen Claudians in *De raptu Proserpinae*", in: *Philologus* 93, 352–376.
Burges Watson, S.E. (2015), Review of Schelske (2011), in: *Classical Review* 65, 412–415.
Cecchetti, V. (2013), Review of Schelske (2011), in: *Prometheus* 39, 299–302.
Colavito, J. (2011), *The Orphic Argonautica. An English Translation*, Albany, NY.
Danek, G. (1998), *Epos und Zitat. Studien zu den Quellen der Odyssee*, Vienna.
Dorandi, T. *et al.* (2019), *L'antre des nymphes dans l'Odyssée*, Paris.
Duff, J.D. (1934), *Silius Italicus. Punica, Volume II: Books 9–17*, Cambridge, MA/London.
Elliger, W. (1975), *Die Darstellung der Landschaft in der griechischen Dichtung*, Berlin.
Fairclough, H.R/Goold, G.P. (1999), *Virgil. Eclogues, Georgics, Aeneid 1–6 (vol. 1), Aeneid 7–12 (vol. 2); ed. and trans. by H.R. Fairclough; rev. by G.P. Goold*, Cambridge, MA/London.
Feeney, D. (1991), *The Gods in Epic. Poets and Critics of the Classical Tradition*, Oxford.
Gärtner, U. (2005), *Quintus Smyrnaeus und die Aeneis. Zur Nachwirkung Vergils in der griechischen Literatur der Kaiserzeit*, Munich.
Hinds, S. (1998), *Allusion and Intertext: Dynamics of Appropriation in Roman Poetry*, Cambridge.
Hofstetter, E. (1997), "Seirenes", in: *LIMC* VIII.1, 1093–1104.
Hopkinson, N. (2015), Review of Schelske (2011) in: *Gnomon* 87, 362–363.
Hunter, R. (1999), *Theocritus, A Selection: Idylls 1, 3, 4, 6, 7, 10, 11 and 13*, Cambridge.
Hunter, R. (2005), "Generic Consciousness in the Orphic *Argonautica*", in: Paschalis (2005), 149–168.
Hunter, R. (2015), *Apollonius of Rhodes, Argonautica Book IV*, Cambridge.
Jesnick, I.J. (1997), *The Image of Orpheus in Roman Mosaic*, Oxford.
Kalachanis, K. *et al.* (2017), "The Argonautica Orphica Version for the Voyage of the Argonauts: A Geo-Analysis", in: *Mediterranean Archaeology and Archaeometry* 17.2, 75–95.
Karanika, A. (2017), "Agonistic Perspectives in the Orphic Argonautica", in: A.N. Michalopoulos/S. Papaioannou/A. Zissos (eds.), *Dicite Pierides. Classical Studies in Honour of Stratis Kyriakidis*, Newcastle upon Tyne, 124–136.
Kayachev, B. (2017), "The Sphragis of Vergil's *Georgics*: Constructing Identity through Intertextuality", in: A. Gavrielatos (ed.), *Self-Presentation and Identity in the Roman World*, Newcastle upon Tyne, 70–81.

Kersten, M. (2019), "Mythical Places in Ancient Epic", in: C. Reitz/S. Finkmann (eds.), *Structures of Epic Poetry*, Volume II.2: Configuration, Berlin, 359–405.
Lee, M.O. (1996), *Virgil as Orpheus, A Study of the Georgics*, Albany, NY.
Luiselli, R. (1993), "Contributo all'interpretatzione delle Argonautiche orfiche: studio sul proemio", in: A. Masaracchia (ed.), *Orfeo e l'Orfismo*, Rome, 265–307.
Madeła, A. (2020), "The Hidden Third Siren of the *Orphic Argonautica*", in: *Mnemosyne* 73, 112–122.
Mynors, R. (1969), *P. Vergili Maronis Opera*, Oxford.
Mynors, R. (1990), *Virgil, Georgics, edited with a Commentary*, Oxford.
Nakassis, D. (2004), "Gemination at the Horizons: East and West in the Mythical Geography of Archaic Greek Epic", in: *Transactions of the American Philological Association* 134, 215–233.
Nelis, D. (2005), "The Reading of Orpheus. The *Orphic Argonautica* and the Epic Tradition", in: Paschalis (2005), 169–189.
Norden, E. (1927), *P. Vergilius Maro, Aeneis Buch VI*. Third Edition, Leipzig.
Nünlist, R./Bäbler, B. (2001), "Sirenen", in: *Der Neue Pauly* 11, 593–594.
Ottaviano, S./Conte, G.B. (eds.) (2013), *P. Vergilius Maro: Bucolica; Georgica*, Berlin.
Paschalis, M. (ed.) (2005), *Roman and Greek Imperial Epic*, Herakleion.
Petrain, D. (2000), "Hylas and Silva: Etymological Wordplay in Propertius 1.20", in: *Harvard Studies in Classical Philology* 100, 409–421.
Platnauer, M. (1922), *Claudian: Volume II*, Cambridge, MA/London.
Race, W.H. (2009), *Apollonius Rhodius, Argonautica*, Cambridge, MA/London.
Rackham, H. (1942), *Pliny. Natural History, Volume II: Books 3–7*, Cambridge, MA/London.
Reitz, C. (2000), "Zur allegorischen Ortsbeschreibung in Ovids *Metamorphosen*", in: *Compar(a)ison* 1, 35–48.
Reitz, C. (2020), "Caesar and the Supernatural. An Interpretation of Lucan 5.504–549", in: *Maia* 72, 404–411.
Reitz, C./Finkmann, S. (2019), "Introduction", in: C. Reitz/S. Finkmann (eds.), *Structures of Epic Poetry*, Volume I: Foundations, Berlin, 1–21.
Richter, W. (1957), *Vergil, Georgica, herausgegeben und erklärt*, Munich.
Rovira Soler, M. (1978), "Datación de la Argonáutica órfica por su relación con la de Valerio Flaco", in: *Cuadernos de Filología Clásica. Estudios Latinos* 14, 171–206.
Sauter, H. (2000), *Studien zum Kimmerierproblem*, Bonn.
Schelske, O. (2011), *Orpheus in der Spätantike: Studien und Kommentar zu den Argonautika des Orpheus: Ein literarisches, religiöses und philosophisches Zeugnis*, Berlin.
Shackleton Bailey, D.R. (2004), *Statius, Volume II: Thebaid, Books 8–12; Achilleid*, Cambridge, MA/London.
Spaltenstein, F. (2002–5), *Commentaire des Argonautica de Valérius Flaccus*. 3 vols., Brussels.
Thomas, R.F. (1988), *Vergil, Georgics*, Cambridge.
van Opstall, E. (2013), "Cave and Cosmos: Sacred Caves in Greek Epic Poetry from Homer (eighth century BCE) to Nonnus (fifth century CE)", in: J. Klooster/J. Heirman (eds.), *The Ideologies of Lived Space in Literary Texts, Ancient and Modern*, Ghent, 16–33.
Venzke, H. (1941), *Die orphischen Argonautika in ihrem Verhältnis zu Apollonios Rhodios*, PhD Dissertation, Berlin.
Vian, F. (1987a), *Les Argonautiques orphiques*, Paris.
Vian, F. (1987b), "Poésie et géographie. Les Retours des Argonautes", in: *Comptes Rendus des Séances de l'Académie des Inscriptions et Belles-Lettres* 131, 249–262.

Vian, F. (1988), "Le périple océanique des Argonautes dans les Argonautiques orphiques", in: F. Jouan/B. Deforge (eds.), *Peuples et pays mythiques*, Paris, 177–185.

Vieillefon, L. (2003), *La figure d'Orphée dans l'Antiquité tardive. Les mutations d'un mythe: du héros païen au chantre chrétien*, Paris.

West, M.L. (1983), *The Orphic Poems*, Oxford.

Wöhrle, G. (1995), *Hypnos, der Allbezwinger. Eine Studie zum literarischen Bild des Schlafes in der griechischen Antike*, Stuttgart.

Sophia Papaioannou
Pantomime Games in the *Dionysiaca* and Vergil's Song of Silenus

Abstract: Contrary to epic tradition, the funeral games celebrated in *Dionysiaca* 19 in commemoration of King Staphylus of Lycia are dominated by a contest on pantomime dancing — the first and only detailed account of a pantomime contest in classical literature. The pantomime contest (*D.* 19.136–286) between Silenus and Maron is informed by the long tradition of pantomime dancing in the Roman empire. Pantomime was very popular in Italy throughout the imperial centuries, and its appeal spread widely in the eastern part of the empire as well, including Egypt. What is more, pantomime in the literary tradition was associated with poetics in Vergil's *Eclogue* 6 where it revolves around Silenus. In the pantomime contest of *Dionysiaca* 19 Nonnus discusses the poetics of epic succession by engaging with earlier tradition, in particular with accounts charged with poetic associations in Latin literature.

Keywords: pantomime; *agon*; *Dionysiaca*; Maron; Silenus; Vergil; *Eclogue* 6.

1 Introduction: Pantomime and pastoral poetry

Nonnus' *Dionysiaca* 19 opens with the funeral games Dionysus organises in honour of King Staphylus of Lycia who earlier in the poem had offered generous hospitality to Dionysus' troops. The games, however, in conspicuous violation of the heroic tradition, involve artistic rather than athletic competitions. They open with a singing contest, in which Erechtheus, the king of Athens, loses to Oeagrus, the father of Orpheus. Immediately afterwards, in *D.* 19.136–286, Maron and Silenus compete in pantomime dancing.[1] This is the first and only detailed account in the literary tradition of a competition in pantomime dancing, and evinces, on the one hand, Nonnus' original appropriation of the epic

---

[1] I have cited the text of Nonnus from Rouse 1940. Translations of the *Dionysiaca* also are from Rouse 1940, with adaptations. The text of Vergil's *Eclogues* is from Mynors 1969; the translation from Kline 2001. Other translations are my own, unless noted otherwise.

athla motif and, on the other, the popularity of pantomime performances in the eastern part of the Roman empire in the fifth century.[2]

Pantomime, according to the evidence of the literary sources, was a solo performance. The dancer performed through gestures and body-movement, without the aid of words and sounds, a story based on some well-known mythological tradition. Pantomime was a Latin form of drama; it was born in Italy by Greek acting professionals in the 1st century BCE,[3] and it became a popular form of public entertainment almost instantly. By the end of the 2nd century CE pantomime performances were held throughout the Roman empire. By the 4th century pantomime actors were performance stars, they had their own claques and most likely their sponsors, and in Constantinople, they were associated with factions. Pantomime dancers were highly trained professionals. Several authors mention their impressive athleticism, their precision with technical movements, their ability to feel the rhythm of the musicians and communicate drama in their act (cf. Libanius, *Oration* 64.103–105). Lucian, who composed an exclusive treatise on pantomime (Περὶ ὀρχήσεως, *On Dancing*), arguably still the most important literary source on ancient pantomime, provides valuable technical information and ascertains the harmonising of narrative, music, and dance during the performance.[4]

Given the popularity of the pantomime in the Roman East in Nonnus' era, and particularly in Egyptian Panopolis, which, according to Lada-Richards, was "a thriving centre of pantomime performances throughout antiquity,"[5] a pan-

---

[2] According to Miguélez-Cavero 2009, Nonnus composed an epic steeped in pantomime vocabulary and imagery.

[3] Specifically, the year 22 BCE; see primarily Jory 1981, listing all relevant literary evidence from antiquity in favour of this date, including Ath. 20d; Jer. *Chron.*, on the year 22 BCE (PL 27, 553–554); Zosim. 1.6.1.

[4] The study of pantomime has seen nothing less than an explosion in recent years. Notable recent works on Roman pantomime and its popularity throughout the Greco-Roman world as late as the 5th century CE, include a series of studies by Lada-Richards, foremost 2007, and also 2004, 2010, 2013, 2016; Zanobi 2008; Wiseman 2008; Ingleheart 2008; Panayotakis 2008; Webb 2002, 2008a, 2008b, and 2012; Garelli 2006 and 2007. Specifically on the epigraphic and papyrological evidence see Tedeschi 2017.

[5] Lada-Richards 2016, 140–141; on the popularity of professional dancing, including pantomime, in Roman Egypt see Vesterinen 2007. On the thriving cultural life of Panopolis itself, assiduously supported by the local élite, see Miguélez-Cavero 2008, 191–263. In the same study, Miguélez-Cavero notes the connection between pantomime librettos and literary texts, and identifies among the library texts in use for pantomime compositions in Panopolis the so-called Barcelona Alcestis, a Latin hexameter poem, possibly of the 4th century; see Miguélez-Cavero 2008, 220; see also n. 12 below.

tomime competition in the context of the unique thematic diversity of Nonnus' epic world, like the swimming contests earlier in the *Dionysiaca*,[6] should not alienate audiences and critics. At the same time, Nonnus' choice of contestants and the theme of their performances capture the many layers whereupon agonistic interaction with the epic tradition is articulated. The identification of the contestants with Maron and Silenus deserves closer look, as do the composition and execution of their performances. In the course of my present study it will be illustrated that the pantomime competition is informed by metapoetics[7] that reach back to the artistic competitions in the Latin tradition, both epic, as conspicuously displayed in the competing artists, singers, and narrators in Ovid's *Metamorphoses*, including the rivalries of Minerva vs. Arachne, Calliope vs. the Pierides, Ulixes vs. Ajax,[8] and pastoral, in the Latin poems of Theocritus and Calpurnius, where the singing contests engage progressively more explicitly with models of competition from other genres (forensic, military, and athletic).[9] The innovative character of the pantomime contest between Maron and Silenus seems to draw inspiration from Vergil, but also from the agonistic theme as elaborated in both the Greek and the Roman tradition: it rivals the metapoetic performers of earlier epics and parodies features of archetypal pastoral rivalries.

Pantomime dancers repeatedly turned to high literary genres, including epic and tragedy, as they sought inspiration or material from them for their next performance. Lucian (*On Dancing* 76) acknowledges that scenes from the Homeric epics were routinely reenacted on the pantomime stage, while Sargent offers comprehensive examination of the argument that Ovid's *Heroides* were the first literary texts composed as libretti for pantomime.[10] In the Hall/Wyles volume (2008), the chapters by Ingleheart (Ovid and the pantomime), Zimmermann (Seneca's tragedy influenced by pantomime), Zanobi, Hall, and Pa-

---

6 Cf. the diving/swimming contest of the satyrs described in *D.* 10.141–174; and the two swimming competitions in *Dionysiaca* 11, the first between Dionysus and Ampelus (1–55), the second between Carpus and Calamus (406–426).
7 On the poetics of pantomime see now Petrides 2013.
8 The bibliography on the poetics that underlies the performances of Ovid's artists is particularly rich; representative studies include (on Arachne and Minerva) Harries 1990; Rosati 1999 and 2002; Oliensis 2004; Johnston 2008; Heath 2011; (on the Pierides vs. Calliope/the Muses) Ziogas 2013, 90–94; (on Ulixes vs. Ajax) Papaioannou 2007; Pavlock 2009.
9 On singing contests and poetics in the Latin pastoral tradition see Karakasis 2011, with detailed earlier bibliography; and recently Baraz 2019, 78–97. On the metapoetic and intertextual character of pastoral poetry across tradition see especially Hubbard 2006.
10 Sargent 1996; referred to in Panayotakis 2008, 190.

nayotakis explore the possibility that as late as the 6th century CE[11] pantomime dancers in both the eastern and the western part of the Roman empire used texts (or extracts from texts) on mythical and tragic themes by Latin authors including Ovid, Seneca, an anonymous Latin poet who adapted the Alcestis theme familiar from Euripides' famous play,[12] and, what is important for the present study, Vergil's *Eclogues*, in particular the staging of *Eclogue* 6.[13] These arguments attest to a long dependence of the genre of pantomime on Latin literature, and reasonably suggest that these performances created a tradition of their own, leading to reproductions in later centuries, both in Italy and beyond, including the Hellenophone eastern part of the Roman empire, whose familiarity with the Latin classics was property of the elite, certainly those who had studied in the famous law school of Beirut and held high offices in the administration of the empire.[14]

According to Panayotakis,[15] there was an ancient tradition that Vergil's *Eclogues* were performed. Servius' testimony at *Ecl.* 6.11 remarks that *Eclogue* 6 was staged by the famous pantomime dancer Volumnia Cytheris, Cornelius Gallus' muse, and that Cicero was among the audience and thoroughly enjoyed

---

[11] "Daphne's transformation was still danced on pagan stages at the turn of the sixth century CE, as emerges very clearly from the Homilies of Jacob of Sarugh": Lada-Richards 2016, 134–136 (the quote from p. 134).

[12] On the Barcelona Alcestis see Hall 2008, 258–282. Critical edition of the text: Lebek 1983 and 1987; Parsons/Nisbet/Hutchinson 1983.

[13] The interaction between pantomime and poetry (but oriented towards the opposite direction, i.e., poetry influenced by pantomime) is strongly attested in Africa and as late as the 5th cent. CE, in Dracontius' *Medea*; while the influence of pantomime, or rather the artful combination of pantomime and miniature epics, is recognisable in other poems by Dracontius; see Dracontius, *Rom.* 10.16-19; Bright 1987, 35–36, discusses another of Dracontius' mimes, *Hylas*, which he, following D'Ippolito 1962, calls a hydro-mime.

[14] The status of Beirut as the pre-eminent centre of legal studies and training in the Latin language and literature in the Roman East from the 3rd through the 6th century is well established: students from all over the empire, during their stay in Beirut, immersed themselves in the study of the Latin language and literature, and the laws of Rome, which changed their self-concept as Romans; on Beirut as centre for the study of Latin in the eastern part of the empire after the 3rd century see Jones Hall 2004, esp. 195–220. Latin was widely used in the courtroom, the army, and the imperial court well into the 6th century, hence it was a high-status language, an asset for those seeking careers and promotion in these fields. On Latin as complementary to legal studies and essential for political advancement see also Szabat 2015, 256–258; Cribiore 2009, 237–238.

[15] Panayotakis 2008, 191–195.

the performance. If this event is true,¹⁶ obviously it refers to an early version of the poem, prior to its finalised literary publication after 39, given that Cicero was dead at that time; if only a fiction,¹⁷ then it attests to the established pantomime tradition of pastoral poetry in Servius' days.¹⁸ Also, prior to Servius, both Tacitus (*Dialogus* 13) and Suetonius (*De Poetis* 103–104, ed. Rostagni [1944]) talk about theatrical performances based on Vergil's poetry.

The success of the *Eclogues* as material appropriate for pantomime-acting logically inspired the forging of a popular tradition that continued as late as at least the later fourth century: shortly before Nonnus' life time, Jerome complains about Christian priests (*sacerdotes*) eager to abandon their study of the sacred texts in order to read comedies instead, and spend their energy in memorising and singing the bucolic love affairs of Vergil (*comoedias legere, amatoria bucolicorum versuum verba cantare, tenere Vergilium*; Jerome, *Epistulae* 21.13.9).¹⁹ The Greek translation of the Fourth *Eclogue* set in chapters 19–21 of the *Oration of Constantine to the Holy Assembly* that is attributed to Eusebius of Caesaria, corroborates the significance of Vergilian poetry in the 4th century, while the

---

16 As argued in Wiseman 2008, 216 "it is not easy to see why these late sources should have invented the idea"; and Panayotakis 2008, 191: "not a figment of Servius' imagination." Also Goldberg 2005, 47 dissociates Cicero from the pantomime performance of the *Eclogues*, which he accepts: "Vergil's *Eclogues* would be set to music and performed in the theater," citing Servius among his sources about the stage performance of the *Eclogues*. More recently Lada-Richards 2019 strengthens Goldberg's argument as she offers a comprehensive reassessment of Servius' anecdote and endorses the view that classical literary texts, including Vergil's *Eclogues*, may well have enjoyed a life on stage in the Late Antiquity: "if Cytheris did perform a theatricalised version of Vergil's sixth *Eclogue*, she would have been doing nothing different from the *cantores* who (again unverifiably) took the *Eclogues* to the stage, the dancers who 'danced' Ovid's 'poems' or the singers who seem to have been rummaging bookstalls in search of appropriate, stage-worthy matter." (p. 94).
17 The most recent argument against the historicity of this anecdote is Höschele 2013, 49: "it strikes me as more likely that the entire incident is the product of a biographer's imagination, intriguingly bringing together the rising literary star of the Augustan age with a notorious femme fatale as well as the most acclaimed author of the late Republic, who immediately recognises the youth's brilliance."
18 How exactly *Eclogue* 6 was transferred on the pantomime stage by Cytheris is not commented upon by the ancient sources; see a modern hypothesis on this in Quinn 1982, 153; also Panayotakis 2008, 194, discussing possible "short dramatic representations which would involve a narrating voice, actors and dancers playing the roles of Tityrus, Meliboeus, Mopsus, Menalcas, and other herdsmen." He acknowledges that the 'amoebaean' *Eclogues* 3, 6, and 7 may provide "excellent opportunities… to a solo dancer wanting to portray fictional characters in passionate situations."
19 Panayotakis 2008, 195; also Horsfall 2000, 250.

fact that the translation is accompanied by ample prose commentary, which often paraphrases material from the poem, postulates the deeper familiarity of elite intellectuals with the Vergilian text.[20] The long Latin tradition of pantomime and the popularity of Vergil's pastoral poetry across the empire may be revisited by the informed reader of the pantomime dancing competition between Maron and Silenus in *Dionysiaca* 19.

2 Epic *athla* revised: Agonistic performance and pantomime contest

The funeral games for Staphylus are atypical, because they celebrate a king who died of old age (this is not unprecedented in light of Vergil's *athla* in *Aeneid* 5 to honour Anchises at the anniversary of his death of natural causes) and include only artistic contests. The choice of these events is explained: the deceased is described as one who "loved to dance" (φιλοσκάρθμῳ, *D.* 19.150), thus Dionysus honoured him by requesting that the *athla* do not feature competitions in athletic disciplines (discus, running, spear; *D.* 19.147–149) but in dance — a pantomime contest. Immediately prior to this contest, the *athla* celebrations began with a song contest, between Erechtheus, the king of Athens, and Oeagrus, the father of Orpheus (*D.* 19.59–117).[21] In this episode Nonnus crafts an intelligent engagement with the Ovidian tradition of deploying the myth of Demeter and Persephone *aliter* and repeatedly, as a statement for alternative generic expression and competing poetics. Erechtheus composes a song that produces yet another version of this widely known epic myth, which at once corrects the Ovidian account (Erechtheus adjusts the Pierides' version of the flight of the Olympians in animal forms during the Gigantomachy) and follows the Ovidian paradigm (by revising tradition and identifying Celeus and Triptolemus as kings of Athens, and the latter as the son of the former). The rival poet composes a similarly complex song that combines well-known material and inventiveness: he sings on an exclusively Nonnian topic, the resurrection of Ampelus; yet by

---

20 The bibliography on the speech is vast: see the items cited in Ziolkowski/Putnam 2008, 491–496; additional material in Girardet 2013; Hadas 2013; Floyd 2001, 57–67; Coronati 1984; Wigtil 1981. Book-length studies on the Greek translation of the Fourth *Eclogue* include: Monteleone 1975; Bolhuis 1950; also Costa 1972, xix–xxi.
21 On the Erechtheus vs. Oeagrus contest and the possible engagement with Ovidian poetics see Carvounis/Papaioannou 2022.

comparing it to that of Hyacinthus whom he claims to have been resurrected by Apollo, his divine lover, Oeagrus innovates on the canonical account of Hyacinthus' story that was celebrated in Ovid's *Metamorphoses* 10, in the poetically-determined song of his son Orpheus. The outcome of the rivalry aside, both songs innovate on firmly established, by Nonnus' times, traditional accounts of myth, hold significant position in Ovid's epic, and are parts of episodes that transcribe Ovid's non-canonical epic poetics. In short, the context represents one other prominent expression of the paradoxical way in which Nonnus treats his sources — both building on and distancing himself from them — and functions as a preamble to the many layers involved in the engagement with the literary sources in the pantomime contest that follows.

This contest is considerably longer (*D.* 19.136–348); the contestants here are Silenus and Maron. Both are tied to poetics and the Latin tradition. Additionally, pantomime dance, with its emphasis on imitation and representation (nicely described in *D.* 19.155–157), encourages reflection on the relationship between form and content, and comparison with the elusiveness of the Nonnian text.[22] The pantomime theme and its association with poetics is established in the literary tradition in Vergil's *Eclogues*: it underwrites the conspicuously programmatic *Eclogue* 6 and revolves around Silenus. In the episode at hand, Nonnus advances through the pantomime contest a statement on the poetics of epic succession, by investing on stories renowned for their treatment in Vergil and Ovid. His treatment is notable for the thematic closeness of the interaction with the Latin poems, which includes the use of the language of writing and drawing, and the associations with the poetics of ecphrasis that the deployment of this language entails.

The rivals are father (Silenus) and son (Maron), a kinship noted explicitly earlier at *D.* 14.96 ff.[23] The two are paired in a quasi-father-son relationship for

---

[22] On pantomime dance reflecting the poetics of Nonnus' idiosyncratic epic see Schlapbach 2017, 251–280; the following quote set early in the chapter encapsulates the author's thesis: "But dance is certainly another source of inspiration for the composition of the *Dionysiaka*, and perhaps a more important one. Pantomime performances also consisted of episodes loosely woven together in associative patterns, and the swift movements and surprising role changes of the dancer arguably offered a model for the quick thematic transitions of the *Dionysiaka*." (pp. 253–254).

[23] Nonnus is the first who makes Maron Silenus' son (along with Lenaeus and Astraeus). Maron's association with Dionysus, however, is recorded often in the earlier tradition: in Hesiod, *Catalogue of Women*, fr. 238 (ed. Merkelbach–West), Maron's father Euanthes is the son of Oenopion, who in turn is the son of Dionysus; note that Homer (*Od.* 19.97–201), who also iden-

the first time in Euripides' *Cyclops*: Silenus, who trails Odysseus into the Cyclops' cave, hears that the hero has brought with him wine from Maron, and exclaims that he used to hold Maron in his hands when the latter was a baby and to dandle him (*Cyclops* 141–142).²⁴ In the *Dionysiaca*, the father/son relationship is seen from a different perspective. Their competition dramatises the victory of the younger poet over the older poet, yet in a contest between two poets that are both, by that time, very old;²⁵ a contest that arguably rewards the artistic sensitivity of an older artist who nonetheless enjoys performing on less traditional topics and, as a result, succeeds to entertain a younger audience.²⁶

In reality, Maron's role in the *agon* is more complex, for it builds on the metaliterary associations that are tied to his status as Dionysus' charioteer. Beyond the well-known symbol for new, pioneering poetics present already in Pindar, Bacchylides, and Parmenides, but canonised in Callimachus,²⁷ the motif of the charioteer thematises a large number of ideas in epic poetry, including the education of the younger, less experienced warrior under the guidance of a seasoned leader.²⁸

At the same time, the name of Maron may recall Vergil, who since the 2nd century CE in the East is better known as Μάρων.²⁹ His status as charioteer ap-

---

tifies Euanthes as Maron's father, does not advance a kinship with Dionysus, but one with Apollo (Euanthes is a priest of Apollo).
24 In his reply (*Cyclops* 143) Odysseus claims that Maron is Dionysus' son.
25 In *D.* 14.96–104, Maron and his two brothers are also very old and move slowly with the help of walking staffs: 100–103, χεῖρας ἐλαφρίζοντες ὀριπλανέος γενετῆρος / γηροκόμοις ῥοπάλοισι· λιποσθενέων δὲ γερόντων / νωχελὲς ἀμπελόεντι δέμας κουφίζετο βάκτρῳ, / ὧν μάλα πουλυέτηρος ἔην χρόνος..., "each with a staff to support the hands of their old father in his travels over the hills. These old men had staffs made of vinebranches to support their slow-moving bodies; and many were the years of their time..." [tr. Rouse 1940 with slight changes].
26 As argued recently in Delavaud-Roux 2009 and (orally) in Whitmarsh 2016; in this presentation Whitmarsh proposes that, for Nonnus, Maron represented the first stage in a process of youthful regeneration of Homeric poetics.
27 Callimachus, *Aetia* fr. 1.25–28 Pfeiffer; Nünlist 1998, 255–264 records additional attestations of the motif, including several earlier parallels. The image of the charioteer has a long history of serving as a metaphor for poetic composition in antiquity; see now Nelson (forthcoming); and particularly with reference to Latin epic, Lovatt 2005 *passim*.
28 Slaveva-Griffin 2003, who argues how Plato appropriated the charioteer allegory initially developed in Parmenides' prologue to his own presentation of the myth of the soul as a charioteer in the *Phaedrus* — or, how a first literary and philosophical appropriation of an earlier literary allegory becomes the "charioteer"/driver for a second and more advanced one.
29 Φλέγων *FGrH* 257 F12, Οὐεργίλιος Μάρων; Dio Cass. 76.10.2, ὅτι ἀχθεσθεὶς τῇ τοῦ πολέμου κακώσει ἔπος τι τοῦ Μάρωνος τοῦ ποιητοῦ παρεφθέγξατο; also, *Anth. Gr.* 16.151.9–10. In addition to Sharrock 2008, 105 see Schlapbach 2017, 256. Vergil himself plays with the homophony

propriates for Nonnus' composition the code for innovative poetics famously tied to the chariot theme. Vergilian critics have focused on the significance of the charioteer theme that opens the Third *Georgic* and its connections to both Roman monuments and the poet's epic designs.[30] The new poetics in Maron is enforced by an allusion to the Homeric Maron of Ismaros — who is associated with Dionysus at least as early as Euripides, as noted above, and features prominently in the Latin dramatic tradition as well, as clearly attested in a fragment from Ennius that refers to a Thracian temple built by Maro and dedicated to Liber[31] — in the likening of the scent exuded by the fawnskin of the Bacchic ambiance to the "Maronian nectar," a simile set in a programmatic place in the prologue to the *Dionysiaca* (*D.* 1.36–37: [νεβρίδα]... Μαρωνίδος ἔμπλεον ὀδμῆς / νεκταρέης). This association is displayed in the pantomime agon. Similarly tied to poetics fully developed in Vergil is Silenus.

Silenus is a leading character in *Eclogue* 6 and is portrayed there as the charismatic pastoral singer who enchants the animate and inanimate world around him — a duplicate Orpheus or Apollo (cf. *Ecl.* 6.82), since, like the archetypal bard, Silenus may draw the Fauns and the beasts to the sound of his song, and also impersonate the enchanting power of Vergil's pastoral poetics.[32]

> *Tum vero in numerum Faunosque ferasque videres*
> *ludere, tum rigidas motare cacumina quercus.*
> *Nec tantum Phoebo gaudet Parnasia rupes,*
> *nec tantum Rhodope miratur et Ismarus Orphea.*
>
> *Ecl.* 6.27–30

> Then you might have seen Fauns and wild creatures dance
> to the measure, then the unbending oaks nodded their crowns:
> no such delight have the cliffs of Parnassus in their Phoebus,
> Rhodope and Ismarus are not so astounded by Orpheus.

Silenus' song comes at the entreaties of young nymphs and satyrs; they have fettered him during his sleep and playfully demand a song for his release. The song is polythematic, truly a compendium of earlier popular literary traditions:

---

between his name and the name of the Homeric Maron: Savage 1965; Mac Góráin 2012–13, 213–214.
30 E.g., Nelis 2008; Meban 2008.
31 Fr. inc. 167 Manuwald (=388–389 Vahlen=352–353 Jocelyn): *o terra Treca ubi Liberi fanum inclutum / Maro locavi*; cf. Mac Góráin 2012–13, 214.
32 On Silenus' Orpheus-like profile see, for instance, Desport 1952, 181–188; Lieberg 1982, 22–26; Scafoglio 2013, 194–200.

it begins with a natural cosmogony (lines 31–40) and continues with the birth of the human race from Deucalion and Pyrrha, and the story of Prometheus and his punishment by Jupiter (41–42). There follow two unhappy love stories: the drowning of the Argonaut Hylas, a story that had been popularised in the Hellenistic tradition, with versions both in Apollonius and Theocritus (43–45), and the unnatural love of Pasiphae, Minos' wife, for the bull sent by Poseidon – a punishment for Minos who refused to perform the sacrifice and decided to keep the bull for himself (46–60). These are followed by the story of the stolen apples of the Hesperides, and the transformation of Phaethon's sisters into alder (poplar) trees, weeping in a row by the river Po that received their brother's body (61–63).

The next story (64–73) revisits the poetics in the programmatic introduction, and the confluence of the Hesiodic and the Callimachean traditions: Silenus' song on the god-sent talent of inspired poetry, symbolically rendered with the pipes of Hesiod, being passed on to Cornelius Gallus, a leading Neoteric poet and a literary ancestor to Vergil, in imitation of *Theogony* 22–34, evokes Apollo, because inspired poetry was a gift by him to Hesiod. The dream of Ennius is now recast as the genius of Cornelius Gallus, the former aspiring to become the Roman Homer, the latter the Roman Hesiod. Callimachus is present, too: the Muses, who at line 72 bid Gallus sing of the "origins of the Grynean grove" (*Grynei nemoris... origo*), urge the Neoteric poet to take on *aitia* poetry, in the pattern of Callimachus, as *origo* is a translation of αἴτιον. Gallus and Vergil are brought next to each other being protegés of Apollo and receiving instruction directly from him, but they are also expected to produce poetry that will honour and delight the Delphic god (11–12~72–73).

Silenus' song closes with two stories of incestuous love, horror, and transformation. The first concerns Scylla, or rather the stories of two Scyllas (the one transformed into a hideous sea monster with six dogs' heads devouring sailors who passed by, and the other transformed into a bird after killing her father), which Vergil expertly interfuses (73–78). The second is that of Philomela, who, in Vergil's account (which again toys with the canonical version of the myth), serves up her son to her husband, Tereus, for dinner when she finds out that he had raped her sister. All three are turned into birds, a hoopoe, a swallow, and a nightingale (79–81). These stories already received treatments in Hesiod and in Hellenistic texts, and they will soon receive a new account in Ovid's *Metamorphoses*. The Vergilian Silenus' song, in sort, is a complex composition, involving a variety of stories that integrate in their narratives a variety of genres and literary traditions, and transformations of various kinds, while they do not seem to follow a naturally developing thematic sequence. A similar diversity in themes and genres is captured in Nonnus' narrative, which, in the programmatic proem, has been described as a *poikilon hymnon* ("diverse song") on the adventures of Dionysus, "in rivalry with both new and old" (*D.* 1.25–27: νέοισι καὶ ἀρχεγόνοισιν ἐρίζων),³³ that is inspired by Proteus, the god of many turns (*polytropos*) who can assume many forms (*poikilon eidos*).

> Μοῦσαι [...] / ἀλλὰ χοροῦ ψαύοντα, Φάρῳ παρὰ γείτονι νήσῳ,
> στήσατέ μοι **Πρωτῆα πολύτροπον**, ὄφρα φανείη
> **ποικίλον εἶδος** ἔχων, ὅτι **ποικίλον ὕμνον** ἀράσσω·
>
> *D.* 1.11, 13–15

> Muses [...] but bring me a partner for your dance in the neighbouring island of Pharos, **Proteus of many turns**, that he may appear in all his **diversity of shapes**, since I strike up a **diverse hymn**.

The song of the Vergilian Silenus itself comes after a conspicuously metaliterary prologue. *Eclogue* 6 opens (6.1–5) with both an invocation to the Muse (personified in Thalia) and Apollo's visitation to the shepherd Tityrus, the aspiring new poet of grand epic (and a persona for Vergil himself), and it interfuses the visitations of the Muses to the shepherd Hesiod, and Apollo to the aspiring poet Callimachus. Subsequently (6–12), Vergil, ready to follow up on both these traditions of alternative reception of grand epic and produce a sophisticated poem (6.5: *deductum carmen*; according to Quintilian 8.2.9, the first occurrence of the soon-to-become technical term for the Callimachean-style Latin poetry³⁴) addresses Varus (6.7, 10), a fellow poet, and by implementing yet another Callimachean trope, the *recusatio*, declines to praise Varus' poetry, because the latter writes traditional heroic epic. Then, Vergil adds a third invocation, to the Muses as a group (6.13: *Pergite, Pierides*! "Pierides, continue!").³⁵ Vergil asks them to take over or acknowledge that the poem about to be unravelled is the Muses' as much as his own composition. All these associations render *Eclogue* 6 a profoundly complex yet clear statement of epigonic poetics, transcribing Vergil's ambitious claim to the Callimachean/Neoteric succession. It is generally held that one of the leading goals of *Eclogue* 6 is to make important statements

---

33 On this line and the question of the claim of novelty in Nonnus' poetry see Verhelst 2017, 4–5; also Miguélez-Cavero 2013, 191–196.
34 Though according to Macrobius 4.4, a similar phrase, *deducta voce*, had already been used by the tragic poet Afranius and the philosopher Cornificus.
35 The opening to the *Dionysiaca* features a tripartite prologue as well: *D.* 1.1–10 addresses the Muse of epic; the second part (*D.* 1.11–33) opens with an appeal to the Muses collectively; the third and final part, at *D.* 1.34–44, opens with an address to the Mimallons (Maenads).

about Vergil's poetry, and also about the poetry of Vergil's friend, Cornelius Gallus, whose poetic initiation is celebrated in lines 64–73. Silenus' opening of his string of tales with a song on beginnings could not have communicated Vergil's expectations more explicitly.

3 Vergil's song of Silenus and pantomime

The binding of Silenus, albeit with garlands of flowers, in order to make him sing, looks back to Menelaus' binding of Proteus in the *Odyssey*.[36] The very episode is mentioned in Nonnus' programmatic prologue in relation with Proteus' ability to transform himself endlessly (*D.* 1.13–33). The Naiad Aegle, who is standing by and inspiring courage to the two timid young satyrs (20: *timidis supervenit Aegle*), recalls the Homeric Eidothea, Proteus' daughter and Menelaus' assistant (*Od.* 4.363–446), in yet another suggestive parallelism between the Vergilian text and the proem to the *Dionysiaca*. Likewise the address to the Mimallons (Maenads), in *D.* 1.33 ff., to wrap around his shoulders a fawnskin "full of the perfume of Maronian nectar" and to leave the rank seal-skins to Homer (*D.* 1.34–38), alludes to the episode in *Odyssey* 4 where Eidothea, Proteus' daughter, who directed Menelaus and his companions to ambush Proteus at the shore, hidden amidst a herd of seals and covered up with sealskins, smeared their nostrils with Maronian nectar to help them withstand the stench (4.435–446).[37] Importantly, in the Second Sophistic period, Proteus is considered a prototypical pantomime dancer in a long speech by Lycinus in Lucian's

---

36 Though Servius (DServ. *Ecl.* 6.13) points out that perhaps Vergil here has in mind a similar story recorded in the historian Theopompus (*FGrH* 115F75C) of the intoxicated Silenus having been captured and bound by some Phrygian shepherds and then led before King Midas, who questioned Silenus on the origin of things and the events of the past. The tradition of Theopompus and the account of Vergil are brought together in Ovid's version of the capture of Silenus in *Met.* 11.90–93; see Hadjittofi 2018, esp. 284–287.

37 On the parallelism between the forced revelations of Proteus to Menelaus and the enforced song of Silenus to the young satyrs Chromis and Mnasyllos, with Eidothea and Aegle offering assistance respectively (and also to the capture and forced revelations of Proteus to Aristaeus in *Georgics* 4 and *Fasti* 1, with Aristaeus receiving assistance from his mother Cyrene), see Clausen 1994, at *Ecl.* 6.18: Vergil "imagines Silenus as a Proteus-like figure, an ancient wizard reluctant and evasive"); Davies 2003, 59; most recently Heyworth 2019, 142 *ad* 293–295; the parallelism was first noted in Keightley 1946, 79.

On Dancing, which defends and praises pantomime performances.[38] Along these lines it has been suggested to consider dancing as part of Proteus' shape-shifting, an idea fully developed in Nonnus, originally suggested in the placement of Proteus and his *poikilia* in the middle of the proem, between the dancing Muses and the dancing Mimallons, by means of an explicit invitation to the Muses to welcome Proteus into their chorus (1.13–14),[39] and fully developed later, in the pantomime contest in *D.* 19.

The close association of Silenus with Apollo at the end of *Eclogue* 6 in combination with the generic diversity and multithematic content of Silenus' song corroborate Silenus' embodying of Vergil's poetics — specifically the reinvention of the bucolic genre in the context of Roman politics. Shortly before the end of *Eclogue* 6, Vergil confesses that Silenus' song had been composed by Apollo (6.82–83), and also that the song does not end with the conclusion of the poem. In the context of Nonnian poetics, the reminiscence of Silenus' association with Apollo should tie him to the canonical tradition. In this way Nonnus' Silenus, contrary to his Vergilian counterpart, embodies the poetic establishment.

If Silenus stands in for the long tradition of informed reception of epic poetics from Hesiod to Vergil, the charioteer Maron, who is an invention of Nonnus, embodies the new epic poetry of *poikilia*. As seen in the programmatic introduction, Nonnus employs a famous metaphor of poetic innovation to turn against the poetics that this metaphor had originally advocated. The charioteer of Dionysus reaches back to the Callimachean significance of the image. His meta-Callimachean poetry of *poikilia*, displayed in a pantomime performance, promises to identify and cut through paths yet untrodden by earlier tradition, including the long Greco-Roman tradition of Callimachean reception.

The competition is tied to Vergil and Vergilian poetics for the additional reason that the pantomime dancing competition features two characters from the pastoral world. As discussed earlier, literary evidence shows that bucolic themes were popular material for pantomime already since the early period of the genre, and they were a staple source of inspiration for the pantomimes staged in Rome during the time of Augustus. According to Plutarch, one of the most popular pantomime dancers of the Augustan era, Bathyllus, preferred to

---

38 On Proteus as a metaphor for the performer see Webb 2005, Lada-Richards 2007, 96–97; and Schlapbach 2008, 314–337.

39 Schlapbach 2017, 259–260, with n. 24 arguing for the accusative ψαύοντα (l. 13) that substantiates the dancing ability of Proteus; see Gigli Piccardi 1993, 230; Agosti 1996, 169 n. 1.

perform bucolic themes: a myth on the dance of an Echo, satyrs, or an Eros.[40] All these themes are celebrated in Vergil's pastoral poetry; they hold prominent presence in Nonnus' pantomime contest as well.[41]

4 Maron vs. Silenus

The poetic resonances in the pantomime agon are manifold: in addition to the performative dimension, the vocabulary used interweaves the politics of writing and drawing, both of them thematic areas of acknowledged poetological significance and core elements of an ecphrasis. Both Maron and Silenus are epic narrators who compose an epic not in writing but in acting; still, their dancing movements remind the audience of writing and drawing.[42] As pantomime dancing is equated to writing, the contest becomes a diatribe on the technology of poetic composition: Maron, who performs a pantomime featuring Ganymede and Hebe, "drew the figure of Ganymede with voiceless hands" (19.216–217: Γανυμήδεως ἔγραφε μορφὴν / χερσὶν ἀφωνήτοισι); and two lines later, when Nonnus wraps up Maron's composition, he significantly notes that Maron "drew his designs in pantomime gestures" (19.219: τοῖα Μάρων ἐχάρασσε πολύτροπα δάκτυλα πάλλων...). Both γράφω and χαράσσω may describe alike writing and drawing.[43] The confluence is both appropriate and paradoxical for describing the narrative of a pantomime performance which is based on a scriptless plot, yet the language of the body and especially the movement of the hands do com-

---

40 Contrary to Pylades, the other great pantomime dancer of the era, who preferred to dance the plots of classical tragedy (Plutarch, *Sympotic Questions* 7.8.3 = *Mor.* 711e-f = T11).
41 Hall/Wyles 2008, 32–33, refer to a work-in-progress by Ruth Webb that discusses the fragmentary Vienna papyrus, no. 123 in Page 1942, 502–507, that records a Greek bucolic poem in hexameter, of anonymous authorship, which involves a musical contest between the satyrs and Pan.
42 The presence of writing has been noted in passing in Shorrock 2001, 157 with n. 165, who further sees the contest between Silenus and Maron as a rivalry on epic poetics (pp. 156–158).
43 On χαράσσω as a) engrave, curve, b) write, inscribe and c) draw, see LSJ s.v., III: e.g., for "engrave, carve": ἐν νομίσματι [Βάττον] χ. (i.e., "stamp" his portrait) Arist. *Fr.* 528; for "inscribe," γράμμα... τοίχοισι χαράξω, Theoc. 23.46; specifically for composing epic: τὸν Τροίης πόλεμον σελίδεσσι χ. *Anth. Pl.* 4.293; for "sketch, draw," μορφὴν χαράξαι *Anth. Gr.* 11.412; on γράφω as "draw" both in terms of weaving and picture-drawing, see LSJ s.v. γράμμα A ("that which is drawn": pl., "lines of a drawing, picture," etc.); see Shorrock 2001, 167 n. 163. Similarly, the verb γλύφω, primarily used for sculpting, may mean also "engrave" and "write" (LSJ s.v.).

pose a script albeit one not put together through letters and characters visually or aurally perceivable.

Maron's performance comes first (D. 19.198–224). Prior to executing this dance, he is reported to have explicitly rejected a pantomime on a theogony or a cosmogony topic, a Typhonomachy or a Gigantomachy, or a creation story:

> οὐδὲ μέν, οἷα **γέρων** Τιτήνιον αἷμα κομίζων, 205
> ἔγραφε **φωνήεντι** τύπῳ Τιτηνίδα φύτλην,
> οὐ Κρόνον ἠὲ Φάνητα **παλαίτερον**, οὐδὲ γενέθλην
> ἠελίου Τιτῆνος **ὁμόχρονον ἥλικι κόσμῳ**·
> ἀλλὰ λιπὼν ξύμπαντα καὶ **ἀρχαίης** χύσιν ὕλης
> οἰνοχόον Κρονίδαο σοφῇ ποίκιλλε **σιωπῇ** 210
> Ζηνὶ δέπας τανύοντα καὶ ἀθανάτων χορὸν ἄλλων
> αἰὲν ἐπασσυτέροισιν εὐφραίνοντα κυπέλλοις,
> ἢ ζαθέην προχέοντα κατὰ κρητῆρος ἐέρσην·
> ἣν δέ οἱ ἁρμονίη γλυκερὸν ποτόν· ἀλλὰ καὶ αὐτὴν
> νέκταρ ἀρυομένην ὠρχήσατο παρθένον Ἥβην· 215
> εἰς Σατύρους δ' ὁρόων Γανυμήδεος ἔγραφε μορφὴν
> χερσὶν ἀφωνήτοισι, καὶ ὁππότε δέρκετο Βάκχας,
> ἥβην χρυσοπέδιλον ἐχέφρονι δείκνυε **σιγῇ**.
> τοῖα Μάρων ἐχάρασσε πολύτροπα δάκτυλα πάλλων,
> καὶ **ποδὸς εὐρύθμοιο σοφὴν ἀνεσείρασεν ὁρμήν**, 220
> **ἀσταθέος τελέσας πολυκαμπέα μέτρα χορείης.**
>
> D. 19.205–221

He did not what an old man of Titan blood might have done, show the Titan race in a speaking picture, not Cronus or Phanes more primeval still, nor the breed of Titan Helios as old as the universe itself: no, he left all the confusion of that ancient stuff. He depicted with wordless art the cupbearer of Cronides offering the goblet to Zeus, or pouring the dew divine to fill up the bowl, and the other immortals in company ever enjoying cup after cup. His poet's theme was the sweet potion. He danced also the maiden Hebe herself drawing the nectar; when he looked at the Satyrs, with voiceless hands he acted Ganymede, or when he saw the Bacchant women, he showed them goldenshoe Hebe in a picture having sense without words. So Maron sketched his designs in pantomime gestures, lifting rhythmic feet with the motions of an artist, as he trod the winding measures of his unresting dance.

Maron's advanced age is incongruent with his thematic choice: his musical performance depicts the erotically suggestive topics of Ganymede and Hebe, instead of grander material that might be considered more appropriate for "an old man carrying the blood of the Titans" (19.205) — material no less popular, but hardly erotic: "the race of the Titans," Cronus, Phanes, the primordial deity preceding the age of the Titans, the Sun and "the confusion of the ancient matter" (ἀρχαίης χύσιν ὕλης) — all of them popular pantomime themes.[44] And yet, these amatory narratives have a precedent in the song of Silenus in *Eclogues* 6,[45] which begins with a cosmogony but soon turns to a long series of episodes that revolve around younger traditions: erotic compositions and transformations, and tragically lost young men. Nonnus' Maron is the opponent to Silenus in this dramatic contest, but seems to have been 'inspired' by Silenus' earlier artistic performance in Vergil's pastoral world; as a result, he is both an antagonist and an heir to the long tradition Silenus represents.

The poetics in Maron's performance is expressed with a series of verbs that may designate both writing and artistic composition — painting or designing: "he depicted (ποίκιλλε) with wordless art the cupbearer of Cronides offering the goblet to Zeus, ... he danced (ὠρχήσατο) also the maiden Hebe herself drawing the nectar" (210–211; 214–215). These are not isolated terms: throughout the pantomime of Maron, Nonnus uses metaphorically expressions related to both writing and art-drawing: 200: χαράσσων; 206: ἔγραφε φωνήεντι τύπῳ; 216: ἔγραφε, etc. Through Maron, Nonnus reaches back to the Horatian *ut pictura poesis* — his pantomime is not a written composition but an artistic representation, even an ecphrasis, subtly acknowledged in the phrase σοφήν... ὀρμήν, which Rouse translates "the motions of an artist." The original meaning of σοφία (according to the LSJ) is "skill in handicraft and art"; it occurs in Homer,[46]

---

[44] Lucian, *On Dancing*, offers a list of popular themes of pantomime performances, with themes from the theogonic/cosmogonic cycle; these include Cronus and the Titanomachy (37), the Titans and Zagreus (39); Cronus eating his children (80); the battle between Cronus and Zeus (47); and Phaethon (55); cf. Gerbeau/Vian 2003/1992, 92 n. 3. On popular pantomime themes across the Greco-Roman antiquity see Gerbeau/Vian 2003/1992, 92–93.

[45] Maron's rejection of a cosmogony or theogony song juxtaposes him to the Vergilian Silenus; the juxtaposition is ascertained on two other occasions in Maron's song: a) his explicit confession that he has always been a disciple of Bacchus and has never received instruction by Apollo in his songs and musical compositions (*D.* 19.182–184) clashes against Vergil's confession at the end of *Eclogue* 6 that Silenus' song had been composed by Apollo (6.82–83); b) his pantomimes do not choose mythological themes that have associations with Apollo, including the myth of Phaethon's death and mourning by the Heliades (*D.* 19.184–186), the theme of another of the Vergilian Silenus' songs (6.62–63).

[46] Ammonius, Commentary on Porphyry's *Introduction to Aristotle's Categories* iv (3), 9: "They applied the term *sophos* (wise, clever) to anyone who pursued any kind of skill ... So Homer (quoted in Clemens, *Strom.* 1.25.1: 'when the clever builder had constructed it')": West 2003, 294–295.

and throughout archaic poetry to refer to skilled artists, including poets,[47] but also to the audience who has the ability to comprehend this skilled poetry.[48] Nonnus once again turns to incongruence as he stresses his allegiance to archaic poetics while at the same time he opts for themes that direct his composition to a different tradition. He also raises the significance of the theme of artistry for assessing the pantomime contest properly, by suggesting to interpret it as an ecphrasis in performance.

The ecphrastic association to pantomime directs the informed reader back to *Eclogue* 6 and to the 'ecphrastic' character of the song of Silenus. Breed (2000) has convincingly pointed out that Vergil's description of the singing voice of Silenus is compared to the description of a visually perceived artifact or an ecphrasis. Vergil does not report Silenus' actual song but the echo of his song; the echo in Latin is rendered with the phrase *imago vocis*, suggestively placing the reflection of the sound next to a visual reflection. This reflective effect of the voice is set both at the beginning and at the conclusion of the song of Silenus: Tityrus opens his narrative on the content of Silenus' song with a description of the captivating effect the sound has over the inanimate and animate worlds, echoing the vocabulary and thematic preference (opening with a cosmogony) of Orpheus' song in Apollonius (*Arg.* 1.496–511) which generates similar marvelling results. Admiration as the reaction to superior artistry typically accompanies ecphrases; while Tityrus in effect performs an ecphrasis of Silenus' song, when he uses verbs, descriptors, and positional indicators similar to those Vergil would later adopt in the *Aeneid* for the presentation of the ecphrasis on the shield of Aeneas, and reactions of delight and pleasure similar to those experienced by Achilles upon admiring the ecphrastic narrative on his own, archetypal shield.[49] Then, *Eclogue* 6 concludes with an explicit mention of the echo of the song of Silenus which ascribes presence to the voice of Silenus within the pastoral world but also within Vergil's audience. "As *imago vocis* an echo is an image, likeness, or reflection of a sound; these are visual metaphors for describing an auditory phenomenon, and there is inscribed in the Latin an implicit comparison with modes of visual representation."[50] Maron, then, may

---

[47] Pindar, *N.* 7.20–21; Theognis 218, with Nagy 1990, ch. 14 §§ 24–26. For the meaning of the term σοφία in Pindar see Svoboda 1952, 108; Bowra 1964, 4–7; Snell 1978, 44–52. Hesiod first and then Pindar use "sophia" to refer to the intellectual competence of the poet; on the evolving conception of "sophia" in archaic thought and poetry see especially Maehler 1963, 66–68, 94–96.
[48] Nagy 1990, ch. 14 §32.
[49] Breed 2000, 333–334.
[50] Breed 2000, 331.

utilise the ecphrastic character of a performance such as the one recorded in Vergil's Silenus to draw inspiration for the pictorial illusion generated by his pantomime composition, in order to combat Silenus' Nonnian counterpart!

When his turn arrives, Silenus performs the competition between Dionysus and Aristaeus as to which of them serves the more enjoyable drink to the gods, wine (Dionysus) or mead (Aristaeus) (19.225–264). Silenus' pantomime dance is both longer and more complex than Maron's own, yet like Maron, he, too, seems to reach backwards to Vergil for inspiration. Aristaeus (etym. from ἄριστος, "the best") is a complex character transcending the boundaries of a mortal's existence (as he is the son of Apollo, according to Pindar *P.* 9.1–75), with a long tradition behind him, close associations to many gods, including Dionysus since the archaic era, and pivotal contribution to human intellectual and cultural progress. His many associations to culture and technological progress (he is the inventor of much rural technology; he learnt the art of prophecy and healing from the Muses, according to Apollonius) justify his frequent presence in didactic and learned Greek poetry from Hesiod onwards (including among others Callimachus, Apollonius, Euphorion, pseudo-Oppian, and Nonnus), occasionally accompanied by mythological digressions (Hesiod, Aratus, and Nicander).[51] In Nonnus, *Dionysiaca* 5, Aristaeus' role in the Theban legend, being the husband of Autonoe and the father of Actaeon, receives detailed treatment, as does his identity as the inventor of a series of agricultural innovations and especially technological devices associated with apiculture (including the linen gauze beekeeper's mask and the technique of smoking the hive, described at *D.* 5.242–257).

Silenus' decision to perform a pantomime on an agon between Dionysus and Aristaeus addresses epic metapoetics on several levels: Dionysus and Aristaeus are interchangeable characters in their association to culture and technology.[52] Silenus in this respect composes his pantomime as a mise-en-abyme at once of Dionysus' contest against the rival earlier (didactic) epic tradition and of his own present contest against Maron, who himself may be considered interchangeable to Silenus, being the latter's son and rival contestant. Also, inspired by Maron, Silenus points the informed reader to Vergil, not only for the association of Aristaeus to the technology of bee-keeping, but because in Vergil's account Aristaeus is linked to Orpheus. In Vergil's epyllion-like conclusion to the Fourth *Georgic*, an episode of 244 lines (315–558), Aristaeus is responsible for

---

51 Schachter/Folkerts 2020.
52 On Aristaeus as culture hero and benefactor of mankind see Perkell 1989, 70–79; also Campbell 1982.

the death of Eurydice: the latter, while trying to escape from Aristaeus' pursuit, failed to see a huge snake (458). This connection of Aristaeus and Orpheus, otherwise unattested, may have been invented by Vergil[53] and seems to have appealed to Nonnus' Silenus, who aspires to rival Maron and the latter's engagement with themes celebrated in the Latin tradition, specifically Vergil, in his quest for effective symbolisms tied to poetics.

The structure of Silenus' performance is different from Maron's own, but like Maron, he makes the point to frame the pantomime with expressions of writing and drawing, eliciting anew the same associations to ecphrastic compositions. The introduction of the pantomime runs as follows: Σειληνὸς δ' ἐχόρευε. πολυστρέπτοιο δὲ τέχνης / **σύμβολα** τεχνήεντα **κατέγραφε** σιγαλέη χείρ. / καὶ παλάμαις τότε τοῖος ἔην **τύπος**, ... "Silenus then began his dance. The silent hand traced skilful signs of the whirling art. And such was the impression he made with his palm" (225–227). Vocabulary such as σύμβολα, κατέγραφε, τύπος, are standard words referring to the act of writing or drawing, even though the performance opens with a verb meaning "dancing". Similarly, the conclusion to the pantomime is marked by ring composition noted by means of a phrase that echoes the vocabulary of artful composition — only, in the conclusion, writing and drawing have been replaced with their alternative art of weaving: τοῦτο σοφῇ παλάμῃ κερόεις Σειληνὸς ὑφαίνων / δεξιτερὴν μὲν ἔπαυσε..., "these things horned Silenus wove with a skilled hand, and he stopped his right hand..." (263–264).

Silenus' choice of theme, the victory of Dionysus over Aristaeus, may be read allegorically as anticipating the superiority of Nonnus' inventive epic over traditional epic, embodied in Aristaeus on account of his descent from Apollo and his conspicuous role in the epyllion that closes Vergil's earlier poetic compositions. As such, it should secure for Silenus the victory in the pantomime.[54] In the end, however, the winning prize is awarded to Maron. To this contributed jointly the clarity and full control of motions during the execution of the dance.

---

[53] Prior to the *Georgics*, the extant tradition describes Aristaeus as neither inventor of the *bougonia* nor victim of Orpheus; see Klingner 1967, 329–333; Bettini 1991, 240–246; on the several levels of Aristaeus' close relationship to Orpheus in *Georgic* 4 see, e.g., Anderson 1982, 25–50; Neumeister 1982; Perkell 1989, 67–88.

[54] It seems that Silenus really tries to influence Dionysus' decision not only by performing the victory of the god over Aristaeus but also by nearly repeating Dionysus' own words: as he points out that in the competition between Dionysus and Aristaeus, "there was no boxing, no running, no quoit" (229–230), his audiences, including Dionysus, are invited to recall that the same line has been part of Dionysus' introductory speech before the pantomime contest (147–149); Schlapbach 2017, 267.

In Maron's pantomime the audience never loses track of the character of the performance — the actor dances two different mythological themes to two different audiences: to the satyrs he dances the myth of Ganymede, to the Maenads that of Hebe. Silenus, on the contrary, despite being introduced as a wise artist, launches a performance that is better suited to a song than to a pantomime. Pointedly, this performance opens with a line that echoes the opening of the *Iliad* and the strife between Achilles and Agamemnon: ὥς ποτε πολλὴ / υἱέι Κυρήνης ἔρις ἔμπεσε καὶ Διονύσῳ / ἀμφὶ πότου, "how once a great wrath arose between Cyrene's son and Dionysos over their cups" (*D*. 19.227–229) ~ ἐξ οὗ δὴ τὰ πρῶτα διαστήτην ἐρίσαντε / Ἀτρεΐδης τε ἄναξ ἀνδρῶν καὶ δῖος Ἀχιλλεύς, "from the moment that Atreus' son, the king of men, parted in wrath from divine Achilles" (*Il*. 1.6–7). The story subsequently leads to a description of the contest of the two, while the other gods have gathered to watch and later to participate as they become the testing subjects of the two competing potions. The articulation of the performance as a pantomime is vague, for Nonnus nowhere describes how Silenus' dancing and gesturing actually represents the rivalry between the two deities or the reactions of the attending divine spectators, their satiety of the mead, and their thirst for more wine. In Schlapbach's words, "the form of this dance loses its contour, and the immersion in the myth takes place at the expense of the vehicle that represents it" (2017, 267). Nonnus' Silenus seems to offer a song much in the pattern of his Vergilian counterpart in *Eclogue* 6, instead of the pantomime dance the contest under way calls for: the dancing performance without a theme that follows does not belong to the domain of the pantomime either, for it involves the dancing element but not the narrative context required in conjunction. And lacking a theme, the dance becomes an unscripted series of movements of leaping, twisting, bending, and turning (263–295), that elicit memories of the satyrs' dances depicted on Attic vase iconography, and extract a heavy toll over the aged body of Silenus, who eventually collapses and virtually disintegrates by liquidation (19.287: ποταμὸς μορφοῦτο, "he turned into a river"). Silenus has no control over his body movements, and his fall in a way dramatises an unintentional pantomime dance.[55] This lack of control draws Silenus next to other similarly uncontained

---

[55] Detailed discussion in Schlapbach 2017, 267–271; Schlapbach points out that the minute detail devoted to the liquidation of Silenus' body (at 287–293) balances the lack of body language expected during the execution of his pantomime dance. "Silenus becomes water, the element that best represents flexibility and malleability, and the element that is associated with many shape-shifting and dancing divinities such as Proteus, Nereus, and Thetis, to name but the best-known ones" (p. 271).

aspiring artists, including Marsyas (*D.* 19.317–319), whose demise was mentioned significantly in the programmatic prologue to the *Dionysiaca* (1.42–44) and, according to Shorrock, set a clear example for Nonnus to avoid.[56]

Silenus' continuation of his pantomime with an acrobatic dance of no particular narrative sequence may be explained only in the aftermath of his transformation into a river — a conclusion that criticism has seen as "a reminder that artistic skill needs to live up to the project undertaken, and that passion or temerity alone does not guarantee a successful outcome" (Schlapbach 2017, 275). Schlapbach raises an interesting point when she compares the collapsing and liquidating Silenus to Phaethon, whose excess and passion similarly transgressed boundaries and proved catastrophic (Schlapbach, *op. cit.*), and led the youth to his deathly and forcible plunge into the Eridanos river. The comparison is tempting, since on both occasions the liquid grave that embraces the heroes' bodies is identically characterised as ἀγκύλον ὕδωρ (38.431 and 19.346). Even more compelling to this direction is the tradition of the plunging Phaethon in Roman pantomime, clearly popular in Nonnus' times. This is explicitly noted in the *Dionysiaca*, in a passage during the Indian war, that describes the death of a pantomime dancer, a certain Phlogius, a soldier in the army of Dionysus, in battle against the Indian prince Morrheus (30.108–116). According to Nonnus, this pantomime dancer specialised in performing the deathly plunge of Phaethon:[57]

καὶ Φλόγιον Στροφίοιο πολύστροφον υἷα κιχήσας
ἔκτανεν, ὀρχηστῆρα φιλοσκάρθμου Διονύσου,
ὅς τις ἀδακρύτοιο παρ' εἰλαπίνῃσι Λυαίου   110
ἀνταιτύπων ἑλέλιζε πολύτροπα δάκτυλα χειρῶν,
καὶ θάνατον Φαέθοντος ἐχέφρονι χειρὶ χαράσσων[58]
δαιτυμόνας ποίησεν ἀήθεα δάκρυα λείβειν,
ψευδαλέου Φαέθοντος ἐπικλαίοντας ὀλέθρῳ·
καὶ νέον αἰθαλόεντα καὶ αὐτοκύλιστον ὑφαίνων   115
λευγαλέον πόρε πένθος ἀπενθήτῳ Διονύσῳ.

D. 30.108–116

---

[56] Shorrock 2001, 157–158; Schlapbach 2017, 272, though her identifying Maron with the Odyssean Maron, the provider of the Maronian wine to Odysseus, is incorrect, but anticipated, even deceptively elicited, by Nonnus himself (see my discussion on Nonnus' programmatic prologue and Maron's evocation of Vergil, pp. 164–165 above).

[57] Lada-Richards 2016, 139–141 is the most detailed discussion on the use of the Phaethon and the Heliades myth as popular pantomime theme; her argument is based on Nonnus' Phaethon narrative in *Dionysiaca* 38.

[58] Vian's correction of the mss. τινάσσων; cf. the use of χαράσσων repeatedly to describe the pantomime performances of Maron and Silenus in *D.* 19.200; see Vian 1997, 119.

> He caught Phlogius the son of Strophius rolling about and killed him; that dancer of springheel Dionysus, who at the banquets of tearless Lyaios, used to flicker the twisting fingers of his mimicking hands. He would engrave Phaethon's death with sensitive hand, until he made the feasters weep with tears quite out of place, mourning the death of an imaginary Phaethon; as he depicted the young man blazing and hurtling down, he would bring painful grief upon Dionysus who feels no grief.

The description of Phlogius' plunge anticipates Phaethon's own graphic death, which, in this way, is cast in light of a pantomime performance and undermines the supposed tragic tone of the episode.[59] At the same time, it revives the long Latin tradition of pantomime enactments of Phaethon's myth, including the song of Silenus in *Eclogue* 6, which alludes to Phaethon's tragic destiny in his reference to the transformation of Phaethon's mourning sisters at 62–63.

The mention of a pantomime tradition of Phaethon's plunge in the *Dionysiaca* does not necessarily suggest direct interaction with the pastoral Vergil, but it is worth pointing out that the Vergilian Silenus' song alludes to Phaethon's death in the reference to the mourning Phaethontiades. The Phaethontiades identify with their tears and are connected to the river element – they come to mind upon reading Nonnus' Silenus and his eventual transformation into a river following a dancing route marked by lack of control. Silenus' fate is reflected in the fate at once of Phaethon and of Phaethon's sisters. Moreover, Lucian's reference to the Phaethon legend as a pantomime topic (*On Dancing* 55) includes the transformation of his sisters into mourning and amber-weeping poplars (θρηνοῦσαι καὶ ἤλεκτρον δακρύουσαι), reaching back to Vergil's Silenus' account of the story and affirming the association of the two.[60]

The performances of Vergil's Silenus and his Nonnian counterpart close (or rather refuse to close) in comparable ways: even though evening comes, and the time arrives for the cows to come home, Silenus in *Eclogues* 6 continues singing till the stars come out. His open-ended song is revisited in the Nonnian Silenus' interminable performance – a dance to his end by transformation into water, an element in turn ever moving and ever eluding, and which, like wine, has been connected to poetic inspiration since Callimachus.[61] Both closures are tied to poetics. This distinct conclusion that replaces closure with elusiveness, firmness with fluidity, is characteristic of the treatment of earlier tradition in the

---

59 See the similarity in vocabulary and tone in the description of Phaethon in *D.* 38.91–93; 38.410–411.
60 Lada-Richards 2016, 140, points out Nonnus' self-consciousness at evoking pantomime in his description of the fall of Phaethon and the lament of the Heliades.
61 Detailed discussion in Knox 1985.

Dionysiaca. Nonnus' text leads to many different directions and resuscitates an increasing variety of intertexts — expectedly so in a poet that celebrates Dionysus, the god of transformation and elusiveness. Familiarity with the Latin tradition may enlighten and inspire alike. The popularity of the pantomime, a Roman genre of comic performance, across the Eastern Empire during the Late Antiquity, justifies the attractiveness of the Latin tradition in the East, and may become a preamble to a more systematic methodology of interlingual literary appropriation across genres.

Bibliography

Agosti, G. (1996), "Ancora su Proteo in Nonno, *Dion*. 1, 13 sgg.", in: *Prometheus* 22, 169–172.
Anderson, W.S. (1982), "The Orpheus of Vergil and Ovid", in: J. Warden (ed.), *Orpheus: The Metamorphoses of a Myth*, Toronto, 25–50.
Baraz, Y. (2019), "*Certare alterno carmine*: the Rise and Fall of Bucolic Competition", in: C. Damon/Ch. Pieper (eds.), *Eris vs. Aemulatio: Valuing Competition in Classical Antiquity*, Leiden, 78–97.
Bettini, M. (1991), *Anthropology and Roman Culture: Kinship, Time, Images of the Soul*. Engl. tr. by J. van Sickle, Baltimore/London.
Bolhuis, A. (1950), *Vergilius' vierde Ecloga in de Oratio Constantini ad Sanctorum Coetum*, Ermelo.
Bowra, C.M. (1964), *Pindar*, Oxford.
Breed, B. (2000), "Silenus and the *Imago Vocis* in 'Eclogue 6'", in: *Harvard Studies in Classical Philology* 100, 327–339.
Bright, D.F. (1987), *The Miniature Epic in Vandal Africa*, Norman, OK/London.
Campbell, J.S. (1982), "Initiation and the Role of Aristaeus in *Georgics* Four", in: *Ramus* 2, 105–115.
Carvounis, K./Papaioannou, S. (2022), "Rivalling Song Contests and Alternative Typhonomachies in Ovid and Nonnus: Revisiting the Issue of Latin Influence on Greek Poetry in Late Antiquity', in: B. Verhelst/T. Scheijnen (eds.), *Greek and Latin Poetry of Late Antiquity. Form, Tradition, and Context*, Cambridge, 13–30.
Clausen, W.V. (1994), *A Commentary on Virgil, Eclogues*, Oxford.
Coronati, L. (1984), "Osservazioni sulla traduzione greca della IV ecloga di Virgilio", in: *Civiltà Classica e Cristiana* 5, 71–84.
Costa, G. (1972), *La leggenda dei secoli d'oro nella letteratura italiana*, Bari.
Cribiore, R. (2009), "The Value of a Good Education: Libanius and Public Authority", in: P. Rousseau (ed.), *A Companion to Late Antiquity*, Malden, MA, 233–249.
Davies, M. (2003), "Proppian Light on the Aristaeus Episode", in: *Prometheus* 29, 57–64.
Delavaud-Roux, M.-H. (2009), "La Danse dionysiaque, un modèle d'expression pour les personnes âgées ? (Nonnos, *Dionysiaques*, XIX, 159–224)", in: *Les Etudes Classiques* 77, 3–22.
Desport, M. (1952), *L'incantation virgilienne*, Bordeaux.
D'Ippolito, G. (1962), "Draconzio, Nonno e gli idromimi", in: *Atene e Roma* 7, 1–14.

Floyd, E.D. (2001), "Eusebius' Greek Version of Vergil's Fourth *Eclogue*", in: R. Blumenfeld-Kosinski/L. von Flotow/D. Russell (eds.), *The Politics of Translation in the Middle Ages and the Renaissance*, Tempe, AZ, 57–67.

Garelli, M.-H. (2006), "Pantomime, tragédie et patrimoine littéraire sous l'Empire", in: *Pallas* 71, 113–125.

Garelli, M.-H. (2007), *Danser le mythe: La pantomime et sa réception dans la culture antique*, Leuven.

Gerbeau, J./Vian, F. (2003/1992), *Nonnos de Panopolis: Les Dionysiaques Chants XVIII-XIX* (v. 7), Paris.

Gigli Piccardi, D. (1993), "Nonno, Proteo e l'isola di Faro", in: *Prometheus* 19, 230–234.

Girardet, K.M. (2013), "Die Christianisierung der 4. Ekloge Vergils durch Kaiser Konstantin d. Gr.", in: *Gymnasium* 120, 549–583.

Goldberg, S.M. (2005), *Constructing Literature in the Roman Republic: Poetry and its Reception*, Cambridge.

Hadas, M. (2013), "Christians, Sibyls and *Eclogue* 4", in: *Recherches augustiniennes et patristiques* 37, 92–109.

Hadjittofi, F. (2018), "Midas, the Golden Age Trope, and Hellenistic Kingship in Ovid's *Metamorphoses*", in: *American Journal of Philology* 139, 277–309.

Hall, E. (2008), "Is the 'Barcelona Alcestis' a Latin Pantomime Libretto?", in: Hall/Wyles (2008), 258–282.

Hall, E./Wyles, R. (eds.) (2008), *New Directions in Ancient Pantomime*, Oxford.

Harries, B. (1990), "The Spinner and the Poet: Arachne in Ovid's *Metamorphoses*", in: *Proceedings of the Cambridge Philological Society* 216, 64–82.

Heath, J. (2011), "Women's Work: Female Transmission of Mythical Narrative", in: *Transactions of the American Philologial Association* 141, 69–104.

Heyworth, S.J. (2019), *Ovid: Fasti Book 3*, Cambridge.

Horsfall, N. (2000), *A Companion to the Study of Virgil*, Leiden.

Höschele, R. (2013), "From Ecloga the Mime to Vergil's 'Eclogues' as Mimes: 'Ein Gedankenspiel'", in: *Vergilius* 59, 37–60.

Hubbard, T.K. (2006), "The Pipe That Can Imitate All Pipes: Longus' *Daphnis and Chloe* and the Intertextual Polyphony of Pastoral Music", in: M. Skoie/S. Bjørnstad-Velázquez (eds.), *Pastoral and the Humanities: Arcadia Re-inscribed*, Exeter, 101–106.

Ingleheart, J. (2008), "*Et mea sunt populo saltata poemata saepe* (*Tristia* 2.519): Ovid and the Pantomime", in: Hall/Wyles (2008), 198–217.

Johnston, P. (2008), *Ovid Before Exile: Art and Punishment in the Metamorphoses*, Madison.

Jones Hall, L. (2004), *Roman Berytus: Beirut in Late Antiquity*, London.

Jory, J. (1981), "The Literary Evidence for the Beginnings of Imperial Pantomime", in: *Bulletin of the Institute of Classical Studies* 28, 147–161.

Karakasis, E. (2011), *Song Exchange in Roman Pastoral*, Berlin.

Keightley, T. (1846), *Notes on the Bucolics and Georgics of Virgil*, London.

Kline, A.S. (2001), *Virgil. The Eclogues*. Online at: https://www.poetryintranslation.com/PITBR/Latin/VirgilEclogues.php.

Klingner, F. (1967), *Virgil: Bucolica, Georgica, Aeneis*, Zurich.

Knox, P.E. (1985), "Wine, Water and Callimachean Polemics", in: *Harvard Studies in Classical Philology* 89, 107–119.

Lada-Richards, I. (2004), "*Mythōn Eikōn*: Pantomime Dancing and the Figurative Arts in Imperial and Late Antiquity", in: *Arion* 2.2, 17–46.

Lada-Richards, I. (2007), *Silent Eloquence: Lucian and Pantomime Dancing*, London.
Lada-Richards, I. (2010), "Corporeal Technologies in Graeco-Roman Pantomime Dancing", in: M.-F. Garelli/V. Visa-Ondarçuhu (eds.), *Corps en jeu de l'Antiquité à nos jours*, Rennes, 251–269.
Lada-Richards, I. (2013), "*Mutata Corpora*: Ovid's Changing Forms and the Metamorphic Bodies of Pantomime Dancing", in: *Transactions of the American Philological Association* 143, 105–152.
Lada-Richards, I. (2016), "Dancing Trees: Ovid's *Metamorphoses* and the Imprint of Pantomime Dancing", in: *American Journal of Philology* 137, 131–167.
Lada-Richards, I. (2019), "On Taking our Sources Seriously: Servius and the Theatrical Life of Vergil's *Eclogues*", in: *Classical Antiquity* 38, 91–140.
Lebek, W.D. (1983), "Das neue Alcestis-Gedicht der Papyri Barcinonenses", in: *Zeitschrift für Papyrologie und Epigraphik* 52, 1–29.
Lebek, W.D. (1987), "Die Alcestis Barcinonensis: Neue Konjekturen und Interpretationen", in: *Zeitschrift für Papyrologie und Epigraphik* 70, 39–48.
Lieberg, G. (1982), *Poeta Creator: Studien zu einer Figur der antiken Dichtung*, Amsterdam.
Lovatt, E. (2005), *Statius and Epic Games*, Cambridge.
MacGóráin, F. (2012–13), "Apollo and Dionysus in Virgil", in: *Incontri di filologia classica* 12, 191–238.
Maehler, H. (1963), *Die Auffassung des Dichterberufs im fruehen Griechentum bis zur Zeit Pindars*, Göttingen.
Meban, D. (2008), "Temple Building, Primus Language, and the Proem to Virgil's Third Georgic", in: *Classical Philology* 103, 150–174.
Miguélez-Cavero, L. (2008), *Poems in Context: Greek Poetry in the Egyptian Thebaid, 200–600 AD*, Berlin/New York.
Miguélez-Cavero, L. (2009), "Gesture and Gesturality in the *Dionysiaca* of Nonnus", in: *Journal of Late Antiquity* 2.2, 251–273.
Miguélez-Cavero, L. (2013), "Rhetoric Novelty in the *Dionysiaca* of Nonnus of Panopolis", in: R. García-Gasco/Sergio González Sánchez/D. Hernández de la Fuente (eds.), *The Theodosian Age (AD 379–455). Power, Place, Belief and Learning at the End of the Western Empire*, Oxford, 191–196.
Monteleone, C. (1975), *L'egloga quarta da Virgilio a Costantino: critica del testo e ideologia*, Manduria.
Mynors, R.A.B. (1968), *P. Vergili Maronis Opera*. Oxford Classical Texts, Oxford.
Nagy, G. (1990), *Pindar's Homer: The Lyric Possession of an Epic Past*, Baltimore.
Nelis, D.P. (2008), "Caesar, the Circus, and the Charioteer in Vergil's *Georgics*", in: J. Nelis-Clément/J.M. Roddaz (eds.), *Le Cirque Romain et Son Image*, Bordeaux, 497–520.
Nelson, T.J. (forthcoming), "Équitation, Char/Horsemanship, Chariot-riding", in: J.-P. Guez/F. Klein/J. Peigney/É. Prioux (eds.), *Dictionnaire des images du poétique dans l'Antiquité*, Paris. Preprint in Academia.edu: ttps://www.academia.edu/36860942/Metapoetic_Horse_and_Chariot-Riding_in_Roman_Literature.
Neumeister, C. (1982), "Aristaeus und Orpheus im 4. Buch der *Georgica*", in: *Würzburger Jahrbücher für die Altertumswissenschaft* 8, 47–56.
Nünlist, R. (1998), *Poetologische Bildersprache in der frühgriechischen Dichtung*, Stuttgart.
Oliensis, E. (2004), "The Power of Image-Makers: Representation and Revenge in Ovid *Metamorphoses* 6 and *Tristia* 4", in: *Classical Antiquity* 23, 285–321.
Page, D.L. (1942), *Greek Literary Papyri I: Poetry. With an English translation*, London.

Panayotakis, C. (2008), "Vergil on the Popular Stage", in: Hall/Wyles (2008), 185–197.
Papaioannou, S. (2007), *Redesigning Achilles: 'Recycling' the Epic Cycle in the 'Little Iliad'*, (Ovid, *Metamorphoses* 12.1–13.622), Berlin.
Parsons, P.J./Nisbet, R.G.M./Hutchinson, G.O. (1983), "Alcestis in Barcelona", in: *Zeitschrift für Papyrologie und Epigraphik* 52, 31–36.
Pavlock, B. (2009), *The Image of the Poet in the Metamorphoses*, Madison, WI.
Perkell, C. (1989), *The Poet's Truth: A Study of the Poet in Vergil's Georgics*, Berkeley/Los Angeles.
Petrides, A. (2013), "Lucian's *On Dance* and the Poetics of the Pantomime Mask", in: G.W.M. Harrison/V. Liapis (eds.), *Performance in Greek and Roman Theater*, Leiden, 433–451.
Quinn, K.P. (1982), "The Poet and his Audience in the Augustan Age", in: H. Temporini/ W. Haase (eds.), *Aufstieg und Niedergang der römischen Welt* II.30.1, Berlin, 75–180.
Rosati, G. (1999), "Form in Motion: Weaving the Text in the *Metamorphoses*", in: P. Hardie/ A. Barchiesi/S. Hinds (eds.), *Ovidian Transformations. Essays on the Metamorphoses and its Reception*, Cambridge, 240–253.
Rosati, G. (2002), "Narrative Techniques and Narrative Structures in the *Metamorphoses*", in: B. Weiden Boyd (ed.), *Brill's Companion to Ovid*, Leiden, 271–304.
Rouse, W.H.D. (1940), *Nonnos: Dionysiaca*. With an English translation; mythological introduction by H.J. Rose, and notes on textual criticism by L.R. Lind. In three volumes, Cambridge, MA.
Sargent, J.L. (1996), *The Novelty of Ovid's Heroides*, PhD Dissertation, Bryn Mawr College.
Savage, J.J.H. (1965), "The Wine of Maron", in: *Transactions and Proceedings of the American Philological Association* 96, 375–401.
Scafoglio, G. (2013), "From Tamarisks to Stars: Cosmic Inspiration in Vergil's *Eclogues*", in: *Acta Antiqua Academiae Scientiarum Hungaricae* 53, 185–209.
Schachter, A./Folkerts, M. (2020), "Aristaeus[1]", in: *Brill's New Pauly*, Antiquity volumes, H. Cancik/H. Schneider (eds.), English ed. by C.F. Salazar; Classical Tradition volumes ed. by M. Landfester, English ed. by F.G. Gentry. Consulted online on 19 March 2020.
Schlapbach, K. (2008), "Lucian's *On Dancing* and the Models for a Discourse on Pantomime", in: Hall/Wyles (2008), 314–337.
Schlapbach, K. (2017), "Elusive Dancers and the Limits of Art in Nonnus' *Dionysiaka*", in: K. Schlapbach, *The Anatomy of Dance Discourse: Literary and Philosophical Approaches to Dance in the Later Greco-Roman World*, Oxford, 251–280.
Shorrock, R. (2001), *The Challenge of Epic: Allusive Engagement in the Dionysiaca of Nonnus*, Leiden.
Shorrock, R. (2008), "The Politics of Poetics: Nonnus' *Dionysiaca* and the World of Late Antiquity", in: *Ramus* 37.1–2, 99–113.
Slaveva-Griffin, S. (2003), "Of Gods, Philosophers, and Charioteers: Content and Form in Parmenides' Proem and Plato's *Phaedrus*", in: *Transactions of the American Philological Association* 133, 227–253.
Snell, B. (1978), *Der Weg zum Denken und zur Wahrheit: Studien zur frühgriechischen Sprache*, Göttingen.
Svoboda, K. (1952), "Les idées de Pindare sur la poésie", *Aegyptus* 32, 108–120.
Szabat, E. (2015), "Late Antiquity and the Transmission of Educational Ideals and Methods", in: W.M. Bloomer (ed.), *A Companion to Ancient Education*, Malden, MA, 267–278.
Tedeschi, G. (2017), *Spettacoli e trattenimenti dal IV secolo a.C. all'età tardo-antica secondo i documenti epigrafici e papiracei*, Trieste.
Verhelst, B. (2017), *Direct Speech in Nonnus' Dionysiaca: Narrative and Rhetorical Functions*, Leiden.

Vesterinen, M. (2007), *Dancing and Professional Dancers in Roman Egypt*, Helsinki.
Vian, F. (1997), *Nonnos de Panopolis: Les Dionysiaques Chants XXX-XXXII* (v. 10), Paris.
Webb, R. (2002), "Female Entertainers in Late Antiquity", in: P. Easterling/E. Hall (eds.), *Greek and Roman Actors: Aspects of an Ancient Profession*, Cambridge, 282–303.
Webb, R. (2005), "The Protean Performer: Mimesis and Identity in Late Antique Discussion of Theater", in: L. Del Giudice/N. van Deusen (eds.), *Performing Ecstasis: Music, Dance and Ritual in the Mediterranean*, Ottawa, 3–11.
Webb, R. (2008a), "Inside the Mask: Pantomime from the Performers' Perspective", in: Hall/Wyles (2008), 43–60.
Webb, R. (2008b), *Demons and Dancers: Performance in Late Antiquity*, Cambridge, MA.
Webb, R. (2012), "The Nature and Representation of Competition in Pantomime and Mime", in: K. Coleman/J. Nelis-Clément (eds.), *L'organisation des spectacles dans le monde romaine*, Geneva, 221–256.
West, M.L. (2003), *Greek Epic Fragments: From the Seventh to the Fifth Centuries BC*, Cambridge, MA.
Whitmarsh, T. (2016), "Maronian Nectar: Nonnus, Homer and Vergil", paper delivered at the SCS Annual Meeting. Abstract available on line at: https://classicalstudies.org/annual-meeting/147/abstract/maronian-nectar-nonnus-homer-and-vergil.
Wigtil, D.N. (1981), "Toward a Date for the Greek Fourth *Eclogue*", in: *Classical Journal* 76, 336–341.
Wiseman, T.P. (2008), "Ovid and the Stage", in: T.P. Wiseman (ed.), *Unwritten Rome*, Exeter, 210–230.
Zanobi, A. (2008), "The Influence of Pantomime on Seneca's Tragedies", in: Hall/Wyles (2008), 227–257.
Ziogas, I. (2013), *Ovid and Hesiod: The Metamorphosis of the Catalogue of Women*, Cambridge.
Ziolkowski, J.M./Putnam, M.C.J. (eds.) (2008), *The Virgilian Tradition: The First Fifteen Hundred Years*, New Haven/London.

Helen Lovatt
Nonnus' Phaethon, Ovid, and Flavian Intertextuality

Abstract: By comparing Nonnus' reworking of Ovid's Phaethon story with the complex intertextual tactics used in Flavian epic (Valerius Flaccus, Silius Italicus, and Statius), this chapter makes a case for a both/and reading of the relationship between Greek imperial epic and Latin poetry. Since Knox's argument that Nonnus' Phaethon showed stronger links with his own poetry and various Greek models, the consensus has remained that Ovid was not important for a reading of Nonnus' Phaethon. But Nonnus' idiosyncratic version shares a clear kinship with Ovid, both in the emphasis on succession and play, the artful ecphrastic framing of the myth, and in its relationship with the surrounding storyline. Nonnus creatively reworks the tradition, a tradition which seems by the 5th century to be highly Ovidian, by avoidance, tangential reference, playful and ironic gestures such as miniaturisation, expansion, reversal, in a way that is very similar to the complexity of Flavian intertextuality.

Keywords: Phaethon; playfulness; framing; intertextuality; Nonnus; Ovid; Flavian epic.

Flavian and imperial Greek epic have been presented similarly by critics: late, long, complex, and avoidable.[1] Assessments such as 'low quality' and 'derivative' frame them as 'unnecessary' texts, and also reduce the parameters for what is considered convincing creative imitation. If there are any small differences between versions of an episode, then they cannot have been related to each other, since the only relationship they could have with the literary past is one of direct copying.[2] It follows then that the reassessment of both groups of texts

---

[1] Agosti 2016 discusses the episodic nature of the *Dionysiaca*, responding to D'Ippolito 1964. Flavian epic was also characterised as episodic, cf. Vessey 1973, 55. The idea of a baroque aesthetic, for instance, in D'Ippolito 1987, matches the emphasis on 'mannerism' in Flavian epic: Vessey 1970.

[2] For instance, Knaack 1886, 27 argues that the passage describing Phaethon's toy chariot must have come from an Alexandrian original, because Nonnus could not have invented it: *neque enim persuadere mihi potero hosque lepores nativa simplicitate conspicuos ab eodem homine profectos esse, qui tot frigidissima intempestivae doctrinae commenta ambagibus longinqui poematis inspersit.* ("For I could not persuade myself that such conspicuous charms with

requires a reassessment of their relationship: both Flavian epic and Greek imperial epic are appreciated as rich, complex engagements with literary traditions. There is much to learn from comparing their intertextual tactics.[3]

This paper takes as a case study the relationship between Ovid's and Nonnus' Phaethon episodes, read alongside the Ovidianism of Silius Italicus' *Punica*, Statius' *Thebaid*, and Valerius Flaccus' *Argonautica*.[4] The fact that Valerius, Statius, and Silius were writing in Latin means that it is assumed they had read and engaged with Ovid.[5] By looking at the Flavian epicists' complex intertextual tactics, we can see whether it is possible or likely that Nonnus was 'engaging' with Ovid's poetry in a similar way, and what interpretative gains we might make if we read the two traditions together. All four poets have been read as re-working Ovid's Phaethon episode. In particular, this chapter will be engaging with Peter Knox's interpretation of Nonnus by comparing with recent approaches to Flavian Ovidianism.[6] Knox argues that it is much more likely that Nonnus was drawing on existing Greek material, as well as using ideas, lan-

---

their inborn simplicity could have come forth from the same man who scattered so many extremely cold elements of inappropriate learning into the windings of his lengthy poems" — my translation).

3 Despite its title, *Roman and Greek Imperial Epic*, Paschalis 2005 mostly keeps the two areas separate. Only Nelis 2005 compares the *Orphic Argonautica* with Valerius Flaccus, but without making any assumptions of an allusive connection.

4 Paschalis 2014 takes Knox's conclusions as current orthodoxy, and instead offers a comparative reading. Comparative approaches which leave open the question of intentional relationships have much to recommend them. Paschalis argues that metamorphosis is a central concern of Nonnus, but Nonnus takes a very different approach to Ovid. This could well be a reaction against Ovid.

5 On Ovid and Flavian epic, much work is currently under way. Recent contributions include: Keith 2002; Newlands 2004; Keith 2014a; Keith 2016; Bernstein 2016; Marks 2020.

6 Knox 1988 maintains a dominant position on this debate, as can be seen in the useful summary provided by Agosti 2016. Agosti's position is: "La conclusione, che sembra dunque prevalente negli studi nonniani, è di un deciso scetticismo o quantomeno di un non liquet: ed è anche l'opinione che personalmente mi sento di condividere." ("The conclusion, which therefore seems prevalent in Nonnian studies, is for a decided scepticism or at least an 'it is not clear': and this is also the opinion which I feel I personally can share" — my translation). Schiesaro 2019, 177 refers to Nonnus in his Actaeon episode as "writing independently from Ovid's *Metamorphoses*," which he also emphasises "does not presuppose ignorance." This wording also shows the remaining shadow of "derivative" or "dependent" interpretations of literary traditions. This paper uses a comparative method to highlight how the assumption of a relationship (as with the Flavian poets) licenses a wider range of interpretative moves, and argues that Knox still retains assumptions of inferiority that limit his appreciation of Nonnian intertextuality.

guage, and imagery from his own previous books of poetry, rather than creatively engaging with Ovid's Phaethon in composing his own version.⁷ Since Knox's article, Ovid's Phaethon has been reinterpreted persuasively, especially in its relationship to the *Metamorphoses* as a whole and to the wider literary and philosophical traditions.⁸ If, as Schiesaro argues, Ovid's Phaethon episode represents a polemical destabilisation of Lucretian poetry and philosophy, this increases the likelihood of significance in anti-Ovidian moves by later authors.

The chapter will begin by exploring models of intertextuality, and by thinking about the different types of intertextuality encountered in Flavian epic.⁹ Second, it will explore the tradition of the Phaethon story and Ovid's place in it. It will then lay out Knox's arguments against seeing the Ovidian Phaethon as a hypotext for Nonnus' Phaethon episode and address some of his assumptions. Finally, it will investigate two aspects of kinship between Ovid's Phaethon and that of Nonnus, first the complex framing of the episode, using ecphrasis and prophecy, and second the poetics of playfulness, temporality, childhood, and succession, key themes in both versions.¹⁰ It will conclude by suggesting further similarities and ways of approaching the relationship, and wider interactions between Latin epic and imperial Greek epic.

1 Intertextuality

The Kristevan model of intertextuality suggests that all texts are constituted of recombinations of other texts, whether intentionally or not.¹¹ Classicists have long been more interested in allusion, the deliberate reference to previous texts,

---

7 For a detailed explanation and assessment of Knox's arguments see below, especially n. 45. Creative engagement, or intertextuality, may not necessarily imply a detailed re-reading of the Latin text of Ovid at the point of writing. There are many ways that texts are recalled in other texts, both conscious and unconscious, mediated and unmediated.
8 See in particular Schiesaro 2014 and Feldherr 2016.
9 For recent approaches to intertextuality in Flavian epic see Coffee/Forstall/Galli Milic/Nelis 2020.
10 Framing is difficult to pin down in intertextual terms, like structure, but is an important aspect of how literary texts work: for recent discussion of frames in their breaking see Matzner/Trimble 2020. Lovatt 2020a addresses the difficulties of analysing structural intertextuality, along with the importance of narrative transitions.
11 Kristeva 1980 [1966]; see further Martínez Alfaro 1996. The introduction to Coffee/Forstall/Galli Milic/Nelis 2020 contains useful reflection on Kristeva's concept and its use in studies of Greek and Latin literature.

which explicitly positions the author in dialogue with their predecessors, and negotiates a place in a tradition.¹² The question of whether or not the author intended an allusion can always be reinterred in studies of intertextuality through the question of which coincidences of verbal choice and ideas are considered significant. This question, though, does place more power in the hands of readers, both reconstructed ancient readers and actual traditions of reading texts, even if both often stand in for the personal judgements of the critics themselves.¹³ As canons are diversified, and communities of readers formed for less well-studied groups of texts, possibilities open up for intertextual significance formerly considered unlikely, unimportant or too difficult. The question of whether Nonnus could or did read Ovid will always remain unprovable: but the text of the *Dionysiaca* and the text of the *Metamorphoses* will always attract readers to consider them together. Given the enormous amount of Latin and Greek literature that did not survive, it is always possible that other texts were also present in these intertextual webs.¹⁴ This does not rule out meaningful similarities between extant texts, however. Just as texts which do not have a secure chronological relationship can still be read meaningfully together, and produce enriching narratives of their relationship, so can intertextuality between traditions that may share common ancestors.¹⁵ The complexity of addressing allusion between different languages adds to this challenge: current digital tools do not straightforwardly support this, but undoubtedly allusion and intertextuality does exist between different languages, whether through the medium of translation or not.¹⁶

Intertextuality can also function as a type of reception. As Hardie 2013 shows, traditions, especially conscious references, show how earlier texts are read and received (and valorised), as first-century-CE epic shows the early Ver-

---

12 Most importantly, Hinds 1998 discusses the differences. Hardie 1993 is a case study in epic poets as self-conscious successors.
13 Fish 1980 argues for the importance of communities of readers in authorising interpretations.
14 Netz 2020 estimates that 2% of Greek literature survives; Gibson (forthcoming) suggests that only 5% of pre-200 CE Latin literature survives, but that it is a relatively good sample of literary culture (that prestige and popularity largely coincided). Ovid is clearly popular and prestigious in late antique Latin literature and visual culture, so despite the possibility of unattested lost versions of the Phaethon episode, there is still reasonable likelihood that writers and readers would be aware of Ovid's version, even if through oral or visual culture rather than reading it themselves.
15 The case for 'productiveness' as a measure of a meaningful relationship is made for Statius and Silius in Lovatt 2010.
16 On interlingual intertextual analysis see Hinds 2020 and Jolowicz 2021.

gilian reception.[17] It is therefore also worth thinking about patterns of behaviour in constructions of literary traditions.[18] Crucially, citation practices do not necessarily reflect actual influences and use of material. Authors, consciously or unconsciously, are much more likely to acknowledge and explicitly cite texts that are perceived as high status and authoritative, 'classic' texts, or 'code models,' while not explicitly acknowledging low status proximate or competitor texts, unless to assert their superiority to them.[19] So Silius explicitly signals his allegiance and debt to Vergil's *Aeneid* but does not explicitly acknowledge his use of Valerius Flaccus and Statius to anywhere near the same degree, even though it is widespread and important.[20] Ovid takes an interesting position in this tradition, a classic, but a subversive classic.[21] Imperial Greek epic, then, may well be using Latin epic without signalling its use.[22] Creators of cultural products are themselves idiosyncratic readers, often aware of their audience's reluctance or resistance.

Flavian epic is particularly useful and interesting for this exercise, because its intertextuality is complex, varied, and thematically similar to that of Nonnus. Silius, for instance, is much less reliant on direct verbal allusion than others, practising tactics of avoidance and tangential echo, while signalling allegiance in other ways. For instance, Wilson characterises Silian intertextuality as follows:

---

[17] Reception theory offers many metaphors and approaches for thinking about indirect or complex relationships between cultural products, including masked reference, shadows, and recognisable images. For a useful recent summary, see Apostol and Bakogianni 2018.

[18] On scholarly canon formation see Grafton/Most 2016. On the function of canons as justifying avoidance of texts see Most 1990. For a quantitative analysis of ancient literary culture see Netz 2020.

[19] For instance, in the Argonaut tradition, later writers are much more likely to acknowledge Apollonius or Robert Graves in paratextual material, and much less likely to mention Apollodorus or Nathaniel Hawthorne. At different periods, different versions are considered authoritative, for instance the *Heroides* in the late medieval and early modern period, or the *Orphic Argonautica* for Charles Kingsley, who considered it to be an authentically early text. On Kingsley see Lovatt 2020b; on the Argonaut tradition generally, Lovatt 2021. See also Kersten, this volume, on the complexity of the ancient Argonaut tradition.

[20] On the interrelationships of Flavian epic see Manuwald/Voigt 2013.

[21] On Ovid and repetition: Fulkerson/Stover 2016; for an overview of the reception of Ovid see Miller/Newlands 2014, including articles on later epic poetry, Keith 2014b, and Late Antiquity, Fielding 2014; the focus is on the Latin tradition, as in the edited volume Consolino 2018, including Roberts 2018 on the Phaethon episode. Ovid's widespread presence in late antique Latin culture is clear.

[22] Gärtner 2005 argues that possible Vergilian echoes in Quintus Smyrnaeus should be examined on a case by case basis.

[Silius] tends to eschew signposting his intertexts by the technique of 'quotation,' that is, by repeating complete phrases or other word collocations from earlier poems. He prefers to signal the intertextual connection by alternative means, in particular, by coincidence of situation and detail rather than wording and, occasionally, by more explicit hints. Most of the time he has multiple intertexts in mind, prose as well as verse.[23]

Silian Ovidianism is complex and multi-faceted, and can provide a useful model for thinking about complex possible relationships between imperial Greek epic and earlier Latin traditions.[24] In some circumstances, Silius takes material from Ovid, and re-writes a scene or story already told by the Augustan poet, such as his re-use of Ovid's story of Anna Perenna (8.44–201) from *Fasti* (3.523–696).[25] On other occasions, he takes Ovidian elements and modes, but uses content not in Ovid, such as the origin of Falernian wine (*Pun.* 7.166–211), which brings together elements from the Baucis and Philemon episode (*Met.* 8.624–724) with Ovid's account of Hyrieus (*Fasti* 5.495–544). Silius also transforms non-Ovidian material into Ovidian shapes, such as the myth of the rape of Pyrene (3.415–441) or reuses Ovidian ideas and phrasing in non-Ovidian contexts, as we will examine below in the way that Pacuvius' speech at Capua adapts Phoebus' advice to Phaethon.

2 The Myth of Phaethon

The myth of Phaethon is resonant for both poetics and politics: Apollo as the god of poetry drives the chariot of song. Phaethon desires to legitimate his status as a true son of Apollo, an image of both poetic and political inheritance.[26] This chapter focuses on the poetics of inheritance, repetition, and control in the

---

[23] Wilson 2004, 226. See also Gärtner's contribution to this volume, which assesses the situation in the light of more recent research and evaluates the productiveness of different approaches.

[24] Bernstein 2016 broadly substantiates Wilson's position, using quantitative analytical methods, which show that after Vergil, Ovid and Lucan are the Latin poets whose words are most often echoed by Silius. Lucan and Silius are also the most Ovidian in language of Ovid's Latin epic successors (Bernstein suggests that the high scores for Ausonius' *Mosella* and the *Ilias Latina* result primarily from shared re-use of Vergil). Silius' relationship to his contemporary epic poets is closest with Statius' *Achilleid* (possibly an outlier due to its short length); their intermediate position between heavy re-use and the dissimilarity of other genres (satire, for instance) suggests his studied avoidance of too much verbal reminiscence.

[25] On the Anna Perenna episode in Silius and Ovid see McIntyre 2019.

[26] On Phaethon imagery and Roman imperial politics see Closs 2020, 13–15.

Phaethon episode. Ovid's Phaethon episode is well-known and influential. Set as it is across the boundary of books 1 and 2 of the *Metamorphoses*, it plays with poetic structure, and showcases Ovid's cosmic reach.[27]

The story of Phaethon is "surprisingly absent" from early extant sources of Greek myth.[28] There is no mention of this Phaethon in the Hesiodic *Catalogue of Women*, although Hyginus attributes the motif of the tears of his sisters turning into electrum to Hesiod (*Fab.* 154).[29] Fragments survive of a *Heliades* of Aeschylus, probably set in the court of Helios. Euripides' lost *Phaethon* shows many points of contact with the Ovidian version, including Phaethon's location among the *Aethiopes* ("Aethiopians"), his need for reassurance on his parentage, the favour owed by Helios, the fateful drive, with Helios advising. Most of the early evidence is compatible with Ovid's version, so it is hard to point to anything that is distinctively Ovidian in the mythemes of the preserved tradition (but this could be because Ovid has so dominated the interpretation that other versions have been suppressed). For instance, Hyginus, *Fab.* 152A preserves a very different story, where Phaethon is the legitimate son of Helios, and steals the chariot without his father's permission, helped by his sisters, and falls out of the chariot in terror rather than being struck down by a thunderbolt. Gantz suggests that this could reflect an early version, as it corresponds with hints elsewhere of mixture and combining versions, and he prefers an Aeschylean rather than a Hesiodic origin.[30] The lack of pre-Roman artistic evidence for the Phaethon story might also suggest Ovid's importance in popularising the story.[31]

Euripides' *Phaethon* focuses more on marriage than paternity and chariot-driving, as far as one can tell. It is set in the kingdom of Merops amongst the Aethiopes, and hinges on Clymene's concealment of Phaethon's divine paternity, which seems to be leading towards a potentially incestuous marriage. The

---

27 Feldherr 2016 reads Ovid's Phaethon episode as a play on representation and reality, which reconfigures Ovid's presentation of poetic temporality. Previous important readings include: Schiesaro 2014 on Ovid's intertextual rivalry with Lucretius; Barchiesi 2009 on Ovid's licentious vision and monstrosity; Holzberg 1998 on book divisions; Brown 1987 on the palace of the Sun.
28 Gantz 1993, 31–34.
29 There is a mention in Hesiod's *Theogony* 986–991 of a Phaethon who is the son of Eos and Cephalos and is abducted by Aphrodite, but the consensus now follows Diggle 1970, 3–32, 180-220 who argues that the two Phaethontes are separate mythological figures. The wedding song at 227–239 of Euripides' *Phaethon* does hint at a connection with Aphrodite beyond that of her role as sponsor of love and marriages in general, though, perhaps suggesting that the two Phaethontes were at least sometimes conflated. The hymn to the Dawn in the first surviving choral ode might also evoke this alternative parentage.
30 Gantz 1993, 33.
31 Gantz 1993, 34.

denouement involves Merops' discovery of Phaethon's death and his parentage, and Oceanus' rescue of Clymene herself, whose life is under threat. While many features of Ovid's plot match Euripides' version of the myth, his narrative focus seems to be very different. Aeschylus' *Heliades*, in contrast, is much more fragmentary but seems to have been set in the court of Helios. It is hard to tell if Ovid drew his narrative framework from Aeschylus, but Phaethon's journey across the boundaries of book 1 and 2, the emphasis on his failed attempt to pass into adulthood, and his lack of interest in erotic themes seem to mark him out from previous extant versions.

Ovid's Phaethon episode is a key part of his self-fashioning as an epic poet.[32] Phaethon's quest is one for both legitimacy and knowledge, the quest of one who fails to follow in the footsteps of his father. He enters the world of didactic poetry made concrete, as the monsters in the stars come to life.[33]

Cuppo Csaki argues that both the Euripidean version, and possible Hellenistic versions, as alluded to in Catullus and Vergil, portray Phaethon as a young man, about to be married. There seems to have been a tradition where he was best known for his love of his companion Cycnus. Ovid's Phaethon is distinctly more child-like: his quarrel with Epaphus arises over a game; he is at first dependent on his mother for his self-esteem, and then transfers this dependency onto Apollo. His lightness in the chariot makes it impossible for him to drive effectively. Ovid's main theme is not the death of a young but capable charioteer, cut off in his prime in the moment before he is married, but the irresponsible ambition of a boy to rival his father, who himself is unable to refuse the request. Ovid's version is characterised by a playful tone, emphasising the callous and capricious nature of the universe. The ecphrasis of the Palace of the Sun brings out the importance of imagery of order and chaos, especially the Seasons and ordered temporality.

The cosmic significance of Phaethon, cause of the apocalypse by fire which matches the flood of book 1, is also developed in Flavian epic, especially Valerius Flaccus, who constantly brings out the cosmic and historic nature of the Argonauts' voyage (which itself has close connections with Phaethon, both by passing near the location of his fall, and by his descent from Helios, shared with Aeetes).[34]

Flavian receptions of Phaethon bring out Ovid's distinctive focus and themes: inheritance and degeneration; cosmic disorder; ecphrasis and framing;

---

32 Schiesaro 2014, 74.
33 Barchiesi 2009, 164.
34 On Valerius' cosmic poetics see Krasne 2018.

repetition and succession. Valerius Flaccus includes the Phaethon episode in his ecphrasis of the temple of the sun in book 5 (407–456). This ecphrasis describes the viewing experience of Jason and the Argonauts, concealed in mist as they arrive in Colchis, after meeting Medea, who here functions as a mixture of Vergil's Venus and the Homeric Nausicaa, and before meeting Aeetes in the temple itself. The description of the temple evokes Ovid's palace of the Sun: for instance, 5.408–410 describes the overwhelming brightness of the building as reflecting the face of the god himself, and then moves on to the description of the engraved double doors (416–418). Ovid too emphasises the brightness of the palace:

> *clara micante auro flammasque imitante pyropo,*
> *cuius ebur nitidum fastigia summa tegebat,*
> *argenti bifores radiabant lumine valvae.*
> *Met.* 2.2–4

> gleaming with bright gold and imitating flames with red-gold bronze,
> whose highest peaks shining ivory covered,
> and the doubled doors were glittering with silver.[35]

Then, he moves on to describe the double doors. Ovid's Phaethon too is overwhelmed by the brightness of Phoebus' face, and cannot go too close (*Met.* 2.22–24). Phaethon is present in the description of the doors, bridging the transition from the origins of Colchis to Vulcan's portrayal of the Argonautic expedition itself. As a version of Vergil's Icarus, Phaethon provides an image of the dead beautiful boy, which here foreshadows the death of Apsyrtus:

> *flebant populeae iuvenem Phaethonta sorores*
> *ater et Eridani trepidum globus ibat in amnem;*[36]
> *at iuga vix Tethys sparsumque recolligit axem*
> *et formidantem patrios Pyroenta dolores.*
> VF 5.429–432

> The poplar sisters were weeping for young Phaethon
> and the black ball was hurtling towards the terrified river Eridanus,
> but Tethys scarcely gathered together the yoke and the scattered axle
> and the horse Pyroes, fearful of paternal griefs.

---

35 Translations of ancient texts are my own unless otherwise noted.
36 The image of Phaethon's body as *globus*, while showing his objectification in death, also suggests his role as an alternative solar god, setting in the waters of the river Eridanus and setting them visually on fire. See *OLD* 2a on *globus* as the sphere of a heavenly body.

Valerius highlights grief and mourning, in line with this ecphrasis' focus on horror and loss, and Ovid's emphasis on the grief of Phoebus (*Met.* 2.381–400): both the Colchians and the Minyae respond negatively (VF 5.454: *odere*; VF 5.455: *Minyas operum defixerat horror*), in ignorance echoing Aeneas' response to his shield, in misery reversing Aeneas' response to the temple of Juno. The fear of the chariot-horse Pyroes at the grief of Phoebus is an intertextual memory of Sol's anger and savagery towards his horses in Ovid as he gathers them back together (*Met.* 2.398–400).[37] Cosmic imagery persists in Valerius' description of Tethys gathering together *iuga* ("chariot yoke," "equinox") and *axem* ("axis," "axle"), the coming together of sun and ocean. So Valerius combines and compresses different elements of Ovid's episode to incorporate it in miniature as a work of art in his own poem. Similarly, he incorporates the previous episode of the *Metamorphoses*, the story of Io, in the previous book, as a song of Orpheus, sung while the Argo passes through the Bosphorus (VF 4.344–422). Structurally, the two stories cover moments of liminality, transgression, and arrival. Likewise, Ovid's Phaethon straddles the first two books, and portrays a failed initiation into adulthood and divinity, along with a potential undoing of the cosmic order created in book 1.

Ovid's emphasis on failed emulation, poor substitutes, and degenerate descent is also characteristic of the apotropaic humble-bragging of Flavian epic poetics, exemplified by the figure of Polynices in Statius' chariot race (*Thebaid* 6), another version of Phaethon.[38] Polynices is twice compared to Phaethon, in similes that signal the intertextual relationship (6.320–325; 12.413–415). In book 6, Polynices is about to take over driving his father-in-law Adrastus' horses in the chariot race. Adrastus offers him advice on how to control the horses, but, like Phaethon, Polynices is fated not to learn (6.316–320). The lead horse Arion stands in for all four, and the horses immediately recognise that Polynices is not their accustomed driver. At 6.424–431, Arion actively flees from Polynices, whom he perceives to be truly the son of Oedipus, not the son of Adrastus. Polynices' attempt to become Argive and Adrastus' heir fundamentally fails: his failure to control the chariot foreshadows his failure to control the expedition. But Statius also reverses the Phaethon episode: Apollo here is actively opposing Polynices, who is racing against his two favourites, Admetus and Amphiaraus. It is Phoebus' monstrous effigy that causes Polynices' near fatal chariot wreck (6.491–512). Statius laments that Polynices lives, imagining an alternative future in which he had died here, the war was prevented, and his grave was wor-

---

37 Ovid uses the name Pyroes at *Met.* 2.153, along with Eous, Aethon, and Phlegon. Wijsman 1996, 210 points out that this name is picked up by Claudian in his *Amores* (*Carm. min.* 25.140).
38 On Polynices and Phaethon see Lovatt 2005, 32–39.

shipped (6.513–517). This anti-immortalisation foreshadows the final Phaethon simile in book 12 where Argia (his wife) and Antigone are compared to the Heliades as they wash Polynices' body and make him beautiful again (12.413–415). This plays with the combined tragic traditions of Phaethon as bridegroom who is also brother. In combination, these two similes cast the whole poem as a "Phaethontic failed initiation," in which Polynices begins by journeying to a new palace and ends as a corpse to be lamented. Throughout, Statius looks through Ovid to his Greek predecessors, especially Euripides, but also Homer (Nestor's advice to Antilochus), by recasting Phaethon as part of a chariot race.

Ovid has long been seen as a key influence on Silius, and Bruère argues that Ovid's Phaethon episode underpins a father's attempt to dissuade his son from assassinating Hannibal in Capua (11.303–368).[39] He bases his argument on both verbal and structural similarities. At the very beginning of the episode, programmatically, Silius' text evokes Ovid's take-home point, his epitaph for Phaethon:

Hic situs Phaethon currus auriga paterni
*quem si non tenuit **magnis tamen** excidit **ausis***
    Met. 2.327–328

Here lies Phaethon, driver of his father's chariot
which if he did not hold straight, nevertheless fell out with great daring.

neque enim, iuvenis non digne sileri,
tramittam tua coepta libens famamque negabo
*quamquam imperfectis, **magnae tamen** indolis **ausis**.*
    Pun. 11.304–306

For I will not willingly pass over your undertakings, young man
Not worthy of silence, and I will not deny you fame
Although unfinished, nevertheless your darings showed inborn greatness.

This verbal reminiscence is clear, in the same metrical position, and consisting of three matching words.[40] A further signal comes with his transitional use of the name Phaethon at the dawn of the next day: *postera lux Phaethontis equos*

---

39 Bruère 1959.
40 Nonnus also adapts the epitaph of Phaethon, outside his Phaethon episode, for the Indian Orontes, at 17.313–314, as Carvounis/Papaioannou (forthcoming, 2022) 142–143 argue, by including an explicit formulaic epigram, with the "here lies" formula, for a character who falls into a river and is lamented by nymphs. The tangential nature of this intertextual relationship is very similar to that of Silius, including Orontes' use of Clymene in his speech to Helios. This adaptation arguably reconfigures Phaethon's mission as suicidal.

proferre parabat ("the next day was preparing to send out the horses of Phaethon," *Pun.* 11.369). Bruère suggests that "Phaethon lingers in Silius' memory" here.⁴¹ The similarities of structure, rhetoric, and repeated motifs are also persuasive.

Pacuvius attempts to dissuade his son in two speeches (332–350 and 353–360), just as Phoebus makes two speeches to Phaethon (50–102 and 126–149), first pleading with him not to risk his life, then accepting his decision and advising him.⁴² The end of Pacuvius' first speech is strikingly similar to Ovid, but without re-using words: *parce oro, et desine velle* ("hold off, I beg, and cease to want," *Pun.* 11.348); *sed tu sapientius opta* ("but you, desire more wisely," *Met.* 2.102). Silius' evocation of Ovid's Phaethon episode is disputed in similar terms to that of Knox's dismissal of Nonnus' connection to Ovid. Matier disagrees with Bruère, arguing that Silius' mention of Phaethon and the circumstantial details are not enough to make the link with Ovid in particular.⁴³ Given Silius' deep engagement with Ovid, however, Bruère's argument is persuasive, even if intertextuality cannot be proved. Strikingly, Silius uses the resemblance to Phaethon primarily to reverse it. Pacuvius emphasises the overwhelming nature of Hannibal's divine gaze, as of an Apollo (337–340), which will extinguish the fiery gaze of Pacuvius' son (327–328), who cannot in the end go through with his assassination. Silius ironically links this back to Phaethon with a reference to his failed daring and lack of fame: *amisit quantam posito conamine* **laudem**, / *cui tantum est* **voluisse** *decus!* ("how much praise did he lose when he set aside this undertaking, him for whom even wanting such a great thing was glorious," *Punica* 11.365–366).

We can see here many different modes and ploys of intertextual engagement: hypotexts are contained within the main narrative as ecphrases, similes or inset stories, even temporal references; predecessors are miniaturised, set up as underlying paradigms, reversed, tangentially referenced, ironically avoided. Often we lack a smoking gun to determine without reasonable doubt that it is Ovid's Phaethon which these references evoke, rather than the Phaethon story, or the tradition as a whole. But given the prominence and importance of Ovid's works in Flavian epic, we can gain powerful and productive metapoetic narra-

---

41 Bruère 1959, 233.
42 This two-speech structure is also present in Nonnus, but is dismissed by Knox as a potential reference to Ovid because of its similarity to the structure of the same scene in Euripides' *Phaethon*.
43 "But this proves nothing. The story of Phaethon is well known in Roman poetry." Matier 1979, 381.

tives by putting the two together. If Ovid uses Phaethon as an antitype of his own poetic flight, an avatar of imperial ambition destroyed, Valerius sets his Argonauts in the same context of unwarranted confidence, in company with Statius' Polynices; Silius' reversal and transference is the most oblique and difficult to interpret, perhaps suggesting that the real Phaethon of his *Punica* is Hannibal, trying unsuccessfully to inhabit a divine role.

3 Knox's arguments against Ovidian intertextuality in Nonnus' Phaethon episode

Peter Knox sets out to disprove the argument that Nonnus used Ovid in the composition of his Phaethon episode, a case made by Braune in 1935.[44] Throughout he displays a dismissive attitude towards Nonnus.[45] His fundamental argument is that similarities with Ovid, even proposed verbal parallels, are not enough to prove intentional allusion because they could equally have been drawn from other sources. He usefully outlines the way that Nonnus creates thematic coherence and strong intratextual links between this episode and other parts of his own poem. However, intratextuality does not exclude intertextuality: why could not Nonnus have evoked the same moment in Ovid more

---

44 Knox 1988; Braune 1935.
45 Knox 1988: for instance, Nonnus "contrives" a different opening (538); Clymene's blush is an "infelicitous recasting" of 18.352–353 (539), which he also calls "indiscreet borrowing." He casts doubt on whether Nonnus can be held to have an original vision: "Nonnus' own imagination (if that is the proper word)" (539). This disparagement seems often to be juxtaposed with and slip into assertions that Nonnus cannot have a relationship with Ovid: such as on *Met.* 2.260–262, where Ovid's Helios emphasises that even Jupiter could not drive the chariot, and Nonnus at 38.200–211 expands the idea into a list of gods who could not handle his role. Knox observes that "Nonnus' wordy account contributes nothing to the point" and calls the passage "a pastiche of words and phrases repeated from other points in the *Dionysiaca*" (245–246). Here Nonnus emphasises and expands the divine element in Ovid's account, as Paschalis 2014 demonstrates, in relation to Nonnus' portrayal of metamorphosis. Later Knox argues that Nonnus' astronomy is a "simple display of erudition, irrelevant to the progress of the narrative," and for this reason cannot be prompted by Ovid's, since Ovid "accurately portrays the route Phaethon must take." Broadly the underlying argument seems to be that Nonnus is not as good as Ovid, therefore he cannot have been inspired by Ovid. This is perhaps an uncharitable interpretation, since the article starts by asserting that previous scholarly traditions overestimated Nonnus' reliance on Ovid because they were dismissive about his poetic skills and originality, but the tradition of dismissiveness is hard to shake off.

than once? Similarly, showing that Nonnus' version of Phoebus' speeches to Phaethon draws on Euripides does not preclude these speeches also drawing on (or evoking) Ovid, just as showing that some of Ovid's conceits are paralleled in Greek epigram does not preclude evocation of Ovid as well. Some readers may prioritise one similarity, others may primarily see the other. The concept of window allusion is useful here, where Nonnus may be referring to Euripides through Ovid.[46] It seems likely that Nonnus' poems would appeal to both monolingual and bi/multilingual readers, both in the ancient world and in later periods. The fact that Ovid's reference to the fire of love in competition with the fires of the sun is embedded in a Phaethon narrative might well make it more likely to come to mind than a stand-alone epigram. Knox also points out Nonnus' use of descriptions in prose works of astrological phenomena: but intertextuality can be seen as a web, with different threads combined in creative tension with each other; one joy of its complexity comes from the combination of different materials.[47] It is true that there are many differences between the two versions, but these differences, too, help to generate meaning in comparison.

4 Avoidance, tangential connections, and miniaturisation

In fact, avoidance of exact repetitions suggests a keen awareness of the other version. Nonnus avoids not just Ovid's catalogues of mountains set on fire and rivers dried up, he also steers clear of Apollo's grief and the transformation of the Heliades, even though Hermes' initial description of the story suggests that this is the main point of the retelling. We can see this in Hermes' introduction to the story of Phaethon:

"τηλίκον οὔ ποτε θαῦμα γέρων τροφὸς ἤγαγεν Αἰών,   90
ἐξ ὅτε δαιμονίοιο πυρὸς βεβολημένος ἀτμῷ
κύμβαχος Ἠελίοιο φεραυγέος ἔκπεσε δίφρου
ἡμιδαὴς Φαέθων, ποταμῷ δ' ἐκρύπτετο Κελτῷ·
καὶ θρασὺν ἡβητῆρα παρ' ὀφρύσιν Ἠριδανοῖο
Ἠλιάδες κινυροῖσιν ἔτι στενάχουσι πετήλοις."   95

---

46 The concept of a window allusion or window reference, through one text to an earlier text, is itself an Ovidian intertextual tactic: see Thomas 1986; McKeown 1987, 37–45; Cowan 2017, 17.
47 Smolenaars 1994 persuasively sets out the multiplicity of Statian intertextuality in his introduction.

Ὣς φαμένου Διόνυσος ἐγήθεεν ἐλπίδι νίκης·
Ἑρμείαν δ' ἐρέεινε, καὶ ἤθελε μᾶλλον ἀκοῦσαι
Κελτοῖς Ἑσπερίοισι μεμηλότα μῦθον Ὀλύμπου,
πῶς Φαέθων κεκύλιστο δι' αἰθέρος, ἢ πόθεν αὐταὶ
Ἡλιάδες παρὰ χεῦμα γοήμονος Ἠριδανοῖο   100
εἰς φυτὸν ἠμείβοντο, καὶ εὐπετάλων ἀπὸ δένδρων
δάκρυα μαρμαίροντα κατασταλάουσι ῥεέθροις.

D. 38.90–102

"So great a marvel ancient eternal Time our foster-father has never brought, since Phaethon, struck by the steam of fire divine, fell tumbling half-burnt from Helios's lightbearing chariot, and was swallowed up in the Celtic river; and the daughters of Helios are still on the banks of Eridanus, lamenting the audacious youth with their whimpering leaves." At these words, Dionysos rejoiced in hope of victory; then he questioned Hermes and wished to hear more of the Olympian tale which the Celts of the west know well: how Phaethon tumbled over and over through the air, and why even the daughters of Helios were changed into trees beside the moaning Eridanus, and from their leafy trees drop sparkling tears into the stream. (tr. Rouse 1940)

This tangential connection from the ominous eclipse to the Phaethon story, via the agency of Time, is highly Ovidian. Ovid connects together the Io story and the Phaethon story through the equal ages of Epaphus and Phaethon, which leads to their quarrel over divine ancestry, and seems to have been Ovid's invention. Hermes' summary of the Phaethon story, focusing on the fall of Phaethon's burnt-up body, like a comet, and his sisters' grief, bears remarkable similarity to Valerius' ecphrastic summary, suggesting it equates to ancient perceptions of the main point of Ovid's version. But the end of Hermes' (and Nonnus') long inset narrative in fact miniaturises and avoids this aspect of the story, just as Ovid miniaturises and avoids his epic predecessors (for instance, Catullus 64 or the *Aeneid*). This marked avoidance suggests to me that Ovid was an important reference point. Nonnus' story of Phaethon runs from 38.105 to the end of the book at 38.434, so is substantial at over 300 lines, but the death of Phaethon and the transformation of the Heliades take only two and three lines respectively (38.410–411; 38.432–434; 2.340–366 in Ovid). This miniaturisation stands in the final few lines of the book, capping Phaethon's own transformation into the constellation Auriga (38.424–428) along with that of the river into the Milky Way (429–431), making metamorphosis the final point, but not Ovid's metamorphoses. Nonnus takes a different track from Ovid. Silius also uses the intertextual tactic of miniaturisation, for instance when he turns the whole of Statius' *Thebaid* into two brothers fighting, killing, and refusing to stop hating each other even in death, in his games (*Punica* 16.546–548).[48] The poetics of expansion and contraction, immeasurable size and inconsequential smallness, are prominent in Flavian epic, for instance in Statius' Opheltes episode, where a baby replaces an epic hero.[49]

5 Framing and ecphrasis

The ending of Nonnus' Phaethon story resembles Ovid's in some ways (by finishing with a collection of different metamorphoses) but not in others (all the metamorphoses are performed by Zeus, Helios' grief is absent, and the overwhelming tone is one of joy at order restored). In Ovid, too, Jupiter tours the *cosmos* re-establishing order, but this is included in the narrative to allow his predatory gaze to fall on Callisto, leading into the next episode. Ovid's ending of the Phaethon episode, then, matches Nonnus' beginning, where Phoebus falls in love with Clymene when he catches sight of her in the ocean.

The beginning of *Dionysiaca* 38 also evokes Ovid and Flavian epic, as Nonnus plays with narrative frames. Book 37 features a set of epic games, which are held in honour of a dead character called Opheltes, like those of Statius in *Thebaid* 6. As in Statius, the games finish at the end of the book, and the following opening section reflects on the delay of the poem's central war:

> ἐπεὶ τότε κυκλάδι νύσσῃ
> Μυγδονίου πολέμοιο καὶ Ἰνδῴοιο κυδοιμοῦ
> ἀμβολίην ἐτάνυσσεν ἕλιξ χρόνος· οὐδέ τις αὐτοῖς
> οὐ φόνος, οὐ τότε δῆρις· ἔκειτο δὲ τηλόθι χάρμης
> Βακχιὰς ἑξαέτηρος ἀραχνιόωσα βοείη.
>
> *D.* 38.10–14

For then Time rolling in his ambit prolonged the truce of combat and strife between Indians and Mygdonians; there was no carnage among them then, no conflict, and the shield which Bacchus had borne for six years lay far from the battle covered with spiders' webs. (tr. Rouse 1940)

---

48 See further Lovatt 2010.
49 The poetics of expansion and contraction are already important in earlier Greek literature, such as Pindar and Callimachus, both of whom were influential on Statius. See Brown 1994, McNelis 2007, and Soerink 2014. Nonnus takes it to new levels: it would make sense to see him building on Ovid and Flavian poetry in his expansion of the sublimity of contrasting size.

The motif of delaying the war is central to the beginning of *Thebaid* 7, where Jupiter forcibly re-starts it, by sending Mercury to the palace of Mars in the far North, evoking Ovid's transitional ecphrasis from books 1 to 2 via the palace of the Sun. Similarly, the *Aeneid* moves from the games in book 5 to the ecphrasis of the temple at Cumae at the beginning of book 6, delaying the Trojans' arrival at Latium. These lines of Nonnus gesture towards possible transitional ecphrases: the shield lies unused (already re-worked by Nonnus in book 25) covered in the threads of Arachne (whose weaving Dionysus admires like a tourist at 40.298–303).

Instead, omens and prophecies frame this delay as a new beginning: dawn and a new year (the seventh of the war) are marked first by an eclipse of the sun (here called *Phaethon*, 38.19) accompanied by meteor showers (that foreshadow Phaethon's disintegrating chariot), storms, and Hyperion's eventual return, stronger than before. This omen is doubled by another of an eagle and a snake, in which the flying eagle drops the snake into the river Hydaspes.[50] These two omens, both apparently negative, are then interpreted by the prophet Idmon, whose expertise comes from his knowledge of the cosmos, particularly the sun and moon. These scenes are reminiscent of the sequence in Valerius Flaccus 1, where Jason first responds to the dark and ominous ecphrasis of the Argo, then sees an omen of an eagle carrying off a lamb, which he interprets as an endorsement of his plan to persuade Acastus to join the expedition, and then mediates between the double prophecies of Mopsus and Idmon as they interpret a pyromancy.[51] Mopsus presents a dark, incomprehensible, and maddened interpretation, while Idmon is the avatar of optimism, calm, and knowledgeable. This double prophecy is not in either Apollonius or the *Orphic Argonautica*, but is matched by Statius' duo of augurs in *Thebaid* 3.[52] Valerius introduces Idmon as untrembling: *sed enim contra Phoebeius Idmon / non pallore virens, non ullo horrore comarum / terribilis, plenus fatis Phoeboque quieto* ("but then in replying Idmon, Phoebus' son, not pale with sickly fear, nor terrible to look upon with

---

[50] This omen probably originates from the Homeric omen at *Iliad* 12.200–209, where an eagle carrying a monstrous snake drops it after being bitten. Polydamas interprets it as a negative omen for the Trojans. Nonnus reverses it by interpreting it as negative for Dionysus' enemy, not for him.

[51] Zissos 2008, 198 points out that Valerius follows Apollonius in making him son of Apollo. The idea that he was known as son of Abas, but was really the son of Apollo, combines the other tradition of his parentage, first attested in Herodorus (*FGrH* 31F44).

[52] Lovatt 2012. In the *Orphic Argonautica* at 187–191, Idmon is both son and pupil of Apollo. Livrea 2014 argues that *Orphic Argonautica* was before Nonnus, but also that the evidence for direct influence of the *Orphic Argonautica* on Nonnus is weak.

upstanding hair, but replete with fate and the calm influence of Phoebus...," VF 1.228–230).⁵³ Nonnus' Idmon too is not afraid:

> καὶ τρομερὴ νήριθμον ὅλον στρατὸν εἶχε σιωπή·
> Ἴδμων δ' αἰολόμητις, ἐπεὶ μάθεν ὄργια Μούσης
> Οὐρανίης εὔκυκλον ἐπισταμένης ἴτυν ἄστρων,
> ἄτρομος ἵστατο μοῦνος, ἐπεὶ μάθεν Ἴδμονι τέχνῃ
> συμπλεκέος Φαέθοντι κατάσκια κύκλα Σελήνης
>
> D. 38.30–34

> Trembling silence held all that innumerable host. Idmon alone stood untrembling, Idmon the treasury of learned lore, for he had been taught the secrets of Urania, the Muse who knows the round circuit of the stars: he had been taught by his learned art the shades on the Moon's orb when in union with the Sun... (tr. Rouse 1940)

The calm and optimism of his approach are founded in his expertise, which here is primarily cosmic. His optimistic interpretation of the cosmic phenomena and the omen is doubled by Erechtheus' request for further explanation (58–69), which gladdens the audience.

This prophecy is then further ratified, expanded, and trumped by Hermes, appearing to Dionysus alone to foretell his victory (78–95). This leads into the story of Phaethon. The figure of Hermes plays multiple roles. He encourages Dionysus to continue his battle, as Statius' Mercury restarts the Theban war of *Thebaid* 7, and Vergil's Mercury restarts Aeneas' mission to Italy in *Aeneid* 4, and takes on the role of storyteller that he plays in Ovid's Io episode of *Metamorphoses* 1. In that episode, the one immediately before Ovid's Phaethon, Hermes' story is a ruse to put Io's guard Argus to sleep, so he can kill him. He begins but does not finish the story of Pan and Syrinx, which is summarised by the narrator. The redundancy of Hermes' story in Nonnus' version plays with the unfinished nature of his story in Ovid, where his role in putting Argus to sleep contrasts with his role as awakener in *Aeneid* 4. There is irony too in the length of his story, which like Statius' version of the Lemnian women told by Hypsipyle, creates narrative delay. While Hypsipyle is traditionally known for delaying the Argonauts and has every reason to want the attention and sponsorship of her Argive listeners, Hermes should be encouraging Dionysus to restart his war, not creating yet more delay, in a chiastic play on Statius' delaying tactics (story-games; games-story). We could see in both of these a glance back

---

53 Zissos 2008, 198–199 points out that 231–233 draw on Apollonius (A.R. 1.144–145), but does not identify a Greek predecessor for 228–230, which he connects rather with the Latin epic tradition, especially Lucan.

to Phoenix's story of Meleager which attempts to persuade Achilles to return to battle in *Iliad* 9, but this thematisation of delay works much more effectively if we view Homer through both Statius and Ovid.

The multiplicity of transitional and framing devices is typical of Nonnus' poetics, and of both Ovidian and Flavian epic. The blurring of the Phaethon story into the surrounding frames creates a sort of osmotic metalepsis which is also highly Statian. Distancing and delay are thematised, reflecting on the belatedness that characterises both Greek and Latin imperial epic. Omens, ecphrasis, and inset stories all share a requirement for intradiegetic interpretation. The obliqueness of Nonnus' Phaethon episode is Ovidian: it is juxtaposed with the games and their Phaethontic chariot race, but it foreshadows Dionysus' victory with a story of defeat and loss. We are not sure why the story is here and how it works thematically. Is Dionysus contrasted with Phaethon or like him? Phaethon is catasterised as Auriga at the end, which turns Phaethon into a potential positive exemplum for Dionysus, memorialised in the heavens.[54] Characteristic of Nonnus is movement to a purely divine level, with Hermes and Dionysus taking the climactic position as narrator and narratee, Zeus taking charge of the concluding metamorphoses, and the confidence of the optimistic interpretations, which ultimately erase the tragic legacies so prevalent in Ovid and Flavian epic. Reading Latin and imperial Greek epic together enriches both.

6 Childhood, playfulness, and descent

One of Ovid's most likely adaptations to the Phaethon tradition is to portray Phaethon as younger and more child-like. Cuppo Csaki argues persuasively that Ovid's Phaethon is likely to have been different from previous versions in his immaturity.[55] Phaethon is introduced as "equal in spirits and age" to Epaphus, son of Io (*animis aequalis et annis*, *Met.* 1.750), and the quarrel that starts the narrative suggests boyishness in its abruptness. Phaethon's response to Epaphus' insult is to blush and carry his anger and shame to his mother, suggesting a reliance on her. The emphasis on marriage in Euripides' *Phaethon* suggests an older young man of marriageable age. The tradition of his love relationship with Cycnus also suggests sexual maturity. Visual representations show him as a

---

[54] The Auriga metamorphosis is not prominent in Ovid, but it is in Claudian, and Loos 2006 argues that Ovid too may have been alluding to it.
[55] Cuppo Csaki 1995, 75–79.

relatively mature youth.⁵⁶ Ovid in contrast emphasises his boyishness: Sol refers to his "boyish years" (*puerilibus annis*, *Met.* 2.55) which make him even less likely to be able to drive the chariot; his physical lightness warns the horses that he is not their true driver (2.150). Cuppo Csaki also points out his emotional volatility: first he is embarrassed and then angry and ashamed at Epaphus' taunt. Then his response to his mother's suggestion that he should go to Sol's palace is characterised by hastiness: *emicat extemplo laetus* ("he flashed up immediately happy," 1.776) and *concipit aethera mente* ("he grasps the heavens in his mind," 1.777), showing his intensity and impulsiveness.

Ovid is particularly interested in children, play, and child-like activities, as Morgan and Cowan have shown.⁵⁷ Morgan argues that "the mode Ovid deploys is typically [epic didacticism's] polar opposite: flippant, playful, and given to puerile sexual humour."⁵⁸ A key example is Ovid's description of Actaeon's viewing of Diana in her bath, which Morgan presents as characterised by "an ethos of mischievous impudence, in the face of figures conventionally deserving of respect: a great man, a goddess, Vergil, Homer" (69). Nonnus chooses to begin his Phaethon episode with the bath of Clymene and continue it with an extensive description of Phaethon's childhood play and his childish replica of the chariot of the sun. Knox argues that this beginning is fundamentally un-Ovidian (there is no version of it in Ovid's account), but in many respects (tone, theme, multiplicity, openness to allegorical reading) it is highly Ovidian. Ovid's 'puerility,' his 'boyisms,' were staples of criticism of his poetry, especially the *Metamorphoses*. The complexity of tone in Ovid is a feature also seen in Flavian epic: an interesting example of this is Silius' catalogue of burnt ships at 14.567– 579.⁵⁹ As in Ovid's catalogue of Actaeon's dogs, or the destruction caused by Phaethon, the aural beauty and order of the catalogue form contrasts with the subject matter of chaos and destruction. Silius mixes the Homeric catalogue of ships, with the burning of ships in both Homer and Vergil, creating an innovative form of the *Todeskette* ("death list") in an Ovidian manner.⁶⁰

Nonnus avoids Ovid's tendentious beginning to the Phaethon episode and the whole theme of inauthentic paternity, but he also avoids Euripides' focus on marriage, potential incest, and the grief of Phaethon's sisters. Instead, he por-

---

56 Cuppo Csaki 1995, 76 citing the Casa Farnesina, Domus Aurea, sarcophagi.
57 Morgan 2003 and Cowan 2017.
58 Morgan 2003, 68.
59 On the poetics of Statius' Opheltes episode see Brown 1994 and Soerink 2014.
60 On this passage as *Todeskette* see Augoustakis 2020.

trays the union between Sun and Ocean, through Tethys' daughter Clymene, as a cosmic phenomenon. He describes Phaethon's play similarly:

> Πολλάκι παιδοκόμοισιν ἐν ἤθεσιν ἁβρὸν ἀθύρων   155
> Ὠκεανὸς Φαέθοντα παλινδίνητον ἀείρων
> γαστρὶ μέσῃ κούφιζε, δι' ὑψιπόρου δὲ κελεύθου
> ἄστατον αὐτοέλικτον ἀλήμονι σύνδρομον αὔρῃ
> ἠερόθεν παλίνορσον ἐδέξατο κοῦρον ἀγοστῷ,
> καὶ πάλιν ἠκόντιζεν· ὁ δὲ τροχοειδέι παλμῷ   160
> χειρὸς ἐυστρέπτοιο παράτροπος Ὠκεανοῖο
> δινωτῇ στροφάλιγγι κατήριπεν εἰς μέλαν ὕδωρ,
> μάντις ἑοῦ θανάτοιο·
>
> D. 38.155–163

Often in the course of the boy's training Oceanus would have a pretty game, lifting Phaethon on his midbelly and letting him drop down; he would throw the boy high in the air, rolling over and over moving in a high path as quick as the wandering wind, and catch him again on his arm; then he would shoot him up again, and the boy would avoid the ready hand of Oceanus, and turn a somersault round and round till he splashed into the dark waters, prophet of his own death. (tr. Rouse 1940)

The boy Phaethon's playful relationship with his grandfather reflects the sun's light interacting with ocean waves, the glitter and fire of sunlight on sea. His erratic motion foreshadows his future chariot-driving, and his fall into water, his death to come. Nonnus gives a playful prelude to the tragic story, just as Statius' games sweat out the war in advance (*quo Martia bellis / praesudare paret... virtus*, "in which martial masculinity prepares to foresweat for battle," Statius, *Theb.* 6.3–4).

We see Nonnus' Phaethon growing through various stages, but he too remains child-like. From conception to birth, to toddler games, we then see him as a "boy hardly grown up and still with no down on his lip" (167-168), creating his own play-chariot:

> πῇ δὲ καὶ αὐτῆς
> Θρινακίης λειμῶνα μετήιεν, ᾗχι θαμίζων
> Λαμπετίῃ παρέμιμνε, βόας καὶ μῆλα νομεύων ...   170
> πατρὸς ἑοῦ ζαθέοιο φέρων πόθον ἡνιοχῆος,
> ἄξονα τεχνήεντι συνήρμοσε δούρασι δεσμῷ,
> κυκλώσας τροχόεντα τύπον ψευδήμονι δίφρῳ·
> ἀσκήσας δὲ λέπαδνα καὶ ἀνθοκόμων ἀπὸ κήπων
> πλέξας λεπταλέοισι λύγοις τριέλικτον ἱμάσθλην   175
> ἀρνειοῖς πισύροισι νέους ἐπέθηκε χαλινούς·
> καὶ νόθον εὐποίητον Ἑωσφόρον ἀστέρα τεύχων
> ἄνθεσιν ἀργεννοῖσιν, ἴσον τροχοειδέι κύκλῳ,

θῆκεν ἑῆς προκέλευθον ἐυκνήμιδος ἀπήνης,
ἀστέρος Ἠῴοιο φέρων τύπον· ἀμφὶ δὲ χαίταις   180
ὄρθιον ἔνθα καὶ ἔνθα φεραυγέα δαλὸν ἐρείσας
ψευδομέναις ἀκτῖσιν ἑὸν μιμεῖτο τοκῆα,
ἱππεύων στεφανηδὸν ἁλίκτυπον ἄντυγα νήσου.

D. 38.168–183

sometimes travelled even to the meadows of Thrinacia, where he would often visit and stay with Lampetie, tending cattle and sheep … There he would long for his father the charioteer divine; made a wooden axle with skilful joinery, fitted on a sort of round wheel for his imitation car, fashioned yoke-straps, took three light withies from the flowering garden and plaited them into a lash, put unheard-of bridles on four young rams. Then he made a clever imitation of the morning star round like a wheel, out of a bunch of white flowers, and fixed it in front of his spokewheeled wagon to show the shape of the star Lucifer. He set burning torches standing about his hair on every side, and mimicked his father with fictitious rays as he drove round and round the coast of the seagirt isle. (tr. Rouse 1940)

Nonnus emphasises the materials of the chariot and their impermanence and lightness (wood, light willow branches, flowers for the morning star). The reference to Thrinacia may also activate the *Odyssey*, perhaps the scene where Odysseus skilfully makes his wooden vessel, also using withies (*Od.* 5.228–262).[61] Where Odysseus reconstructs his identity by therapeutic building, Phaethon expresses his longing to be his father.[62] This reading is enriched by adding Ovid. Phaethon's fake chariot is itself a metaphor for mimicry and emulation, fragile and mortal in comparison with Ovid's ecphrasis of the chariot of Helios:

ergo, qua licuit, genitor cunctatus ad altos   105
deducit iuvenem, Vulcania munera, currus.
aureus axis erat, temo aureus, aurea summae
curvatura rotae, radiorum argenteus ordo;
per iuga chrysolithi positaeque ex ordine gemmae
clara repercusso reddebant lumina Phoebo.   110

Met. 2.105–110

Therefore the father, who had delayed as much as was allowed, led down the
Young man to the high chariot, gift of Vulcan.
Its axle was golden, its pole golden, golden were
Curves of the high wheels, and silver was the array of spokes;

---

61 Ships and chariots are similarly risky forms of transport (Roman chariot crashes are referred to as shipwrecks, Vergil swaps his chariot race for a ship race in *Aeneid* 5), as well as both acting as metaphors for poetic production and control. See Lovatt 2005, 29–32.
62 On Odysseus' therapeutic building see Christensen 2020, Introduction.

Along the yoke were set chrysolites and jewels in a row
Which sent back the bright light when struck by Phoebus.

Ovid's chariot is made by Vulcan, golden, silver and jewelled, precious and permanent. Ovid then follows this ecphrasis with a description of the palace of Aurora and the setting of Lucifer. Nonnus' Phaethon adds additional elements with yoke straps, reins, and rams for horses, but also attempts to replicate the morning star going beforehand with flowers, and the light from the jewels with flaming torches. This fabrication thematises the process of artistic and poetic imitation. The inadequacy of Phaethon's chariot works in apposition to both Odysseus' ship, itself inadequate against ocean storms, and the real chariot of Helios as presented by Ovid.

Nonnus' Phaethon remains child-like as he supplicates his father: even though he is now described as "in the fair bloom of youth" by this point, he still has a "little hand" and is a "playful boy" enjoying petting the horses. He sits on his father's lap and cries imploring tears (190–191), and Helios thinks of him still as "young son" (195). Nonnus intensifies the pathos of the story by making his Phaethon even younger than Ovid's.

The poetics of playfulness subverts masculinity and generic authority: in Nonnus, Dionysus himself is characterised as playful, and the association of child-likeness with mysticism brings out its closeness to the divine. We can see this in both ancient and modern constructions of childhood, exemplified by the famous words of Jesus: "suffer little children and forbid them not to come unto me, for of such is the kingdom of heaven" (New Testament, Matthew 19.14). Nonnus goes beyond Ovid in emphasising the youth and playfulness of his Phaethon, which is also a reflection of Phaethon's fiery character. His impulsiveness is further emphasised by his overuse of the whip.

7 Conclusions

Comparison of the two accounts reveals a rich play of similarity and difference. Limitations of space and time prevent me from detailing more: the way Nonnus' Helios is relatively unmotivated in comparison to Ovid's (Why does he agree to Phaethon's ride, given he knows Phaethon will die? Does this lack of motivation suggest a reliance on more clearly delineated motivation from earlier in the tradition?); the way Ovid's Phaethon is immediately terrified and overwhelmed, and his lack of control causes the horses to run wild, while Nonnus' Phaethon drives the horses too hard, and that is what sends him off course; the way

Nonnus' Phaethon enjoys the divine gaze and takes in the world below him, while the narrator's gaze focuses on the stars and cosmos thrown into disarray, in contrast to Ovid's Phaethon, too overwhelmed and terrified to look, and Ovid's narrator, focusing on the devastating effects on the world below. Might these differences reflect self-conscious correction or deliberate variation? We could also look at how each Phaethon account plays with the Euripidean pleading scene, and each re-works the Homeric scene in which Nestor advises Antilochus how to drive in the chariot race of *Iliad* 23. There is undoubtedly a strong kinship between these two tellings of the myth of Phaethon. Does it actually matter whether they are siblings, cousins or father and son?[63]

Knox concludes that "the onus of proof" remains with those who "maintain" that Nonnus had a "deep and fruitful" interest in Ovid. There is a fundamental problem with the idea that intertextuality can be 'proved.' Two texts relate to each other, and some readers perceive those relationships and find them meaningful. Knox also seems to work on the basis that intertextuality is a zero-sum game, a problematic premise. If words, phrases, and ideas are so common as to be ubiquitous, texts that share these elements may not relate to each other. But reasonable frequency does not preclude a relationship. If Nonnus was reusing his own phrases, referring back to Euripides, or drawing on common tropes and ideas from amatory epigram or other Greek sources, it does not follow that his poem did not, or cannot, have drawn on Latin traditions as well. Both texts are part of a broad cultural context that also involved visual culture and prose literature in both languages. Nonnus' version shows considerable kinship with Ovid's, and bears out the impression gained from other sources that the Ovidian Phaethon had become the most prominent version in the tradition.[64] On the other hand, a 'lost source,' such as Aeschylus' *Heliades* or a proposed Hellenistic epyllion, is convenient in an argument, because its influence can never be disproved. We must always acknowledge the vast amount of material we do not have, but its absence makes all reference to it speculative. We have Ovid, Ovid's Phaethon is the longest and most prominent surviving adaptation of the story, and given the similarities of tone, narrative structure,

---

[63] Paschalis 2014 takes a comparative approach to the relationship, and productively analyses Ovid and Nonnus together without insisting on a deliberate allusive relationship; see also nn. 5 and 45 above.

[64] We should also acknowledge that Ovid's popularity in later receptions of Greek myth can lead to assumptions of ancient prominence. For instance, Murnaghan/Roberts 2017 show the dominance of Ovid in myth collections for children.

theme, and intertextual framing, it seems perverse to exclude Ovid from comparison.

What do we gain from reading Ovid and Nonnus together as part of the wider Greco-Roman literary tradition, alongside Flavian epic? The two versions weave together the cosmic and the playful, thematising wayward narrative connections and over-reaching poetic ambition. Nonnus shares with Ovid (and surpasses him in) a poetic *jouissance*, a fullness, (almost) excessive pleasure in exploring and developing ideas, which is fundamentally un-Callimachean. The complex intratextuality of this episode, its wide-ranging connections with other parts of the *Dionysiaca*, far from invalidating connection with Ovid, is itself Ovidian, and shows that this episode typifies the poetics of Nonnus.

There are good reasons why scholars of Greek epic prefer to ignore Latin epic. But there is a middle ground between requiring it and rejecting it: if we think about intertextuality as under the power of the reader rather than in the mind of the author, can we consider how many of the elite readers engaging with a text like Nonnus' *Dionysiaca* would have been (at least) bilingual and bicultural (like Josephus, Plutarch, Claudian, or Apuleius)? Even if the current community of readers of Greek Imperial epic feels this group of ancient readers would be a relatively small proportion, should we only privilege ancient readers? Does treating Nonnus as part of Greco-Roman epic actually open his text up to a different readership? A permissive, playful, expansive model of reading seems appropriate.

Bibliography

Agosti, G. (2016), "L'epillio nelle Dionisiache? Strutture dell'epica nonniana e contesto culturale", in: *Aitia* 6; online at: https://journals.openedition.org/aitia/1579.

Apostol, R./Bakogianni, A. (eds.) (2018), *Locating Classical Receptions On Screen: Masks, Echoes, Shadows*, Cham.

Augoustakis, A. (2020), "Collateral Damage? Todeskette in Flavian Epic", in: Coffee/Forstall/Galli Milic/Nelis (2020), 169–186.

Barchiesi, A. (2009), "Phaethon and the Monsters", in: P. Hardie (ed.), *Paradox and the Marvellous in Augustan Culture*, Cambridge, 161–188.

Bernstein, N.W. (2016), "Revisiting Ovidian Silius, along with Lucretian, Vergilian and Lucanian Silius", in: Fulkerson/Stover (2016), 225–248.

Braune, J. (1935), *Nonnos und Ovid*, Greifswald.

Brown, J. (1994), *Into the Woods: Narrative Studies in the Thebaid of Statius with Special Reference to Books IV-VI*, PhD Dissertation, Cambridge.

Brown, R. (1987), "The Palace of the Sun in Ovid's *Metamorphoses*", in: M. Whitby/P. Hardie/M. Whitby (eds.), *Homo Viator: Classical Essays for John Bramble*, Bristol, 211–220.

Bruère, R.T. (1959), "Color Ovidianus in Silius' *Punica* 8-17", in: *Classical Philology* 54, 228–245.
Carvounis, K./Papaioannou, S. (forthcoming, 2022), "Nonnus' Dionysiaca and the Written Word", in: B. Verhelst (ed.), *Nonnus of Panopolis in Context IV: Poetry at the Crossroads*, Leuven, 133–149.
Christensen, J.P. (2020), *The Many-minded Man: The Odyssey, Psychology and the Therapy of Epic*, Ithaca, NY.
Closs, V. (2020), *While Rome Burned: Fire, Leadership and Urban Disaster in the Roman Cultural Imagination*, Ann Arbor.
Coffee, N./Forstall, C./Galli Milic, L./Nelis, D. (eds.) (2020), *Intertextuality in Flavian Epic Poetry: Contemporary Approaches*, Berlin.
Consolino, F.E. (ed.) (2018), *Ovid in Late Antiquity*, Turnhout.
Cowan, R. (2017), "Ovid, Virgil and the Echoing Rocks of the Two Scyllas", in: *Cambridge Classical Journal* 63, 11–28.
Cuppo Csaki, L. (1995), *The Influence of Ovid's Phaethon*, PhD Dissertation, Fordham University.
Diggle, J. (1970), *Euripides, Phaethon*, Cambridge.
D'Ippolito, G. (1964), *Studi nonniani: L'epillio nelle Dionisiache*, Palermo.
D'Ippolito, G. (1987), "Straniamento ossimorico e mitopoiesi nel barocco letterario tardogreco", in: M. Giacomarra/E. Marchetta (eds.), *Mito, storia e società (Atti del III Congresso internazionale di studi antropologici siciliani. Palermo, 7-9 dicembre 1981)*, Palermo, 347–357.
Feldherr, A. (2016), "Nothing like the Sun: Repetition and Representation in Ovid's Phaethon Narrative", in: Fulkerson/Stover (2016), 26–46.
Fielding, I. (2014), "A Poet Between Two Worlds: Ovid in Late Antiquity", in: J.F. Miller/C. Newlands (eds.), *A Handbook to the Reception of Ovid*, Malden, MA, 100–113.
Fish, S. (1980), *Is There a Text in This Class? The Authority of Interpretive Communities*, Cambridge, MA.
Fulkerson, L./Stover, T. (eds.) (2016), *Repeat Performances: Ovidian Repetition and the Metamorphoses*, Madison, WI.
Gantz, T. (1993), *Early Greek Myth: A Guide to Literary and Artistic Sources*, Baltimore.
Gärtner, U. (2005), *Quintus Smyrnaeus und die Aeneis. Zur Nachwirkung Vergils in der griechischen Literatur der Kaiserzeit*, Munich.
Gibson, R. (forthcoming), "Classical and Later Latins: Quantity, Canon and the Shape of the Field", in: R. Gibson/C. Whitton (eds.), *The Cambridge Critical Guide to Latin Literature*, Cambridge.
Grafton, A./Most, G. (eds.) (2016), *Canonical Texts and Scholarly Practices: A Global Comparative Approach*, Cambridge.
Hardie, P. (1993), *The Epic Successors of Virgil. A Study in the Dynamics of a Tradition*, Cambridge.
Hinds, S. (1998), *Allusion and Intertext. The Dynamics of Appropriation in Roman Poetry*, Cambridge.
Hinds, S. (2020) "Pre- and Post-digital Poetics of 'Transliteration': Some Greco-Roman Epic Incipits", in: Coffee/Forstall/Galli Milic/Nelis (2020), 421–446.
Holzberg, N. (1998), "*Ter quinque volumina* as *carmen perpetuum*: The Division into Books in Ovid's *Metamorphoses*", in: *Materiali e Discussioni per l'Analisi dei Testi Classici* 40, 77–98.
Jolowicz, D. (2021), *Latin Poetry in the Ancient Greek Novel*, Oxford.

Keith, A.M. (2002), "Ovidian *personae* in Statius' *Thebaid*", in: *Arethusa* 35, 381–402.
Keith, A.M. (2014a), "Ovidian Geographies in Flavian Mythological Epic", in: M. Skempis/
    I. Ziogas (eds.), *Geography, Topography, Landscape: Configurations of Space in Greek and Roman Epic*, Berlin, 349–372.
Keith, A.M. (2014b), "*Poetae Ovidiani*: Ovid's *Metamorphoses* in Imperial Roman Epic", in: Miller/Newlands (2014), 70–85.
Keith, A.M. (2016), "Ovidian Itineraries in Flavian Epic", in: Fulkerson/Stover (2016), 196–224.
Knaack, G. (1886), *Quaestiones Phaethonteae*, Berlin.
Knox, P.E. (1988), "Phaethon in Ovid and Nonnus", in: *Classical Quarterly* 38, 536–551.
Krasne, D. (2018), "Valerius Flaccus's Collapsible Universe: Patterns of Cosmic Disintegration in the *Argonautica*", in: L.D. Ginsberg/D. Krasne (eds.), *After 69 CE: Writing Civil War in Flavian Rome*, Berlin, 363–386.
Kristeva, J. (1980 [1966]), "Word, Dialogue and Novel", in: L.S. Roudiez, *Desire in Language: A Semiotic Approach to Literature and Art*, New York, 64–91.
Livrea, E. (2014), "Nonnus and the *Orphic Argonautica*", in: Spanoudakis (2014), 55–76.
Loos, J.X. (2006), "How Ovid Re-mythologises Greek Astronomy in the *Metamorphoses*", in: *Mnemosyne* 61, 257–289.
Lovatt, H.V. (2005), *Statius and Epic Games: Sport, Politics and Poetics in the Thebaid*, Cambridge.
Lovatt, H.V. (2010), "Interplay: Statius and Silius in the Games of *Punica* 16", in: A. Augoustakis (ed.), *Brill's Companion to Silius Italicus*, Leiden, 155–178.
Lovatt, H.V. (2012), "Competing Visions: Prophecy, Spectacle and Epic in Valerius Flaccus *Argonautica* 1 and Silius Italicus *Punica* 4 and 5", in: A. Augoustakis (ed.), *Religion and Ritual in Flavian Epic*, Oxford, 53–70.
Lovatt, H.V. (2020a), "Meanwhile Back at the Ranch: Narrative Transition and Structural Intertextuality in Statius *Thebaid* 1", in: Coffee/Forstall/Galli Milic/Nelis (2020), 21–41.
Lovatt, H.V. (2020b), "Didactic Heroes: Masculinity, Sexuality and Exploration in the Argonaut Story of Kingsley's *The Heroes*", in: R. Bryant Davies/B. Gribling (eds.), *Pasts at Play: Childhood Encounters with History in British Culture, 1750-1914*, Manchester, 71–95.
Lovatt, H.V. (2021), *In Search of Jason and the Argonauts*, London.
Manuwald, G./Voigt, A. (eds.) (2013), *Flavian Epic Interactions*, Berlin.
Marks, R. (2020), "Searching for Ovid at Cannae: A Contribution to the Reception of Ovid in Silius Italicus' *Punica*", in: Coffee/Forstall/Galli Milic/Nelis (2020), 87–106.
Martínez Alfaro, M.J. (1996), "Intertextuality: Origins and the Development of the Concept", in: *Atlantis* 18, 268–285.
Matier, K.O. (1979), *A Commentary on the Eleventh Book of the Punica of Silius Italicus*, PhD Dissertation, Rhodes University.
Matzner, S./Trimble, G. (eds.) (2020), *Metalepsis: Ancient Texts, New Perspectives*, Oxford.
McIntyre, J.S. (2019), "Calendar Girl: Anna Perenna Between the *Fasti* and the *Punica*", in: G. McIntyre/S. McCallum (eds.), *Uncovering Anna Perenna: A Focused Study of Roman Myth and Culture*, London, 37–53.
McKeown, J.C. (1987), *Ovid Amores: Text, Prolegomena and Commentary*, Leeds.
McNelis, C. (2007), *Statius' Thebaid and the Poetics of Civil War*, Cambridge.
Miller, J.F./Newlands, C. (eds.) (2014), *A Handbook to the Reception of Ovid*, Malden, MA.
Morgan, L. (2003), "Child's Play: Ovid and his Critics", in: *Journal of Roman Studies* 93, 66–91.
Most, G. (1990), "Canon Fathers: Literacy, Mortality, Power", in: *Arion* 1, 35–60.

Murnaghan, S./Roberts, D.H. (2017), "Myth Collections for Children", in: V. Zajko/H. Hoyle (eds.), *A Handbook to the Reception of Classical Mythology*, Malden, MA, 87–104.

Nelis, D. (2005), "The Reading of Orpheus: The *Orphic Argonautica* and the Epic Tradition", in: Paschalis (2005), 169–192.

Netz, R. (2020), *Scale, Space and Canon in Ancient Literary Culture*, Cambridge.

Newlands, C. (2004), "Statius and Ovid: Transforming the Landscape", in: *Transactions of the American Philological Association* 134, 133–155.

Paschalis, M. (ed.) (2005), *Roman and Greek Imperial Epic*, Herakleion.

Paschalis, M. (2014), "Ovidian Metamorphosis and Nonnian *poikilon eidos*", in: Spanoudakis (2014), 97–122.

Roberts, M. (2018), "The Influence of Ovid's *Metamorphoses* in Late Antiquity: Phaethon and the Palace of the Sun", in: Consolino (2018), 267–292.

Rouse, W.H.D. (1940), *Nonnos: Dionysiaca*. With an English translation; mythological introduction by H.J. Rose, and notes on textual criticism by L.R. Lind. In three volumes, Cambridge, MA (Loeb Classical Library 344, 354, 356).

Schiesaro, A. (2014), "*Materiam superabat opus*: Lucretius Metamorphosed", in: *Journal of Roman Studies* 104, 73–104.

Schiesaro, A. (2019), "Nonnus' Actaeon: Destiny in a Name", in: *Philologus: Zeitschrift für Antike Literatur und Ihre Rezeption* 163, 177–183.

Smolenaars, H.J.L. (1994), *Statius Thebaid VII: A Commentary*, Leiden.

Soerink, J. (2014), *Beginning of Doom. Statius Thebaid 5.499–753. Introduction, Text, Commentary*, PhD Dissertation, Rijksuniversiteit Groningen.

Spanoudakis, K. (ed.) (2014), *Nonnus of Panopolis in Context: Poetry and Cultural Milieu in Late Antiquity with a Section on Nonnus and the Modern World*, Berlin.

Thomas, R.F. (1986), "Virgil's *Georgics* and the Art of Reference", in: *Harvard Studies in Classical Philology* 90, 171–198.

Vessey, D.W.T.C. (1970), "Lucan, Statius, and the Baroque Epic", in: *Classical World* 63, 232–234.

Vessey, D.W.T.C. (1973), *Statius and the Thebaid*, Cambridge.

Wijsman, H.J.W. (1996), *Valerius Flaccus Argonautica, Book V*, Leiden.

Wilson, M. (2004), "Ovidian Silius", in: *Arethusa* 37, 225–249.

Zissos, A. (2008), *Valerius Flaccus' Argonautica Book 1*, Oxford.

List of Contributors

Silvio Bär is Professor of Classics at the University of Oslo. His research areas and interests include Greek hexameter poetry (especially of the imperial period), tragedy, lyric, the novel, mythology, rhetoric, the Second Sophistic, intertextuality, transtextuality, diachronic narratology, and the reception of antiquity in English literature and popular culture. He has published widely on Quintus of Smyrna's *Posthomerica*, on the genre "epyllion", and on the character of Herakles in Greek epic and beyond.

Katerina Carvounis is Assistant Professor in Ancient Greek Literature at the National and Kapodistrian University of Athens, Greece, and was previously British Academy Postdoctoral Research Fellow at the Faculty of Classics, Cambridge, and Fellow of Murray Edwards College, Cambridge. Her main research interests include early hexameter poetry and the later Greek epic tradition, and she has published widely in these areas. Most recent works include *A Commentary on Quintus of Smyrna, Posthomerica 14* (Oxford, 2019) and (with Sophia Papaioannou) a series of studies of Latin influence on Nonnus' *Dionysiaca*.

Ursula Gärtner studied Latin, Greek, Medieval Latin, and Hebrew at the universities of Heidelberg, Freiburg, Pittsburgh, and Basel, gained her PhD from the University of Freiburg and completed her Habilitation treatise in Leipzig. She has been Professor of Classics at the University of Potsdam since 2002 and at the University of Graz since 2016. She has written, edited and co-edited books on Valerius Flaccus, Quintus Smyrnaeus and Vergil, Phaedrus, fables, and classics and literary theory.

Emma Greensmith is Associate Professor of Classical Languages and Literature at the University of Oxford and a Fellow of St John's College. She is a member of the Council of the Hellenic Society. She specialises in imperial Greek literature, particularly epic, poetics, and religious culture. Her recent book, *The Resurrection of Homer in Imperial Greek Epic: Quintus Smyrnaeus'* Posthomerica *and the Poetics of Impersonation* offers a new reading of the role of epic and the reception of Homer in imperial Greece. She has also written articles on Nonnus, Triphiodorus, and Colluthus, and has co-edited an international volume on the *Posthomerica* (*Quintus of Smyrna's* Posthomerica: *Writing Homer under Rome*, EUP 2022). Her latest project, *Homer and the Bible,* explores the religious politics of verse in Late Antiquity, and includes recent and forthcoming publications on the Sibylline Oracles and Gregory of Nazianzus. She is also currently editing a new Cambridge Companion to Greek Epic.

Markus Kersten studied Classical Languages and Literature and Mathematics in Rostock, Groningen, and Oxford; he holds a doctoral degree from the University of Rostock. He has published a book on Lucan's reception of the *Georgics* (Göttingen, 2018) as well as several articles on Greco-Roman epic. After working as a school teacher, he is currently a postdoctoral fellow at Basel. In 2020 he was elected a junior member of the Akademie der Wissenschaften und der Literatur, Mainz.

Helen Lovatt is Professor of Classics at the University of Nottingham. She has published on Greek and Latin epic and its reception, including *The Epic Gaze* (Cambridge, 2013), which discussed Nonnus, *Statius and Epic Games* (Cambridge, 2005), and her most recent monograph on the cultural history of the Argonaut tradition, *In Search of the Argonauts* (Bloomsbury, 2021). She has also co-edited two volumes, *Epic Visions*, with Caroline Vout (Cambridge, 2013) and *Classical Reception and Children's Literature*, with Owen Hodkinson (I.B. Tauris, 2018). She is currently working on an Argonaut sequel (*Return of the Argonauts: Prequels, Sequels and Mash-ups, 1990-2020*) and an exploration of negative emotions as catalysts for action (*The Power of Sadness in Virgil's Aeneid*).

Sophia Papaioannou is Professor of Latin Literature at the National and Kapodistrian University of Athens. She is the author of *Epic Succession and Dissension. Ovid, Metamorphoses 13.623-14.582, and the Reinvention of the Aeneid* (Berlin, 2005), and *Redesigning Achilles. 'Recycling' the Epic Cycle in Ovid, Metamorphoses 12.1-13.622* (Berlin, 2007), and she has edited and co-edited numerous volumes, most recently *Intertextuality in Seneca's Philosophical Writings* (London, 2020), *Plautus' Erudite Comedy: New Insights into the Work of a doctus poeta* (Newcastle upon Tyne, 2020), *Elements of Tragedy in Flavian Epic* (Berlin/New York, 2021) and *Comic Invective in Greek and Roman Oratory* (Berlin/New York, 2021). She is currently working on a book on Nonnus' *Dionysiaca* in light of the Latin literary tradition.

Giampiero Scafoglio is Professor of Latin language and literature at the University of Nice-Côte d'Azur and Research Coordinator at CNRS (CEPAM UMR 7264). He works on Homer and the epic cycle, Roman tragedy, Vergil, Late Antique poetry, the Homeric presence in the literature of the Imperial Age, the classical reception in Italian culture. Among his publications are: *Noctes Vergilianae* (Hildesheim/New York, 2010) and *Ajax. Un héros qui vient de loin* (Amsterdam, 2017). As for collective books, he edited *Studies on the Greek Epic Cycle* (vols. I-II, Pisa/Rome, 2015) and *Revival and Revision of the Trojan Myth: Studies on Dictys Cretensis and Dares Phrygius* (with G. Brescia, M. Lentano, and V. Zanusso, Hildesheim/New York, 2018). Since 2019, he is member of the *Conseil National des Universités* (on nomination of the French Minister of University and Research).

General Index

aemulatio 17, 68, 103
Aeneas 21, 23, 55–122 *passim*, 126, 128, 167, 188, 196; *see also* criticism
Aeschylus 12, 117 n.61, 185–186, 202
aetiology 79–96
Alexandrian poetics 12, 21 n.67, 65, 105–109, 131
allusion 3, 8, 9, 12, 18–22, 31, 40, 46, 47, 62, 63, 68, 69, 76, 77, 82–84, 87, 89, 91, 103 n.12, 106, 112, 115, 116, 125, 127 n.18, 159, 180 n.3, 181–183, 191, 192, 202 n.63; *see also* interlingual allusion
anachronism 69, 79, 93–94, 113, 115
Apollonius Rhodius 12, 15, 79–80, 92, 106 n.25, 126–137, 143, 160, 167, 168, 169, 183 n.19, 195, 196 n.53
Argonauts 92, 127–148 *passim*, 186, 187, 191, 196
Aristaeus 134, 162 n.37, 168–169
author 7–26 *passim*

Bauform 126
belatedness 197
bilingual 2, 3, 4, 34 n.15, 85, 95, 203
'bilingual papyri' 11, 32, 103
bilingualism 78 n.12

Calchas 59, 63–64, 69–70, 75, 79, 85–87, 89–90, 113–114
Capua 184, 189
Cassandra 60, 65–66, 101, 115–117
cave(s) 123–149
charioteer theme 158–159, 163
Chiron 123, 126, 135–138, 147
Cicero 154, 155
Cimmerians 123, 126, 143–147
Claudian 4, 11, 24, 31–50, 132–134, 188 n.37, 197 n.54, 203
Clymene 185–186, 189 n.40, 191 n.45, 194, 198–199, 203
Colluthus 12 n.18
contest 24, 38 n.28, 40 n.37, 70 n.50, 151–177
– (singing/artistic) 151, 153–154, 156, 158
– (pantomime) 151–173

– (poetic) 38
cosmos 194, 195, 202
criticism
– of Aeneas' heroism 101, 118–119
– of Roman ideology 118–120

delay 194–197
Dionysius of Halicarnassus 9 n.6, 119 n.67
drawing 157, 164–166, 169

ecphrasis 35, 66, 126 n.16, 138, 157, 164, 166–167, 181, 185–201
empire 11, 34, 57, 70, 75, 79–92, 154–156
Epic Cycle 13, 58, 102, 105–106, 107, 108, 109, 116, 119
Erechtheus 38, 151, 156, 196
erotics 106 n.25, 134 n.58, 139, 165, 166, 186
Euripides 12, 117 n.61, 132 n.45, 154, 158, 159, 185–186, 189–192, 197, 198, 202

Flavian epic 24, 135, 137 n.67, 179–203 *passim*
funeral games 38–40, 151, 156

Hannibal 145, 189–191
Hermes (as narrator) 192–197
Hesiodic sphragis 39–41, 47–49

imago vocis 167
inheritance 83, 90, 184, 186
intentionality 4, 19, 180 n.4, 191
interlingual allusion 24, 173, 182 n.16
intertextuality *passim*
– as kinship 113, 179, 181, 198, 202
– tangential 179, 183, 189 n.40, 190, 192–194

Jerome 155

Laocoon 23, 55–74, 101–120
legitimacy 184–186
liminality 188
Lucan 9, 81 n.28, 136 n.64, 146 n.113, 184 n.24, 196 n.53

Lucian/*On Dancing* 152–153, 162–163, 166 n.44, 172

'many mouths' motif 42 n.46, 48–49
Maron 24, 151–173
marriage 185, 197, 198
Merops 185–186
metalepsis 197
metapoetics 24, 38, 42, 66, 67, 69 n.44, 123, 125, 128 n.23, 134, 138, 153, 168, 190
multiplicity 192 n.47, 197, 198
Musaeus 12 n.18
mythical places 123–148
mytho-chronology 123, 126, 127, 137

Nonnus/*Dionysiaca* 19 151–173
nymphs 123, 126, 131, 138–140, 159, 189 n.40
Odysseus 63–71, 75–96, 109, 111, 126–129, 139, 158, 171 n.56, 200–201
Oeagrus 38, 131 n.41, 151, 156–157
oppositio in imitando 39 n.34, 102, 116, 119
Oracula Sybillina 12 n.18
Orphic *Argonautica* 123–148
Ovid/*Metamorphoses* 4, 23, 32, 55, 77, 80, 143, 153, 157, 160, 180 n.6, 181, 182, 185, 188, 193, 196, 198
Ovidianism 180, 184
pantomime 24, 155–173
Peisander 13
Phaethon tradition 4, 24, 160, 166 nn. 44–45, 171–172, 179 n.2, 184–203
Plutarch 8–9 n.6, 31 n.2, 163, 164 n.40, 203
poetic development 31, 42, 46
poikilia 163
Polynices 188–191
Proclus 13, 119 n.67
programmatic statements 31, 44, 46
prophecy 69, 70, 75, 79, 86–89, 114, 116–118, 168, 181, 195, 196
Ps-Apollodorus 13, 129
Ps-Plutarch 81
Quellenforschung 7–30, 75–76, 96, 123, 125

Quintus/*Posthomerica* 1, 3, 7–26, 38, 39, 55–71, 75–96, 102, 106, 107, 110

reader 7–30, 56, 58, 62, 64, 67–69, 76, 80, 85, 103, 147, 156, 167, 168, 203
reception 4, 10, 15, 17, 20, 21, 25, 58, 76, 88, 132 n.50, 161, 163, 182–183
repetition 63, 124 n.8, 126, 127, 183 n.21, 184, 187
rivalry (poetic; younger vs. older poet) 50 n.76, 157, 161, 164 n.42, 170, 185 n.27

seafaring imagery and poetry 31–48
Second Sophistic 55, 57, 68–71, 78–82, 119, 162
self-fashioning 186
Silenus (song of) 24, 151–173
Silius Italicus 135, 145–146, 179–184, 189–191, 193, 198
Sinon 17, 21, 23, 55–71, 78, 101–120
Sirens 123, 126, 127–130, 134, 147
Sophocles 12
Statius 34 n.13, 35, 44, 47 n.68, 136–143, 183–206
subtext 1, 7, 8, 10–19, 22 n.71, 25

temporality 24, 75–99
testudo 15 n.32, 23, 69, 75, 79, 86, 92–95
Theocritus 15, 140 n.90, 153, 160
transition/transitional 43, 47, 140, 187, 189, 195, 197
Triphiodorus 1, 4, 9 n.8, 12 n.18, 24, 101–120
Troy (sack of) 55–71, 101–120
Troy (escape from) 23, 83–92

Valerius Flaccus 124, 135, 137, 139 n.82, 140, 142–143, 144, 145 n.111, 179, 180, 183, 186, 187, 193
Vergil/*Aeneid* (general) 7–26 and *passim*
Vergil/*Aeneid* 2 55–71, 101–120
Vergil/*Aeneid* 5 128, 156, 200 n.61
Vergil/*Eclogue* 6 4, 24, 151–173

writing 157, 164–166, 180

χαράσσειν 164, 166, 171 n.58

Index Locorum

Apollonius Rhodius
1.23–25	131 n.41
1.26	131
1.496–511	167
2.1047–1089	92
4.145–147	141 n.94
4.214–215	38 n.27
4.898–899	127 n.21

Aristotle
Poetics
1459a30–b2	106

Callimachus
Aetia (Pfeiffer)
fr. 1.25–28	158 n.27
fr. 2.1–2	43, 65

Claudian
Carmina Minora
12.56	33
19.3	33
31.4–6	133
41.13–14	33

De Raptu Proserpinae
pr. 1–12	41–42

Gigantomachia
1–15	36–41

Dracontius
Romulea
2.129–130	139

Ennius
Fr. inc. 167 Manuwald (=388–389 Vahlen =352–353 Jocelyn) 159 n.31

Euripides
Cyclops
141–142	158
143	158 n.24

Eusebius
Oration of Constantine to the Holy Assembly
19–21	155

Hesiod
Catalogue of Women
fr. 238 (Merkelbach-West)	157 n.23

Theogony
22–28	65
22–34	160
30–34	41
304–325	66
986–991	185 n.29

Works and Days
646–662	39–41

Homer
Iliad
1.6–7	170
2.144	38 n.27
2.488–493	38 n.27
4.442–427	38 n.27
12.200–209	195 n.50
14.224–291	140
20.300–308	87–88

Odyssey
2.230–234	91
4.363–446	162
4.435–446	161
5.228–262	200
5.70–71	139 n.84
19.97–201	157 n.23
11.14–19	144
11.15–16	144 n.103

Hyginus
Fab. 152A	185
Fab. 154	185

Jerome
Epistulae
21.13.9	155

Libanius
Oration
64.103–105	152

Livy
43.13.2	7

Lucian
On Dancing
37	166 n.44
39	166 n.44
47	166 n.44
55	166 n.44, 172
76	153
80	166 n.44

Macrobius
4.4	161 n.34
5.2.4	13
5.5.2	109 n.33

Nemesianus
Cynegetica
58–62	44

Nonnus
Dionysiaca
1.1–10	161 n.35
1.11	161
1.11–33	161 n.35
1.13–14	163
1.13–15	161
1.13–33	162
1.25–27	161
1.33 ff.	162
1.34–38	162
1.34–44	161 n.35
1.36–37	159
1.42–44	171
5.242–257	158
10.141–174	153 n.6
11.1–55	153 n.6
11.406–426	153 n.6
13.47–52	48
14.96–104	157, 158 n.25
14.100–103	158 n.25
19.59–117	156
19.106–115	39
19.136–286	24, 151
19.136–348	157
19.147–149	156, 169 n.54
19.150	156
19.155–157	157
19.182–184	166 n.45
19.184–186	166 n.45
19.198–224	165
19.200	166, 171 n.58
19.205	165
19.205–221	165
19.206	166
19.210–211	166
19.214–215	166
19.216	166
19.216–217	164
19.219	164
19.225–227	169
19.225–264	168
19.227–229	170
19.229–230	169 n.54
19.263–264	169
19.263–295	170
19.287	170
19.287–293	170 n.55
19.317–319	171
19.346	171
30.108–116	171–172
38.10–14	194
38.19	195
38.30–34	196
38.90–102	192–193
38.91–93	172 n.59
38.155–163	199
38.168–183	199–200
38.410–411	172 n.59, 193
38.424–431	193
38.431	171
38.432–434	193

Paraphrasis
4.147	38 n.27

Index Locorum

Orphic Argonautica
8–10	124
72–75	130
79–80	133
378–379	135
393–405	135
394	136 n.65
401	136 n.65
415–418	137
435–439	138, 138 n.74
438	137
440–441	138
643–648	139–140
1000	143
1002–1003	143
1004–1012	140, 141
1013–1014	142
1027	143
1112	144 n.103
1119–1128	144
1142	146
1248–1249	146
1264–1290	127
1267	129
1268	129 n.30
1270–1271	129
1373	133 n.55

Ovid
Fasti
3.523–696	184
5.495–544	184

Metamorphoses
1.750	197
2.2–4	187
2.55	198
2.105–110	200–201
2.327–328	189
2.340–366	193
2.381–400	188
2.398–400	188
8.624–724	184
10.86–87	132 n.47
11.90–93	160 n.36
12.21	114 n.52

Pindar
Nemean
3.26–28	37–38
7.20–21	167 n.47

Pythian
9.1–75	168
11.39–40	38

Pliny the Elder
Naturalis Historia
3.61	145–146

Propertius
1.20.33	139, 139 n.81
3.3.21–24	43, 45

Quintus of Smyrna
2.242	70 n.51
3.216	70 n.51
3.284	70 n.51
4.128–170	38
4.423–429	69
5.180–316	70 n.50
5.191	70 n.51
5.485	66
5.487–488	70
6.260–262	66
6.531–536	69
10.353–360	64
11.358–360	24
11.358–366	15 n.32, 23, 92–93
11.358–375	69
11.358–396	75, 79
11.388–396	94
12.1–103	61
12.19–20	94
12.25–45	64
12.35–36	64
12.51–65	64
12.104–156	61
12.163–171	64
12.182–188	64
12.183–184	64
12.217–305	61
12.235	70 n.51
12.245–246	62
12.252–585	23

12.306–313	61, 67	2.178	114
12.307	94	2.182	114 n.54
12.314–352	61		
12.327–328	94	**Silius Italicus**	
12.351	70 n.51	3.415–441	184
12.353–388	61	7.166–211	184
12.363–373	58	11.303–368	189
12.375–386	61, 62, 67	11.348	190
12.377	64	11.365–366	190
12.379	64	11.369	189–190
12.387–388	62 n.22	11.449	135–136
12.389–417	65	12.120–133	145
12.399–415	66	14.567–579	198
12.418–443	61, 65	16.546–548	194
12.444–480	61, 65		
12.447–463	66	**Statius**	
12.452	67	*Achilleid*	
12.463–464	66	1.101–103	136–137
12.480–481	67	1.106–118	136
12.480–499	60, 67	1.110	137 n.66
12.487–488	70	1.110–111	137
12.500–524	61, 65	1.111	137
12.525–585	61, 66	1.120–121	136 n.65
13.300–332	23, 83	1.125	136 n.65
13.333–343	85–86, 89–90	1.187–188	137 n.69
13.333–349	79	*Thebaid*	
13.336–341	69	6.3–4	199
13.338	170	6.23–24	44
13.344–349	89	6.320–517	188–189
13.558	70 n.51	10.141–145	142
14.105–111	64	11.303–368	189
14.107	64	12.413–415	188, 189
14.154–164	22 n.71		
14.474–487	16, 18	**Strabo**	
14.630–631	69 n.44	*Geographica*	
		5.4.5	145 n.111
Quintilian			
8.2.9	161	**Suetonius**	
		De Poetis	
Servius		103–104 (Rostagni 1944) 155	
ad Ecl.			
6.11	154	**Tacitus**	
ad Geo.		*Dialogus*	
3.115	137 n.70	13	155
ad Aen.			
2.148	110		

Theognis

218	167 n.47
969–970	38 n.25

Triphiodorus

1–5	109
109	38 n.27
270–272	111
279–280	111
286–287	112
292–293	110
296–299	113
360	116
376–378	116, 117
412–413	116
417–418	117
651–655	118

Valerius Flaccus

1.228–230	195–196
3.397–401	144
4.344–422	188
5.407–456	187
5.429–432	187
5.454	188
5.455	188
8.74	142
8.83–87	143

Vergil

Aeneid

1.34–87	16, 18
2.10–13	107
2.13–39	59
2.25	61
2.37–38	117
2.40–56	59
2.41	116
2.42	116
2.42–49	56
2.57	62
2.57–198	59
2.63–64	63 n.24
2.69–72	59, 62
2.77–78	110
2.77–104	59, 62
2.97–100	64
2.103–104	112
2.128–129	64
2.108–144	59, 62
2.137–138	112
2.145	62, 110 n.38
2.146–147	62
2.148–149	112
2.148–151	59
2.154–194	59, 62
2.178	114
2.180–182	114 n.51
2.281	114
2.199–231	59
2.232–249	60
2.246–247	116, 117
2.248–249	117
2.250–804	84
2.438–444	15 n.32, 93
3.94–98	88
5.864–866	128
6.460–463	22 n.71
6.893	146
9.434–437	69
9.503–524	69
9.505–518	15 n.32, 89
12.432–441	91

Eclogues

6.1–5	161
6.5	161
6.6–12	161
6.11–12	160
6.13	161
6.20	162
6.27–30	159
6.31–40	160
6.41–42	160
6.43–45	160
6.46–60	160
6.61–63	160
6.62–63	166 n.45
6.64–73	160, 162
6.72	160
6.72–73	160
6.73–78	160
6.79–81	160
6.82	159
6.82–83	153, 166 n.45

Georgics
2.39–46	42–43, 45
4.315–558	168–169
4.458	169
4.507–510	131–132
4.563–566	4

www.ingramcontent.com/pod-product-compliance
Lightning Source LLC
Chambersburg PA
CBHW020230170426

43201CB00007B/380